THE COLLECTION OF THE QUR'ĀN

THE COLLECTION OF THE QUR'ĀN

JOHN BURTON

Senior Lecturer in Arabic in the University of
St. Andrews

CAMBRIDGE UNIVERSITY PRESS

Cambridge

London · New York · Melbourne

CAMBRIDGE UNIVERSITY PRESS
Cambridge, New York, Melbourne, Madrid, Cape Town, Singapore,
São Paulo, Delhi, Dubai, Tokyo, Mexico City

Cambridge University Press
The Edinburgh Building, Cambridge CB2 8RU, UK

Published in the United States of America by Cambridge University Press, New York

www.cambridge.org
Information on this title: www.cambridge.org/9780521296526

First published 1977
First paperback edition 1979
Re-issued 2010

A catalogue record for this publication is available from the British Library

Library of Congress Cataloguing in Publication data

Burton, John, 1929–
The collection of the Qur'ān.

Bibliography: p.
Includes index.
1. Koran – History. 2. Koran – Readings.
3. Islamic law – Interpretation and construction.
I. Title.
BP131.B87 297'.1226 76–27899

ISBN 978-0-521-21439-1 Hardback
ISBN 978-0-521-29652-6 Paperback

Contents

Acknowledgements

I should like to record my gratitude to both the School of Oriental and African Studies in the University of London and the University of St Andrews for grants of study leave with supporting finance which enabled me to consult unpublished manuscript materials in European and Middle Eastern collections, use of which underlies certain aspects of this present study.

I record also with pleasure my debt to my colleague, Dr J. Wansbrough of the School of Oriental and African Studies, who over the years has offered generously both time and encouragement.

The principal debt which must here be acknowledged is to the members of my immediate family whose tolerance and understanding have sustained me and eased the burden of frequent separations.

J. Burton

PART I

The Qur'ān and the Islamic legal sciences

1 Introduction

Classical Islam, as it is referred to by European scholars, may be dated from the stage when Islam first saw itself as a religio-legal system wholly rooted in a divine revelation. As in Judaism the heart of the system was the Law and it has long been a truism for Western scholars that the Law which Islam proclaimed was held by the Muslims to have derived from two co-equal sources, the Islamic Scripture and the Islamic Tradition.

The derivation of the Law had resulted from the labours of a series of individual scholars active in the course of the first two centuries after Muḥammad. To this Law was given the name *šarīʿa*, while the science concerned with its elaboration was called the *Fiqh*.

At an identifiable moment in recent history God had spoken to and through a prophet, Muḥammad (A.D. 570-632). To Muḥammad God had addressed His Holy Book, the Qur'ān, the written law of Islam, *kitāb allāh*. Simultaneously through the Prophet's words and actions, lovingly recorded by Muḥammad's contemporaries, God had further communicated to mankind the unwritten law of Islam, the perfect pattern of divinely approved human conduct, the Sunna. The scholars of the classical age of Islam saw themselves as having inherited a revealed Law securely preserved in two literary sources, the Sunna which had circulated in primarily oral transmissions and the Qur'ān which had been cherished in both oral and written form.

The texts of the Qur'ān had been preserved in two ways. The better to express the Qur'ān's quality as a direct divine revelation independent of earlier revealed religions, Islam portrayed its prophet as doubly illiterate. Despite his personal inability to read and write, during the twenty-odd years of his public activity Muḥammad had employed the services of a series of amanuenses to record at his dictation each of the individual fragments of the revelation immediately he received it.

Others of his followers had devotedly committed the revealed texts to memory. On the death of the Prophet and before the written texts had been assembled, edited and promulgated his Companions had disseminated their knowledge of the Qur'ān texts among the Muslims of the Islamic lands. They simultaneously instructed them in the minutiae of the Sunna. This double body of knowledge became the common heritage of the Muslim faithful.

In time there had arisen throughout the Islamic empire a number of specialists, the scholars of the *Fiqh* to whom especially belongs the merit of having produced a manageable statement of the Law, devising for the purpose a set of techniques known as *uṣūl al fiqh*.

These were the rules governing the extraction of the Law from the twin sources of Qur'ān and Tradition.

Scholars may advance the general stock of knowledge in a

variety of ways: by the discovery and publication of hitherto unknown source materials; by placing their entire subject in a wholly novel perspective on the basis of an extensive re-examination and analysis of available sources; or finally, by applying the new perspective to the elucidation of a single long-recognised problem. The present work is of this last kind. It seeks to re-open the question of the collection of the Qur'ān as seen by the Muslims. Their accounts will be re-examined in the light of studies by Goldziher and Schacht, pre-eminent instances of works of the second type.

Each of these scholars had the fortune and the genius to perceive amid the multiplicity of baffling detail presented in the literatures of Islam the few points of significant meaning which held the clue to an overall pattern and which, properly assessed, offered the key to its interpretation.

Goldziher's contribution to modern Islamic studies lay in his observation that the literature of the Muhammadan Tradition, the *Ḥadīth*, represented less a corpus of information from and about the Prophet as transmitted with verbal fidelity by successive generations after him than a reflection of the social, political and religious ideals of the transmitters themselves and of the societies or groups they served as spokesmen. By Sunna was to be understood, not the inherited instruction of the Prophet, but the *ius consuetudinis* of a group or party, large or small. By *ḥadīth* is meant the vehicle of that sunna, a report, verbal or written, conveying a description of the relevant practice, opinion or custom approved by the disseminators of the report.[1]

Building upon this ingenious suggestion, Schacht has shown in his studies of the Muhammadan legal traditions that, rather than spreading out from an original centre at Medina, Islamic Law originated in the provinces. Reference of the Sunna to the Prophet was the end rather than the beginning of a process. Its purpose was to verify some local legal viewpoint. In other words, the Sunna differed and was differently defined from region to region. Thus, the individual _ḥadīth_ conveys a truth that is theoretical rather than historical. It served as verification by documenting legal conclusions reached by the scholars of a particular locality on the individual topics of the _Fiqh_.[2]

We in our turn are now directed by the findings of these two scholars towards a more detailed consideration of the role played within the broad field of the Islamic Tradition by _uṣūl al fiqh,_ the Islamic source theory.

Our aim shall be to enquire whether and how these _uṣūl al fiqh_ may even have fashioned part of that Tradition, in particular, the part that recounts the history of the collection of the Qur'ān texts. It will be suggested that the available evidence indicates that the Muslim accounts of the history of the collection of their Scripture must now be re-interpreted in the light of a prolonged and highly technical discussion on the role (as opposed to the history) of the revealed book.

The discussion concerned the relative status of Qur'ān and Sunna as legal sources. Although the details of the course of the discussion during the second and third centuries after Muḥammad have long been available to us, they could not hitherto be properly evaluated.

Only one version of the traditions on the collection of the Qur'ān has until now been accepted. This is the version maintained and handed on by Muslim and Western scholars alike. European investigations into Muhammadan accounts of the collection of the Qur'ān texts have hitherto been restricted to the analysis of the accounts as preserved. There is no sign of any realisation that it might be profitable to seek to relate the accounts to the wider background within the totality of the Islamic sciences out of which they had emerged; and nor has there been any effort to enquire whether there might not lurk behind the wording of the accounts some underlying motivation.

We now possess enough information to discover the ideological basis of the accounts and to expose the evolution of the motives which shaped the accounts. The solution lies in an unsuspected yet not improbable quarter.

2 The Islamic legal sciences

Queen of the Islamic sciences and the first to achieve major development was the *Fiqh*. As we now know it the *Fiqh* was constructed mainly in the course of the second century A.H. Since then it has been represented in a number of separately developed and frequently conflicting schools or systems independently established in the main cities of the chief centres of the empire, Iraq and the *Ḥijāz*. Syria also produced a system of law but this was early replaced by the more vigorous systems of the two neighbouring territories.

Mecca, Medina, Baṣra and Kūfa were the homes of schools of law which had been the gradual creation of locally-settled scholarly groups who had inherited from their predecessors, in addition to their Qur'ān and Sunna knowledge, the broad lines of a developing local Qur'ān science.

These schools of *Fiqh* had emerged nearly simultaneously and those who received their training in each local legal tradition grew up in the belief that the achievement of those who had founded the local school or *maḏhab* (pl. *maḏāhib*) had consisted in derivation, in the review in their entirety of the twin constituent source 'documents' of the local expression of Islam, the Qur'ān, and the Sunna. Included under the heading Qur'ān were close textual study, *qirā'a*, and the accumulated masses of interpretation of the individual verses as transmitted in the *ta'wīl* or *tafsīr* of the foregoing generations.

The *Fiqh*, as elaborated locally by the anonymous founders of the several *maḏāhib*, represented to their successors the totality of the *šarīʿa*, the normative Muslim 'way of life' which the commands, prohibitions, exhortations and recommendations of the common sources could be shown to embody.

This outlook of the later adherents of the *maḏhab* was cultivated in a secondary science, *uṣūl al fiqh*, which sought to determine precisely which source materials the founders of the local *Fiqh* had consulted in deriving each clause, *ḥukm* (pl. *aḥkām*) of the Law. The work was to involve the identification of the materials, their authentication as either Qur'ān or Sunna and finally the definition of the relative primacy that the founders of the *maḏhab* had accorded in their derivation of the Law to each of the two primary sources. This, as we see, was a relatively late development posterior to the articulation of the *Fiqh* and presupposes dispute.

Dispute had been occasioned by the fact that the Muslims were indefatigable travellers, frequently covering enormous distances for the purpose of commerce, warfare against the Infidel, study or pilgrimage to Mecca. These movements would have provided individuals with opportunities to realise that there were numerous disagreements between the *maḏāhib*. The word means 'attitudes' or 'interpretations'.

As the *Fiqh* had been originally a local creation, so also each local *maḏhab* evolved its own local science of *uṣūl* al fiqh. Uṣūl must therefore be seen not as a unitary science cultivated in different centres, but as a series of local sciences regionally organised like the Fiqh itself, and continuously developing to serve the function of documenting, verifying and defending the Fiqh taught in the parent madhab. Naturally uṣūl scholars engaged in polemics and apologetics.

As the schools of uṣūl became more sophisticated through the discipline of disputation, it became clear that the madāhib differed not merely in the individual aḥkām propounded by their respective founders, but also in the use that these had apparently made of the basic sources - for that is how the observable conflict between the madāhib on the various legal topics came to be explained. The conflicting local schools of uṣūl science are best seen therefore as having been called into being to provide the necessary retrospective rationalisation of instances of such conflict.

Uṣūl studies were not, however, restricted solely to points of law where the paths of the madāhib had diverged. The entire corpus of legal conclusions now represented in the local body of legal knowledge was the proper sphere of the uṣūlī, and as the content of the science expanded the awakening of interest in the technical aspects of the study led the way to the formulation of axioms and definitions, theorems and rules. Refined by use and practice, and improved by the lessons of debate, the framework of rules enabled uṣūl al fiqh to achieve eventual academic independence to be pursued for its own sake within the confines of each of the several madāhib long after the days of inter-school rivalry, when contention had given way to mutual recognition and a resigned acceptance of differentness. The Muslims never achieved either a unified Fiqh or a unified uṣūl.

Each madhab produced its uṣūl literature, the study of which presents the reader with a series of rationalised justifications of the local school Fiqh. In the analysis of the history and development of the school's agreed set of views, the rationalisations are characterised from madhab to madhab by the varying emphasis placed upon appeal now to the Qur'ān, now to the Sunna.

This differential emphasis affects, however, not only the aḥkām traditionally at issue between the madāhib. It affects also the rationalisation of the aḥkām held in common by all groups of Muslims.

This is especially evident in the treatment of particular aḥkām maintained by a majority of Muslims, which we propose to examine in detail.

Whereas one group of uṣūl writers refers the shared viewpoint to one source, another group refers the same ḥukm to the other source. This had interesting results for the further development of the uṣūl science.

One seldom reads (except in the edited version of a debate penned by his adversary) of a scholar abandoning his original Fiqh or uṣūl viewpoint owing to his finding the representative of the rival madhab adducing more convincing evidence or more cogent logic. Rather one notes a sharpening of the debating techniques and the search for (and discovery of) more impressive Qur'ān or Sunna or interpretative arguments to be used in future.

This prompts the further question: whether it is

possible to understand and interpret all these developments by accepting at face value the insistence of the _uṣūlī_ that he is concerned solely to review the use made of the primary sources by his scholarly predecessors. To what extent would the modern student be justified in adding to Qur'ān and Sunna the local _Fiqh_, bringing the number of actual sources up to three?

A specific case will help to bring out the relevance of the question, which simply proposes that the local _uṣūl_ science, developing its own impetus, created a local methodological tradition on the basis of which it proceeded to the examination of the _šarīʿa_ in the light of its own assumptions.

ibn al ʿArabī (A.H.543) reports from ibn Šihāb that ʿUrwa said

> 'I asked ʿĀ'iša, "What is your view of Q 2.158?: 'There shall be no blame on him who performs _ṭawāf_ between Ṣafā and Marwa.' Surely there can be no blame on anyone who does not perform this _ṭawāf_?"'
>
> ʿĀ'iša replied that were the case as ʿUrwa supposed, the verse would read: 'There shall be no blame on him who does not perform the _ṭawāf_.' The _Anṣār_, feeling certain scruples about this ceremony, on account of the locality's former association with idols, consulted the Prophet. God revealed Q 2.158. The Prophet then laid down the sunna of performing the _ṭawāf_. It is thus incumbent upon pilgrims not to omit it.[1]

In ibn al ʿArabī's view, the point of the _ḥadīth_ is that ʿUrwa took the verse to indicate that the _ṭawāf_ was not obligatory. Yet he observed that the _šarīʿa_ assumed that it might on no account be omitted by those fulfilling their religious obligations.

The Qur'ānic expression: 'there is no blame in doing

it', implies that the performance of an act is legally neutral (mubāḥ). ʿUrwa understood the verse to mean that the omission of the act was legally neutral, but ʿĀ'iša informed him that the verse did not indicate this. Omission of the ṭawāf would have called for a different reading.

Within the terms of the ḥadīth, the discussion first arose following the legal conclusion, for ʿUrwa noted that the šarīʿa assumed the ṭawāf to be required. The discussion occurred at a secondary stage when the Fiqh was already regarded in the circle from which the ḥadīth stems as a relevant source in its own right. That makes three sources: Qur'ān, Sunna and Fiqh.

It is also of interest to note that whereas this discussion contrasts the Sunna with the Qur'ān, there was in fact an intimate connection between the two. The sunna appealed to by ʿĀ'iša is a tafsīr-sunna, that is, a sunna which had clearly originated from a comment upon the relevant verse.

We mentioned above what was included under the heading Qur'ān. We now learn that included under the heading Sunna were materials which had originated in scholarly discussions on the implications of Qur'ān verses. The mechanical contrast between Qur'ān and Sunna, arising originally out of the concerns and methods of the uṣūlīs, was to become absolute. Accustomed to trace this doctrine to the Qur'ān and that doctrine to the Sunna (part of which, as we have just seen, proceeds indirectly from the Qur'ān), some scholars from ingrained habit treated their two sources as formally separate and independent. Regular exercise of the uṣūlī's craft ultimately both conduced to and reinforced this attitude to the sources of the Fiqh.

We have already seen that where a ḥukm could not satisfactorily be traced in any of the statements of the Qur'ān, it was assigned, as an element of the local Fiqh, to an origin in the Sunna.

Where a ḥukm was a matter of contention between two or more maḏāhib, the uṣūlī of one school might trace the differing conclusions arrived at in his own and those arrived at in the rival groups to what he conceived to be their respective origins in the Islamic Tradition. This might point either to a Qur'ān verse, or to the Sunna. The aḥkām being at loggerheads, the two primary sources were before long thought to be also at loggerheads, not simply separate and independent.

In cases where the general source claimed for competing aḥkām was the same, but where the appeal of the maḏāhib, if to the Qur'ān, was to different verses, or, if to the Sunna, was to different ḥadīth reports, the verses or the reports, as the case might be, were also thought to be at loggerheads. The preference apparently shown by the founders of the different maḏāhib for this or that particular source on such occasions of conflict of source was noted and analysed.

As disputes arose, one technique adopted by the uṣūlīs was to question the validity or relative strength of the opposing group's evidence. When the opponent rested his argument on a ḥadīth, the strength of his evidence could be challenged by the rough-and-ready rule of counting ḥadīth reports. The uṣūlī would allege that a greater number of reports, or transmitters for a particular report, could be amassed in favour of his school's view. This technique resulted in classification of hadīth reports according to their 'spread' as: mutawātir (universally acknowledged), mašhūr (widely attested), and khabar al wāḥid (isolate).

More subtle methods of challenging evidence were emerging. One of the most enduring was to be isnād criticism. By isnād (support) is meant the list of guarantors which came to be demanded for all statements as to what constituted the Sunna. To ensure the soundness of information conveyed, all scholars were required to list the names of those persons responsible in each generation for the downward transmission of every individual ḥadīth.

From his knowledge of the maġāzī and sīra sciences, which dealt respectively with the campaigns and the biography of the Prophet and his contemporaries, the scholar might note a discrepancy in the opponent's argument, such as the transmission from a Companion on some topic of a report which could not possibly be authentic, either because the Companion had not been born, or had not yet been converted to Islam, or had already died at the time of the introduction of a particular ruling. The same technique served also to determine 'correctness' as between conflicting views each traced to a different verse of the Qur'ān, for among the masses of information presented in the maġāzī works were frequently to be found also statements as to the date of revelation of this or that Qur'ān passage. Such data, asbāb al nuzūl (the occasion of the revelation of the verses), were eagerly collected.

From statements linking the revelation of particular verses to specific events or individuals, a chronological profile of the Qur'ān could as easily be constructed as the one currently being constructed for the Sunna. We have just seen in ʿĀ'iša's report the confident dating of Q 2.158.

It was then a simple matter to link both timetables and to argue from the relative chronologies which was the earlier of two ḥadīths, two verses, or ḥadīth and verse.

The extent to which asbāb al nuzūl is exegetical is clear from the frequency of the claim that no assistance is greater for understanding the Qur'ān than a knowledge of when and in what circumstances its verses were revealed.

These techniques placed in the hands of the uṣūlīs invaluable instruments for measuring the relative correctness of the choice made between the elements of the Islamic Tradition by the several founders of the Fiqh, the fuqahā', in determining the ḥukm for each legal topic.

Central to our understanding of these developments was the question of the mutual status of Qur'ān and Sunna in the event of apparent conflict between them. Just as information derived from a later Companion came to be held to supersede information from an earlier Companion, so also the ruling based on a later Qur'ān verse came to be held to supersede that derived from an earlier verse.

But what view would be taken in cases where Qur'ān rulings clashed with Sunna rulings? In some instances, the Qur'ān was acknowledged to be the later statement; in others, the later was said to be the Sunna. This could be decided by comparing both sources with the Fiqh. For example, all

Muslims now pray facing towards Mecca. This is the qibla based on the later source, for the obligation to face the Kaʿba was introduced in the Qur'ān. No other qibla is specifically imposed in the Qur'ān, yet the Qur'ān verse imposing the Meccan qibla implies change of direction.[2] The qibla apparently abandoned was assigned by some scholars to the Sunna. The verse in question was the later statement. Few topics were quite so universally agreed upon as the qibla. On other topics confusion and dispute reigned. The Muslims, it will be seen, even here failed to achieve a uniform view on the relative status of Qur'ān and Sunna.

Some scholars trusted to their ability to judge each case of Qur'ān-Sunna conflict on its merits, but the majority preferred to draft formal general principles.

Thus, as all the processes which, so far as the uṣūlī judged, had led to the elaboration of the regional maḏāhib were reviewed in retrospect and in the light of the assumptions adopted in the local science of uṣūl, all instances were noted of conflict of evidence and conflict of sources underlying the conflicting legal views reached in the several Fiqh systems. As a result, in the context of discussions held within and between the several maḏāhib, a significant methodological role can be seen to have been allotted to a number of phenomena referred to collectively as al nāsikh wa al mansūkh.

Conflict was thought to have obtained between: some statement of an opponent's Fiqh and a relevant Qur'ān or Sunna statement; the choices made by the several fuqahā' as between this or that Qur'ān verse, this or that ḥadīth, or a

Qur'ān verse and a *ḥadīth*.

From detailed studies of such conflicts there emerged in *uṣūl al fiqh* a new sub-science on *naskh* or *al nāsikh wa al mansūkh*, devoted to the verification and elaboration of the so-called Muslim theories of abrogation - 'so-called' because, as will be seen in what follows, the expression *al nāsikh wa al mansūkh* conveyed much more to the Muslim than merely abrogation.

In the nature of things, where formal principles of *al nāsikh wa al mansūkh* were adopted, these showed no more uniformity than the parent *Fiqh* had done.

According to the Kufans, certain rulings of the Qur'ān had superseded other rulings established either by the Qur'ān or by the Sunna. Šāfiʿī and his followers held that the Qur'ān had superseded the Qur'ān, but had not superseded the Sunna; and that the Sunna had superseded the Sunna, but had not superseded the Qur'ān.[3]

Very important influences were at play in the shaping of these theories which are directly relevant to our study of the Muslim accounts of the history of the collection of the Qur'ān texts.

The issues involved in the disputes on *naskh* are identified in the slogans circulated: *inna al sunna qāḍiya ʿala al kitāb* (the Sunna is the judge of the Qur'ān); *al qur'ān aḥwaju ila al sunna min al sunna ila al qur'ān* (the Qur'ān has greater need of the Sunna for its elucidation than the Sunna has of the Qur'ān).[4] These clearly enough express one point of view on the question of the relative primacy thought to have been accorded by the *fuqahā'* to the two sources.

We have argued that the differing principles of al nāsikh wa al mansūkh had evolved from the studies of the uṣūlīs on the twin problems of conflict of sources, as this had affected the genesis and development of the local Fiqh; and conflict of evidence, as this now seemed to explain the observable differences between the conclusions historically reached in their own and in the rival madāhib.

We must enquire further into the means adopted by the Muslims to verify the common appeal to naskh and to justify their differing interpretations of the term.

The study of the application of the principle to specific legal problems will clarify the nature of the differences between the principles adopted in the various schools, while throwing light on the evolution of the principles themselves. That will lead us inevitably to ask what, if any, significance the principles of naskh had for the framing of the Muslim accounts of the history of the Qur'ān texts, and when and in what circumstances the texts were envisaged as having been first assembled.

We have suggested that the Muslims were not united in their view of the emphasis that had been placed on the two sources. Indeed, there is evidence in the uṣūl works that as late as the second half of the second century A.H. some questioned that there was more than one legitimate source.[5] These men insisted on the sufficiency of the Qur'ān source and repudiated the role claimed for the Sunna, not least in view of the differing status and different histories behind the transmission of the two.

They were especially opposed to accepting evidence from elsewhere on legal questions referred to in the Qur'ān. In addition, they were inclined to regard any question not referred to in the Qur'ān as having been left deliberately unregulated by the divine Lawgiver.[6]

The Qur'ān was a public document transmitted from generation to generation by the entire community. On the other hand, the Sunna had come down in _ḥadīth_ reports transmitted by one, or possibly two or more individuals. The Sunna did not carry the absolute guarantee of authenticity that marked the _mutawātir_ Qur'ān texts, which, besides, were of divine authorship.

All are agreed, including the Sunna supporters, that no human is quite free from error, not to speak of mendacity. Indeed, the Sunna party themselves not infrequently used this argument, picking and choosing among the reports in circulation. The Sunna party were surely wrong in placing their unbounded trust in reports which they then elevated to the level of the Book of God, granting the Sunna the same source status as the Qur'ān, and, in the derivation of the Law, using it to extend or restrict the rulings of the revealed Book.

This severe attitude could not prosper. Too many matters of urgent concern to the _fuqahā'_ were simply unmentioned in the Qur'ān. Other basic matters alluded to in the Qur'ān, such as prayer, fasting, ritual purification, inheritances, sales and the like, were referred to perfunctorily and in terms too general and imprecise to be of assistance in the extraction of the practical rules required for everyday purposes. That these matters were mentioned in the Book indicated that they were intended to be acted upon. The earlier generations had had to reach for every scrap of exegetical and legal information available in *ḥadīths*.

> Some of us met to exchange *ḥadīth* reports. One fellow said, 'Enough of this! Refer to the Book of God.' ʿImrān b. Ḥuṣain said, 'You're a fool! Do you find in the Book of God the prayers explained in detail? Or the Fast? The Qur'ān refers to them in general terms only. It is the Sunna which supplies the detailed explanation.'[7]

The tendency to exaggerate the sufficiency of the divine revelation provided in the Qur'ān was answered by the tendency to exaggerate man's inability to fathom the intention underlying the divine word without the guidance offered by the community's past practice.

The arguments of the Sunna party are most clearly and in most detail presented in the writings of Šāfiʿī, their greatest spokesman (d. A.H. 204). Stressing the frequency with which Qur'ān verses could be taken in more than one sense, and arguing from the familiar principle that, having taken the trouble after so many centuries of error, ignorance and deviation from the divinely approved path to send His Prophet into the world, God would not then have left mankind in uncertainty, Šāfiʿī insists that God has provided adequate indications of the means by which knowledge of His will on every topic may be secured.

By exegetical subtlety Šāfiʿī wrang from his opponents assent to his view that the Qur'ān imposes upon every Muslim the solemn obligation to obey Muḥammad in all things. References to the *Ḥikma* revealed along with the Book are, he asserts, references to the Sunna. The Qur'ān speaks of the Prophet instructing his people in the Book and the _Ḥikma_ and Šāfi'ī is unaware that Muḥammad had taught his people two things other than the Qur'ān and the Sunna.

The Muslim has therefore no option, he insists, but to seek out the Prophet's decisions and observe them to the letter.

No one scholar is in possession of all the Sunna; but the collective of Sunna specialists are between them aware of all the Prophet's instructions. The Qur'ān's command to obey the Prophet refers precisely to _ḥadīths_, for in no other way can the Prophet's teachings reach us.

The defence and maintenance of the _Fiqh_ renders submission to the Sunna inescapable. Unless we accept the Sunna we cannot counter the arguments of those who challenge certain _Fiqh_ rulings on the ground of their own plausible exegeses. The surest exegesis is that conveyed in a Prophet-_ḥadīth_.

This applies with even greater force to those _Fiqh_ rulings based on the Sunna's indication of which Qur'ān rulings were intended to be general and which specific to the individuals or situations referred to in the verses. That distinction had been vital to the patient elaboration of the Law. The categories of persons whom the Muslims have agreed to exclude from general Qur'ān rulings could not otherwise have been identified than by the relevant rulings transmitted in the Sunna.

Similarly, the only sure indication of the repeal of any Qur'ān ruling and the only reliable pointer to the later, repealing ruling is that afforded by the Sunna. The Sunna served an even wider purpose than merely the elucidation of Qur'ān statements.

In Šāfiʿī's view, it had complemented and even extended the Qur'ān's regulations. The Sunna had independently legislated for the Muslims on matters nowhere referred to in the Qur'ān. But it was the Qur'ān by its insistence on acceptance of the Sunna that had sanctioned this extra-Qur'ānic legislative role of the Sunna. The Qur'ān approved and endorsed the Sunna rulings, otherwise it would have repealed them.

The soundest indication of sound Qur'ān exegesis is the _Fiqh_ on which the Muslims are unanimous. The individual might, but the community cannot, err in the discovery of the divine intention.

No _madhab_ permits unbeliever-believer inheritance; slave-free man inheritance; homicide-victim inheritance. All _madāhib_ accept the testimony of two male witnesses in homicide cases. These and many other agreed principles and procedures are unmentioned in the Qur'ān.

Šāfiʿī asserts that the Sunna is guaranteed. The _Ḥadīth_ specialists impose demands on _ḥadīth_-transmitters more onerous than those imposed upon witnesses. Many a Muslim, acceptable as witness, would be quite unacceptable as _ḥadīth_-transmitter. Witnesses number only two, yet we act without hesitation on their testimony in life-and-death matters. Transmitters are many and security of knowledge is assured when they corroborate each other. We ought to act without hesitation on the information they supply.

Only in certain minor matters have the Muslims been permitted to exercise personal judgment, as in determining the direction of Mecca at prayer time. Different men reach different conclusions. All are right. Each had honestly exercised his judgment. That was all that was required of him. The result must be valid. Only arbitrary decisions are prohibited in Islam. The principle itself is illustrated in a Prophet-ḥadīth which Šāfiʿī adduces in support of his view.[8]

It will be noted that, in the person of Šāfiʿī, the Sunna party directed their propaganda indifferently at two unrelated groups: the strict Qur'ān party and others who appealed, in addition to the Qur'ān, to sources other than the Sunna of the Prophet.

In his discussion of the relative primacy as source of Qur'ān and Sunna, that is, in what would seem to be a discussion on naskh, Šāfiʿī shows himself particularly concerned to argue that the Sunna of the Prophet could not be held to have ever been abrogated because, as the word of a prophet, it could not be thought to have been superseded by the word of any mere mortal. This adds nothing to the discussion on the relative status of Qur'ān and Sunna. His immediate objective would seem, rather, to have been to establish a theoretical basis on which the special class of ḥadīth attributed to the Prophet could be securely placed above reports from other Muslims, namely the Companions and Successors.[9]

The practice adopted in the maḏāhib of ignoring reports from the Prophet in favour of ḥadīths from others particularly provoked Šāfiʿī's invective. The maḏāhib's weakness was in fact their inconsistency. Reference to Prophet-*ḥadīths* whenever these are available provides consistency. Reference to others he unfairly characterises as arbitrary. Only Prophet reports set aside Prophet reports.

To preserve the Sunna, Šāfiʿī ferreted out all Qur'ān references to the obligation to obey Muḥammad. He finally so closely bound up the Sunna with the Qur'ān that to question or reject the one was made to appear tantamount to questioning or rejecting the other. Šāfiʿī delivers assertions on the subject, but in fact he never came to grips with the problem of the relative primacy of the Qur'ān and the Sunna sources. His aim was to establish the legitimacy of reference to the Sunna of rulings absent from, or treated differently, in the Qur'ān.

Conflict between any single Qur'ān text and any single Prophet-*ḥadīth* led to the elaboration of Šāfiʿī's ingenious theory of *takhṣīṣ* (exclusion) which lies quite outside his theory of *naskh*. Conflict between Qur'ān and Sunna is only apparent. To admit otherwise would have led to the wholesale abandonment of numerous *Fiqh* *aḥkām* sustainable only by referring them to the Sunna. The Sunna explains occasional exclusion from general rulings.

The gravity of the challenge from the Qur'ān party lay of course not in the justice of their claim. No Muslim could question the claim that the Qur'ān be seen to be the primary source. Šāfiʿī's work did precisely that, although he thought he was questioning the claim that the Qur'ān was the only source.

Schacht has shown in the parallel case of the impact

upon the madāhib of the challenge from the Sunna party that the real danger to be apprehended by the madāhib was the threat of disturbance to the legal doctrine itself by the demands of the stricter theory. The madāhib responded to the challenge not by rejecting the work of generations and agreeing to jettison elements of their Fiqh. Like Šāfiʿī, they preserved the Fiqh but adjusted its documentation in conformity with the novel theory.

Šāfiʿī met the challenge to the Fiqh represented in the exclusive claim advanced on behalf of the Qur'ān by improving the documentation of the Sunna's claim. Addressing his opponents on their own terms, he extracted from the Qur'ān, often with scant regard for the context, every single verse of service to his thesis that the first ruling that might be derived from the Qur'ān was that a Muslim must accept the Sunna of the Prophet. One of his favourite verses, 'Whatsoever the Prophet gives you accept it; whatsoever he denies you, abandon',[10] occurs in a verse on the division of the spoils of war. Another of his favourite arguments, a ḥadīth which requires acceptance of ḥadīths, is merely circular.[11]

The quality of his arguments makes it plain that, as with the madāhib, Šāfiʿī's concern is to preserve every single ḥukm of his Fiqh. He was determined to yield nothing to the Qur'ān party. He saw that what must be done was so to interweave the Sunna with the divine command to obey Muḥammad that the dangers threatening to wipe out whole areas of the Fiqh could be repelled.[12]

If Qur'ān and Sunna could be shown to be twin aspects of the divine revelation they could never be held to be in actual conflict. The Qur'ān frequently identified the will of Muḥammad with the will of God. Šāfi'ī copied this by identifying the Sunna with the will of the Prophet. His brilliance in tackling a serious challenge to the Fiqh lay in replying to the Qur'ān party in their own language and on their own terms. Insisting upon the Qur'ān source, they would have been deaf to any attempted justification of the Sunna source; indeed there is none other than Šāfi'ī's argument that it is the Qur'ān source itself which commands reference to and adherence to the Sunna source.

Dealing with two incompatible assaults on the Sunna from different directions, he attempted, but failed, to answer additional unrelated questions. Šāfi'ī discovered in the Qur'ān a rationale to secure his school's claims on behalf of reference to the Sunna of the Prophet against attack from both the Qur'ān party and those maḏāhib resting the documentation of the Fiqh upon ḥadīths from persons other than the Prophet. Now that the principle of abrogation had been added to the armoury of the uṣūlī, he perceived the dangers that still threatened the Fiqh. Had the Qur'ān party pressed home the attack, they must have gained the day for the claim that in cases of Qur'ān-Sunna conflict, the Qur'ān source must prevail. Šāfi'ī failed to adduce a conclusive argument that the Qur'ān lacked the force to overcome the Sunna, the corollary he alleged of the argument that the Sunna lacked the force to overcome the Qur'ān. He failed to provide the uṣūlī with unequivocal guidance on the problem of Qur'ān-Sunna conflict. He obscured the issue of Qur'ān-Sunna naskh and his rigidity on the question affected its future discussion.

Šāfiʿī might be said to have ushered in the age of classical uṣūl al fiqh, in the sense that after him the term Sunna is normally a reference to the Sunna of the Prophet. Although not the first to employ the concept of the Sunna of the Prophet, he was the first major scholar to make that concept the corner-stone of a systematic methodology. The emphasis he laid on Qur'ān and Sunna as joint sources of the Fiqh entitles him to be regarded as the first major scholar to treat Islam as a divine revelation in the elaboration of which only revealed sources had a legitimate role to play.

His brilliant response to the threats posed to the Sunna secured the Sunna against any claim that it might be superseded by another source, whether that was ḥadīths from others than the Prophet, or rulings that might be adduced from the Qur'ān. But by arguing that only Qur'ān rulings had superseded Qur'ān rulings, and that Qur'ān rulings had superseded only Qur'ān rulings; that only Sunna rulings had superseded Sunna rulings, and that Sunna rulings had superseded only Sunna rulings, he had unwittingly sharpened the sense of the separateness of the two sources.[13] That in turn emphasised afresh the gulf separating Fiqh and Sunna from the Qur'ān.

Šāfiʿī failed to address himself directly to that problem. Its solution dates from the post-Šāfiʿī period in the renewed discussions on naskh, the course of which, however, was already predetermined by the principles which Šāfiʿī had established.

An extension of the slogans mentioned above, 'The

Sunna is the judge of the Book, it elucidates it', perfectly mirrors Šāfiʿī's position.[14] His uṣūl are based on stressing this definition of the role of the Sunna vis-à-vis the rulings established in the Qur'ān. The principle that the Sunna had not superseded the Qur'ān in fact plays only a very minor role in his theory. Indeed, it is never applied to actual cases, but occurs simply as part of his methodological argument, where he seeks to give the impression that it is based in turn upon a Qur'ān ruling. This suggests that the terms of this passage were forced upon Šāfiʿī by the arguments of the Qur'ān party.[15]

The principle that the Sunna had never superseded the Qur'ān was thus a defensive posture into which Šāfiʿī was forced by opposition to the Sunna. It may be that that principle was the price Šāfiʿī realised he would have to pay to give the corollary principle, that the Qur'ān had never superseded the Sunna, the appearance of having been derived from the same Qur'ān ruling, Q 2.106, which we shall examine more fully below.

Šāfiʿī realised that any claim that the Sunna, even on one topic, had superseded the Qur'ān could with ease have been reversed. His scrupulous abstention from any such claim may account for the frequent complexity and obscurity of his language.

Following and largely owing to Šāfiʿī's brilliant advocacy, the threat posed for the Sunna, and hence for certain elements of the Fiqh, had been averted. The Sunna emerged triumphant and the following generation could busy themselves with the compilation of the great *Ḥadīth* collections.

In reporting Šāfiʻī's debates with the Qur'ān party we noted that his reaction in defence of the *Fiqh* had resulted in an improvement of the technical arguments for appeal to the Sunna. The Qur'ān source was made to appear to require appeal to the Sunna source.

An alternative and simpler technique for placing one's *Fiqh* views under the aegis of the Qur'ān was quite simply to change the Qur'ān texts. This method worked both to defend the local *Fiqh* against other *maḏāhib* and to defend the commonly agreed *Fiqh* against the objections of the Qur'ān party who drew attention to the texts preserved in the book (the *muṣḥaf*).

We earlier handled the case of the *ṭawāf* between Ṣafā and Marwa on which there had been disagreement. The *Fiqh* had, we were told, evolved in a way which suggested that the *ṭawāf* might on no account be omitted. This *ḥukm* was challenged. In a *ḥadīth*, ʻUrwa represented the protest of those who were inclined to argue that the wording of Q 2.158 indicated, on the contrary, that the observance was quite optional. Performance or neglect of the *ṭawāf* was at the discretion of the individual.

However, those who viewed the observance as obligatory, and who are represented in the report by the figure of ʻĀ'iša, justified their view by the bald assertion that the Prophet had established the sunna of performing the *ṭawāf*, whence it was to be regarded as obligatory. The Sunna of the Prophet had settled the dispute as to the interpretation of the verse. Had the divine intention been to declare the *ṭawāf* optional, that would have been indicated by a different reading.

Farrā' (A.H. 207) reports: 'Some Muslims read Q 2.158: "There shall be no blame on him if he do not perform the *ṭawāf*."' He comments that this reading can be explained in one of two ways:

1. That the negative is linguistically inoperative. cf. Q 7.12: '*mā mana'aka an lā tasjuda*', which of course means *an tasjuda*.
2. Alternatively, the *ṭawāf* may be entirely optional. But the first explanation is the basis of the practice.[16]

Ṭabarī (A.H. 310) reports the views of the *maḏāhib*. Šāfi'ī's opinion was that the *ṭawāf* is an essential and indispensable *ḥajj* rite. Anyone omitting it must return to Mecca to perform it.[17]

Mālik, Thawrī and the Ḥanafīs, while not insisting that he return and perform it, would impose on anyone omitting this *ṭawāf* a special sin-offering.

'Aṭā' regarded the *ṭawāf* as entirely optional. This view, Ṭabarī explains, was explicitly derived from the variant reading of Q 2.158 transmitted in the *muṣḥaf* of 'Abdullāh b. Mas'ūd. The same is reported from Anas, ibn 'Abbās and Mujāhid.

Thus, on this topic we are left in no possible doubt that for some the practice was at variance with the Qur'ān. The practice was held to derive from the Sunna. The partisans of a particular *Fiqh* attitude appealed to the Sunna; the opponents appealed to the Qur'ān. This provokes the upholders of the practice to look again at the Qur'ān. As long as the dispute centred upon the words of the Qur'ān, both sides acknowledged a common reading, disputing the exegesis. It is not at this stage self-evident that the practice represents the most natural meaning of the verse, least of all when one considers the gravity of the view taken of omission of the *ṭawāf* by the *fuqahā'*.

The really interesting point is, however, that when the discussion advanced beyond the exegetical stage, the proponents of the practice next seek their support in the Sunna, whereas their opponents improve upon the wording of the Qur'ān, inserting a word and appealing to the authority of a Companion of the Prophet, from whom not merely a variant reading, but a variant Qur'ān had apparently been transmitted. The alleged variant reading unmistakably proceeded from one of two rival and competing interpretations. To that extent the reading arose at a secondary stage.

A practice which does not immediately commend itself to the reader as the most natural meaning of the verse had been challenged by scholars referring to the same verse. After an initial unsatisfactory appeal to the Qur'ān to document the usage, support was finally discovered in the Sunna. Thus usage and Sunna were both placed in conscious opposition to the Qur'ān. The Sunna is guaranteed by 'Ā'iša, a widow of the Prophet, in a Companion-sunna-*ḥadīth*. This appeal to the Sunna is countered by what presumably was thought to be an even stronger argument in favour of the opposite view, that is, renewed appeal to the Qur'ān by means of a

Companion-Qur'ān-*ḥadīth*.

Methodologically expressed, this means that some thought that the Sunna (as the Prophet's implicit exegesis) adequately countered the Qur'ān. Their opponents considered that the Companion variant (as the Companion's report on the Prophet's explicit exegesis) was the 'superior' argument, hence to be preferred in documenting their opinion. Four elements are involved: the practice (*Fiqh*); the Qur'ān; appeal to the Sunna; a second Qur'ān (i.e. counter-appeal to the Qur'ān now suitably amended by interpolation with reference to a Companion-*muṣḥaf*).

The interpolation favours a counter-*Fiqh* and, it must be emphasised, was originally hypothetical: 'Were the case as you allege the verse would read differently.' It next appeared as the reading of certain anonymous Muslims. Finally it emerged as the ascertained reading of a contemporary of Muḥammad. In other words, this reading has always been recognised as at variance with the Qur'ān text. When acceptance of a variant reading had been won, it could nevertheless still be neutralised by further appeal to the Qur'ān. The Companion reading supplies the exegesis of the Qur'ān. Suitably neutralised, the Companion reading is harmonised with the Qur'ān reading and held to be the basis of the practice. One perceives that, throughout, the really significant factor is the practice, that is, the *Fiqh*.

The wheel of argument turned full circle. Some were content to rest the documentation of the practice on the Sunna. Others evinced an irresistible desire to have the Qur'ān appear to be the primary source - that is, although in this instance their effort failed, some sought to use the Qur'ān to counter the Qur'ān.

We had supposed that the Fiqh had derived from the Qur'ān. We now observe how a particular Qur'ān derived from a particular Fiqh.

The implication of the reference to the variant reading ascribed to ʿAbdullāh is that, in the field of the Qur'ān, information reported from the Companions (i.e. appeals to the Companion sources) conflicts in phase with conflicts in the information reported from the Companions in the Sunna field. Both appeals originated from conflicts in Companion information in the legal field.

Anas recited: hiya ašaddu waṭ'an wa aṣwabu qīlan. Someone pointed out that the 'correct' reading was aqwamu; aqwamu, he retorted, aṣwabu, ahya'u - they're all the same![18]

Muḥammad b. Sīrīn said, 'We read, "in kānat illā ṣaiḥa wāḥida." ʿAbdullāh reads, "illā zaqya wāḥida."'[19]

Q 5.89 regulates the penalties for breach of oaths. Among these is a three days' fast and the Ḥanafīs argue that the fast should be consecutive. ʿAbdullāh is said to read, 'a fast of three [consecutive] days'.[20]

Šāfiʿī argued that, as the Qur'ān did not stipulate that it should be consecutive, the Muslim was free to decide whether to fast on consecutive or separate days. The Q 5.89 fast should be read on the analogy of the substitute fast imposed for breach of Ramaḍān. The Qur'ān merely says, 'a similar number of days' (Q 2.183).[21]

Ġazālī argues,

> The fast in expiation for a breach of one's oath need not be consecutive, even if ʿAbdullāh did read, 'three [consecutive] days'. This reading is not universally acknowledged to be the Qur'ān text. Perhaps ʿAbdullāh adduced this reading in order to elucidate what he took to be a justifiable exegesis. Or, perhaps he may have attracted to Q 5.89, by analogy, the word 'consecutive', which does occur in Q 58.4. Abū Ḥanīfa, conceding that the reading is not Qur'ānic, accepted it, but as a _ḥadīth_. The practice however, should be based exclusively on what is explicitly attributed to the Prophet.[22]

Sarakhsī (A.H. 490) a Ḥanafī, argued,

> The fast in expiation of a breach of oath is consecutive on the basis of ʿAbdullāh's reading which was in circulation as late as the time of Abū Ḥanīfa, but did not turn out to be _mutawātir_, the sole criterion for inclusion in the _muṣḥaf_. No one can question ʿAbdullāh's veracity, nor his memory. We can but conclude that the word 'consecutive' was part of the original wording of the Qur'ān and has been preserved in ʿAbdullāh's reading. The word was apparently withdrawn in the lifetime of the Prophet. The Muslims were caused to forget it, with the exception of ʿAbdullāh who was honoured with its preservation, in order to preserve the ruling. The isolate sunna-_ḥadīth_ may establish a practice: the isolate Qur'ān-_ḥadīth_ can do no less.[23]

The same variant reading was attributed to Ubayy who, in addition, was credited with reading Q 4.24, a verse charged with significance for the Muslim law on marriage, in a variant version: _fa mā stamtaʿtum bihi minhunna [ilā ajalin musamman]_.[24]

Although it may have implications for the view that

may be formed of the manner of the textual transmission of the Qur'ān, it matters not a whit to the Qur'ān's revealed status whether one reads aṣwabu, aqwamu, or ahya'u; ṣaiḥa or zaqya. These are more or less synonymous.

On the contrary, it was of the highest significance to the incessant inter-madhhab polemic whether one read Q 5.89 or Q 4.24 with or without ʿAbdullāh's or Ubayy's reported interpolations. Only with the Ubayy interpolation does Q 4.24 sanction the doctrine of mutʿa, or temporary marriage, rejection of which was elsewhere being propounded on the basis of information from a third Companion of the Prophet as a part of the Sunna. Evidently the Qur'ān, in the form of the Ubayy reading, is playing the role of a counter-sunna, rather, a counter-exegesis, the function of the Ubayy interpolation being to gloss and bring out the full meaning of the root of stamtaʿtum, m t ʿ.

The Muslims were fully alive to the import of variant readings: 'The differences in the readings indicate the differences in the legal rulings.'[25]

> Two opposing doctrines - the invalidation of the ritual purity [wuḍū'] and the contrary doctrine - could both be referred to the Qur'ān, according as the contending fuqahā' read: lamastum/lāmastum; or the permissibility of sexual intercourse with the menstruating woman at the expiry of her period but before she has cleansed herself, and the contrary doctrine, according as they read either yaṭhurna or yaṭṭahirna.
>
> There is an interesting discussion on verses yielding two-fold readings. Abū al Laith reported two views: 1. God had uttered them both; 2. God had uttered only one, but permitted the verse to be read

> in two possible ways. Samarqandī's own view was that if each of the two readings was susceptible of a distinct interpretation and legal application, God had uttered both. In such instances, the two readings were the equivalent of two distinct revelations. If the two readings yielded a single meaning, God had uttered only one reading, but permitted the other, owing to the differences between the dialects of the peninsular Arabs.

Q 5.6, the verse imposing the wuḍū' yielded a two-fold reading, the distinction this time residing in the vowelling. 'The verse was revealed to sanction two distinct legal doctrines:
arjulakum - enjoined the washing of the feet
arjulikum - permitted the wiping of the feet.'[26]

Rather, the differences over the Fiqh on this question had called forth the differences in reading. Šāfiʿī (Ikhtilāf, p. 204) stipulates the accusative reading. He bases his Fiqh argument in support of the permissibility of wiping the feet (more precisely, the wiping of the boots), which he simultaneously upholds, exclusively upon an alleged concession documented in the Sunna of the Prophet.[27]

Factors affecting variant readings thus far, are: dialect differences; interpolation; vowel choice; synonyms.

> Abū ʿUbaid [A.H. 224], in his Faḍā'il al Qur'ān, stated that the function of the isolate reading was the elucidation of the mašhūr reading. For example, ʿĀ'iša's reading, which she shared with Ḥafṣa: wa al ṣalāt al wusṭā ṣalāt alʿaṣr.[28]

Compare this with Ṭabarī's reports (Tafsīr, vol. 5, pp. 168-98): ʿAlī, ibn ʿAbbās, Abū Huraira, ʿAbdullāh b. ʿUmar, Abū Saʿīd al Khudrī all interpreted the verse as referring to the ʿaṣr. The reading in ʿĀ'iša's muṣḥaf identified al ṣalāt al wusṭā with ṣalāt al ʿaṣr. Umm Salama and Ḥafṣa both ordered their scribes to write the verse in the same way in their private codices. Finally, we are informed that the Prophet identified the wusṭā with the ʿaṣr.

Another case in point is ʿAbdullāh's reading of Q 5. 38: faqṭaʿū aimānahum (for aidiyahum).

> These and similar instances provide the exegesis of the Qur'ānic texts... By degrees, what was originally exegesis penetrated into the actual reading. This is more common than exegesis and better founded. At the least, the readings show the correctness of the tafsīr.[29]

The variant readings were classed then as isolate and the legitimacy of deriving legal rulings from them was long debated: Šāfiʿī does not have a statement on the question, but

> what may be deduced from his practice is that he thought it not permissible. Those who took his view argued that the isolate reading had been transmitted as Qur'ān, whereas it is not. Those who permit the derivation of a ruling from the isolate reading plead the analogy of the isolate ḥadīth. This line was approved by ibn al Subkī in Jamʿ al Jawāmiʿ, and our madhab adduce as evidence of the legitimacy of basing a ruling on a variant reading the practice of cutting off the right hand of the thief on the ground of ʿAbdullāh's reading, also adduced by Abū Ḥanīfa. He further adduced ʿAbdullāh's reading in arguing that the fast in expiation of the breach of an oath is consecutive. We do not accept this view because that reading has been repealed.[30]

The isolate reading is analogous to the isolate ḥadīth, yet was distinguished from it.

Impeccability of the isnād alone was insufficient guarantee that the reading was Qur'ānic. Further restrictions were imposed upon it, as will be seen.

The majority of the variant readings came to be regarded as little more than exegeses that had gradually crept into the texts transmitted from the Companions. It is reported of Ubayy that he read: kullamā aḍā'a lahum mašaw fīhi [marrū fīhi saʿaw fīhi][31] and from ʿAbdullāh that he read: lilladīna āmanū anẓirūnā [amhilūnā akhkhirūnā].[32]

Related to the reading just attributed to Ubayy, is the statement that the transmission of the reading, famḍū ilā dikr allāh, showed that the meaning of the Qur'ān's fasʿaw is 'go!' rather than 'run!' or 'hurry!'.[33]

In Ṭaḥāwī's view, the frequency of variants was the result of the first generation's inexperience of verbatim oral transmission of texts together with their ignorance of the art of writing.[34]

Like the isolate ḥadīth, the isolate reading had originated with the Companions, and the scholars were divided on the question of alleging a Qur'ānic origin for rulings derived from these isolate readings.

On one aspect of the use of the Qur'ān variants, the scholars were, however, undivided. They are unanimously of the view that use of an isolate Qur'ān reading in the ritual prayer is quite irregular and renders the prayer invalid.

This attitude of the scholars introduces a wedge between the Qur'ān and the Sunna and discloses an awareness that the two sources were not in fact similar in nature or function.

The analogy which permitted some to derive legal rulings from the isolate Qur'ān reading, as they had derived rulings from the isolate _ḥadīth_, had occurred in a context where both types of report were relevant to the use that may be made of the sources of the Law.

The unanimity of the scholars in condemning the use of the isolate reading at prayer occurs, on the contrary, in a context in which the Qur'ān is seen as a document.

Variations have frequently been alleged in the appeals to the Qur'ān source. Deviation has never been permitted from the Qur'ān document.[35]

Impeccability of the _isnād_ was insufficient guarantee that the variant reading was Qur'ānic. The scholars classified two kinds of reading variant:

1. What is transmitted in reliable reports, conforms with Arabic usage and coincides with the written text.
2. Isolate transmissions which conform with Arabic usage but do not coincide with the written text.

The second readings may be accepted but may not be employed at prayer for two reasons: they vary from what has been sanctioned by the consensus (i.e. from the texts recorded in the _muṣḥaf_); and they are based upon isolate reports, whereas the _muṣḥaf_ is _mutawātir_.

The first class of readings consist of minor variations upon the vowel/consonant rendering of the universally acknowledged text. The second class of variants show frank departures from the agreed text.

To deny any of the reported isolate readings is deplorable conduct. To deny any fragment of the universally acknowledged Qur'ān text as transmitted in the *muṣḥaf* is unbelief (*kufr*).[36]

The Qur'ān party by their assault upon the role allotted to the Sunna as a source for the derivation of the Law had provoked two types of reaction from the defenders of the existing *Fiqh*.

They pushed Šāfiʿī to assert that it was the Qur'ān source which enjoined reference to the Sunna source. This attitude is summarised in Šāfiʿī's slogan, 'the *ḥukm* of Muḥammad is the *ḥukm* of God'.[37]

Other scholars reacted by attempting to strengthen the visible links between their legal views and the Qur'ān texts. In other words, they improved the text, a technique that could be applied in defence of their local *Fiqh* against other *maḏāhib*, but also in defence of the commonly agreed *Fiqh* against protests based on the texts as preserved in the universally agreed *muṣḥaf*.

Companion readings of the kind adduced on the occasion of the quarrel over Q 2.158 show that in both Qur'ān and Sunna fields alike, appeals to the Companions conflict, as befits evidence brought to support conflicting legal viewpoints. For the Sunna, there are Companion-sunna-*ḥadīths*; for the Qur'ān, there are variant readings, that is, Companion-Qur'ān-*ḥadīths*. Companion readings vary from the universally acknowledged readings and Companion-*muṣḥafs* vary from the universally acknowledged *muṣḥaf*.

The *mutawātir muṣḥaf* is held to have come into its present form and condition only after the death of the Prophet. Muḥammad, having had no hand in its compilation and collection, the Qur'ān as we know it we owe to the labours of certain of his associates.[38]

Variant readings were attributed to individual Companions, and it came to be assumed that those readings had figured in the personal copies of the Qur'ān which those Companions had drawn up for themselves during the days of the Qur'ān's revelation to the Prophet.

The first stage in the history of the Qur'ān texts had been marked by the circulation in the regions of these parallel, not quite identical, recensions independently prepared by their several owners.

As the Companion-sunna-ḥadīths have come down, each equipped with its isnād, the Companion-Qur'ān-ḥadīths have come down, each equipped with its isnād.

Companion-sunna-ḥadīths, in Šāfiʿī's day and since, have been distinguished from and compared with ḥadīth reports coming down from the Prophet. That was a necessary stage in the definition of the Sunna.

Companion-muṣḥafs have similarly been distinguished from and compared with the mutawātir muṣḥaf coming down from the Companions responsible for its first collection. Since its collection, following the death of the Prophet, there has, however, been no need to define the mutawātir muṣḥaf. It was universally known and it was universally used - at prayer. That is, it was both source and document.

Variant readings reported from Companions played their role in inter-madhab disputes on legal points. Variant ḥadīth reports reported from Companions played their role in the very same disputes. Only the mutawātir Qur'ān text might be solemnly recited; only that text rendered the prayer valid.[39]

The implication of the concern with the *isnād* of the variant Qur'ān reading is quite simply that it was seen by the Muslims as but another element in their Tradition. This brings it into the range of the ideas of Goldziher and Schacht. Production of Qur'ānic evidence responded to the demand of those dissatisfied with Sunna evidence.

With the development of the concept of the Sunna of the Prophet, a device to overcome the difficulty that juridical sunnas reported from a wide variety of Companions tended to contradict each other, one finds Companion-*ḥadīths* evolving into Prophet-*ḥadīths*. It was necessary only to extend the *isnād* by one stage.[40] Having regard to their origin, many *ḥadīths* reported as from the Prophet contradict each other. This led to *isnād* study. *Ḥadīths* transmitted via Companions of later conversion date came to be regarded, since later, as abrogating *ḥadīths* from Companions of earlier date.

One finds, however, no parallel evidence of Companion readings, where these go against the texts of the *mutawātir muṣḥaf*, evolving into Prophet readings.

Rather, one is aware of a consistent sense that the Companion readings are at odds with a vigorous textual tradition, independent of all *maḏāhib* and, to all appearances, not amenable to manipulation. This very inflexibility suggests, indeed, that the reverse of the Sunna situation obtained in the Qur'ān field.

As a document, the Qur'ān had existed and was widely known before it was called upon to behave as the source of the *uṣūlīs* in their inter-regional dispute. We have seen that the *isnād* technique was applied to the reported Qur'ān variants.

The differences between the *madhāhib* centred upon the details of the *Fiqh* doctrines. When the Qur'ān had begun to be demanded as the primary source in the *uṣūlīs'* consideration of the documentation adduced in support of the varying legal viewpoints, each *madhhab* reached for the Qur'ān.

For Sunna documentation purposes, the teachings of the *madhhab* had been traced to the stock of Sunna information transmitted from the Companions under whose aegis the school had placed its *Fiqh*. By analogy, the same technique was now extended into the Qur'ān field. A variant reading was attributed to the school's Companion eponym. But the local *Fiqh* can occasionally be fitted to the Qur'ān texts only by means of an interpolation. Suitable words would be concocted and inserted in the reports on the text of the *muṣḥaf* ascribed to the *madhhab*'s Companion patron.

Like the appeals to the Sunna, the appeals to the Qur'ān from time to time clash. The same remedy, that is, consideration of the *isnād* in terms of the late or early date of a man's conversion, was applied.

Certain of the legal conclusions for which, at this stage in the development of *uṣūl al fiqh* studies, Qur'ān documentation was being peremptorily demanded are quite unmentioned in our Qur'ān texts. These were legal conclusions of a more than merely local or regional character. We have in mind certain _aḥkām_, to be examined in greater detail below which were upheld by the majority of the _maḏāhib_ in all the regions but which were under attack from the Qur'ān party for the very reason that they were nowhere referred to in the Qur'ān, as we know it. In their case, the revelations relevant to their documentation were referred by the _maḏāhib_, not merely to the _muṣḥafs_ of the Companions to whom they traditionally appealed, but to the Qur'ān. Two factors underlay this procedure, one entirely exegetical in origin, the other jurisprudential.

3 The sub-science of *naskh*

The terms *naskh* or *al nāsikh wa al mansūkh*, despite the *uṣūlīs*' habit of treating them in a single chapter, refer not to one but to three methodological principles. They are quite unconnected with each other, and each has evolved from its own evidentiary base to supply three distinct needs in separate Islamic sciences.

That there are indeed three modes of *naskh* has never been the universal view of the Muslims.[1] The majority acknowledged only two modes and this further division of opinion will help solve the mystery of the origin of the third mode.

That the three modes have little in common is best shown by an analysis of the *naskh* formulae.[2]

NASKH AL ḤUKM WA AL TILĀWA

This principle refers to the suppression of both the ruling and the wording. It is of relevance to Qur'ān studies only, since it is impossible to conceive of any *hadīth* whose ruling and wording have both been suppressed but which nevertheless merited discussion.

In the exploitation of the Qur'ān source for *Fiqh* documentation purposes, it might also be supposed that the reference in the formula to the suppression of the ruling would render the material irrelevant. There could be no access to the knowledge of any Qur'ān ruling, any more than to a Sunna ruling, if the wording had been suppressed. But we noted that the Qur'ān, unlike the Sunna, is both document and source. This alerts us to the suspicion that the formula really refers to the allegation that omission from the Qur'ān has occurred. Certain materials, originally part of the revelation, have apparently been omitted from the collected texts.

The rulings have also apparently been suppressed. We are, thus, not discussing naskh at all, and certainly not abrogation. It would seem, therefore, that in their discussions of the Qur'ān and its history, the Muslims eschewed use of the word 'omission', perhaps because omission might suggest either negligence or inadvertence. Neither should be posited of the Prophet or of his Companions by scholars entirely dependent upon that one generation for all their knowledge of the sources. Nor should such words be used of the history of a divine book revealed to a prophet and a generation of saints by the creator of the universe. No man could have been permitted to frustrate the divine design. If so much as a dot has been omitted from the record of the revelation, this can be held to have occurred solely by the intention of the divine author. Omission ought not to be predicated of a divine book, nor inadvertence of its divinely guided recipient.

There are, or there appear to be, references to Muḥammad's forgetting in the Qur'ān:

Q 17.86: If We wished, We could make away with what We have

revealed to you.

Q 87.6-7: We shall teach you to recite it and you will not forget - except what God wills.

Q 2.106 : mā nansakh min āyatin aw nunsi hā na'ti bi khairin min hā aw mithli hā.

Examination of the Muslim commentaries shows clearly that the exegesis of these verses concentrated solely upon the issue of the precise relation between the Qur'ān's references to forgetting and the prophetic office.

For Q 2.106 at least a dozen suggested readings have been recorded - ample evidence of the extent, and hence of the significance, of the dispute as to the meaning. What was eventually settled as the joint exegesis of Q 87 and Q 2 (the interpretation of each of these verses operating upon that of the other) was that there were indeed verses once revealed to Muḥammad as part of the 'total Qur'ān revelation' which, however, have been omitted from the collected texts of the Qur'ān, the muṣḥaf. That had by no means occurred from Muḥammad's having merely forgotten them. Q 87 refers to God's will and Q 2 uses the root n s y in the causative. God had caused Muḥammad to forget in conformity with the mysterious divine intention as to the final contents of the Book of God.

Part of the armoury of those exegetes who had promoted this way of reading Q 87 was a series of ḥadīths designed expressly to give the impression that Muḥammad had forgotten part of the revelations. The reports were specific and detailed enough to identify the actual wording of the verses in question. Anas is reported in the two

Ṣaḥīḥ's as declaring: 'There was revealed concerning those slain at Bi'r Ma'ūna a Qur'ān verse which we recited until it was withdrawn: "Inform our tribe on our behalf that we have met our Lord. He has been well pleased with us and has satisfied our desires."'[3]

That verse had been 'withdrawn'. Concentration upon the divine will, as opposed to mere forgetting, and developments in the exegetical discussion of Q 2.106, where we find both the roots n s kh and n s y in a single context, had led to the accommodation under the general heading of naskh of a type of Qur'ān omission. Muḥammad's supposed forgetting, having been formalised, had been neutralised. A satisfactory means had been found of re-stating a prophet's forgetting in a way that conflicted with no basic theological axiom. The divine revelations had been in no sense hostage to a human weakness. It could be admitted that there were omissions from the muṣḥaf, but those were solely due to the intentions of the divine author.

NASKH AL ḤUKM DŪNA AL TILĀWA

The second mode of naskh alleges the replacement of the ruling of an earlier statement by the ruling of a later statement. This is the only one of the three modes of naskh which properly corresponds to our concept of abrogation. This is par excellence the naskh of the uṣūlīs and the formula is so worded as to adapt it for application to either Qur'ān or Sunna. The Qur'ān abrogates the Qur'ān; the Sunna abrogates the Sunna. On these two principles, the majority of the uṣūlīs were agreed.

As to whether the Qur'ān abrogates the Sunna, or the Sunna abrogates the Qur'ān, unanimity was not achieved. The two principles were readily accepted by the majority, and strenuously resisted by the Šāfi'ites.

We earlier touched upon the technique of alleging abrogation when appeals to the sources conflicted. Since that was the business of the uṣūlīs, it cannot be surprising if, to underpin their assumptions, they once more appeal to the Qur'ān source to verify the general thesis that abrogation has indeed affected the Qur'ān and the Sunna. The appeal to the Qur'ān is indicated by the choice of technical term. The word they hit upon to denote their general theory of abrogation, naskh, was selected precisely on account of its occurrence in Q 2.106 which they interpreted: 'Whatsoever verse of the Qur'ān We abrogate, or cause to be forgotten, We shall bring another like it, or superior to it.'

The charm of their verificatory exegeses is self-evident: consigning to oblivion by causing to forget is presented in the more attractive formal attire of naskh, or conscious suppression, expressed in the theorem: naskh al ḥukm wa al tilāwa. Q 2.106's separate terms n s kh and n s y are here fused into one.

Playing fast and loose with the legal rulings that might be derived from the verses of the revelation to bring them into harmony with the rulings of the Fiqh was similarly made to sound respectable and legitimate by reference to conscious supersession: naskh al ḥukm, the replacement of the Qur'ān ruling, despite the survival in the muṣḥaf of the

Qur'ān's wording.

Use was made of the Qur'ān source to reinforce both modes. The first, suppression, was to be 'proved' by incidental reference to Q 17 and to Q 87, while the second, supersession, was confidently endorsed by appeal to Q 16.101: idā baddalnā āya makāna āya, 'Whenever We substitute one āya for another'. Tabdīl, replacement, an undeniable divine activity, was equated with another undeniable divine activity, naskh. Q 2.106 refers, it was alleged, to substitution, replacement, abrogation.[4]

The development of notions about the Qur'ān's i'jāz, interpreted to mean its literary inimitability, meant that the minority of scholars who objected to the use made of Q 2.106, to 'prove' that the Qur'ān itself proclaimed that one verse had been revealed to supersede another, were able to exploit the same verse. God said that on the naskh of a verse He would bring a better verse. Since the Qur'ān is of divine authorship, and is perfect in construction and style, no verse can be better than another verse. All verses are equally perfect. No sunna, of acknowledged human origin, is similar, let alone superior to any verse in the Book of God.

To both protests, the uṣūlīs could return a single answer: It is precisely because the Qur'ān is inimitable, no one verse being superior to another and no sunna equal, let alone superior to a single verse of the Qur'ān, that the exegetes, following the indications of the Qur'ān and of reason, had appreciated that the abrogation had affected not the wording of the Qur'ān, but only its rulings.[5]

Šāfiʿī, referring to this same Q 2.106, had insisted that in this verse, God had stated unequivocally that only the Qur'ān abrogates the Qur'ān. The Sunna did not have this prerogative of abrogating the Qur'ān. Its function, secondary to that of the Book, was to establish rulings like those imposed in the Qur'ān. Further, it indicated the interpretation of those verses of the Book which were couched in general terms.

The Qur'ān itself, in Q 10.15, denied that Muḥammad had the prerogative to alter any of the verses of the Qur'ān on his own initiative.[6]

We have already seen that Šāfiʿī's exploitation of Q 2.106 had been dictated by the circumstances prevailing in his day. His approach to the question of abrogation had been two-sided. The denial that the Sunna could be held to have ever superseded the Qur'ān was forced upon him by the realisation that resort to naskh implied conflict. The admission that there was actual, rather than apparent, conflict between the Qur'ān and the Sunna spelled great danger for the Sunna, whilst the claim that the Sunna abrogated the Qur'ān could be reversed by the Qur'ān party, not least on the ground of appeal to na'ti bi khairin min hā aw mithli hā. The Sunna, they argued, was not the equal of the Qur'ān. The Qur'ān was unquestionably superior to the Sunna.

Šāfiʿī's second argument, designed to prevent the maḏāhib, who rested the documentation of much of their Fiqh on reports from Companions and others, from using naskh to justify their ignoring or even setting aside Prophet-ḥadīths, again exploited Q 2.106. He made the point that no

Companion was similar or superior to the Prophet. No Companion-ḥadīth could therefore set aside and supersede a Prophet-ḥadīth.

The schools might argue that none would have known the mind and purpose of the Prophet better than those who had spent their lives in his service. When they transmitted rulings at variance with those conveyed in Prophet reports, that could safely be taken to indicate that the Companions were aware that the Prophet had altered one of his own rulings. Šāfiʿī insisted that we may not act on mere presumption. Only a later report from the Prophet himself stating or indicating that he himself had altered his own ruling was acceptable evidence of the abrogation of a sunna. Only the Sunna of the Prophet abrogated the Sunna of the Prophet.

In the face of this insistence, the maḏāhib could not do other than improve the isnāds of their ḥadīths, projecting the threatened Fiqh backwards from the Successors and the Companions to the Prophet.

In constructing his defence of the appeal to the Sunna, and in defining its role, Šāfiʿī had described it as bringing that which is like the Qur'ān rulings. This motif was itself to become a ḥadīth in which the Prophet was made to claim that he had been given the Qur'ān, and along with it its like. But, as we shall see, what is really a subtle appeal to Q 2.106, 'We shall bring that which is better than it, or like it', was to be exploited, once the threat to the Sunna and hence to the Fiqh had been removed, by scholars seeking to free themselves from the rigidity of Šāfiʿī's impossibly mechanistic arguments.

The Qur'ān party's repudiation of the Sunna was likewise cast in ḥadīth form. 'The Prophet said, Compare what I am reported to have said or done with the Book of God. If it agrees, I did actually say it; if it disagrees, I did not say it.'[7]

Šāfiʿī rejected this ḥadīth on isnād grounds, countering with an isnād which he admits is incomplete: 'The Prophet said, "Don't let me find one of you hearing a command or prohibition from me and saying, 'We shall follow what we find in the Book of God.'"'

To those who besought him to alter the Qur'ān Muḥammad replied, 'It is not for me to alter it on my own initiative. I merely follow what is revealed.'[8]

Šāfiʿī exploited this verse to 'prove' that the Sunna had never superseded the Qur'ān. From the Qur'ān source one could show that the Qur'ān had never been abrogated by the Sunna source.

Šāfiʿī was to progress to the view that the Sunna was revealed. The Qur'ān is waḥy matlū, solemnly recited inspiration; Sunna, waḥy ġair matlū, is non-recited inspiration. To that extent, they are alike.[9]

Šāfiʿī's uṣūl doctrine that Sunna does not abrogate Qur'ān was dictated by the prevailing intellectual circumstances. Once those circumstances altered in favour of the uncomplaining acceptance of the Sunna, owing largely it must be said to Šāfiʿī's brilliant defence of the Sunna, and once the Sunna's survival was assured by the completion of the great medieval collections of Ḥadīth, another result of

Šāfiʿī's triumph, the threat to the Sunna receded. Many scholars could now afford to take a more relaxed attitude to the question of whether the Sunna had abrogated the Qur'ān, or the Qur'ān the Sunna. Lists were drawn up of the instances in which this had been seen to occur on the evidence of the Fiqh.

The Qur'ān's rulings on inheritances, for example, had been abrogated by Prophetic rulings prohibiting believer-unbeliever inheritance and slave-free man inheritance. Bequests to parents and nearest kin had been set aside by the Prophetic dictum that no heir might benefit by bequest. The same Sunna ruling barred the widow from benefit, and had thus set aside both Q 2.180 and Q 2.240. The Prophet had forbidden the marriage of the niece to the husband of her aunt, and a woman to her sister's husband. He had in addition extended the forbidden degrees which prevented marriage to include foster relationships as well as blood ties. Muḥammad had modified the general provisions of the Qur'ān's penalty for theft to exclude the stealing of small cattle left unpenned at night, dates left outside the drying-store, the spadix of the palm and all articles valued at less than a quarter dīnār. To prohibited foodstuffs he had added wild beasts and birds of prey. He had modified the rules governing prayer by permitting the shortening of prayers while on a journey, whether or not danger threatened, and had permitted the mounted traveller to take as his qibla the direction in which his mount was heading.[10]

Those who argue that the Sunna abrogated the Qur'ān appeal to Q 53.4, 'He does not speak from mere whim,'

> and to Q 59.7, 'Whatsoever the Prophet brings you, accept it.' They say that the Muslim has no option but to accept Muḥammad's words. Their opponents retort that Q 59.7 is a reference to whatsoever he brings of the Qur'ān. That we must all accept. Q 53.4 similarly refers to that which he recites of the Qur'ān which comes to him from God. Muḥammad did not get it up out of his own head. This interpretation is confirmed by the continuation of the same verse: 'It is but inspiration.' The reply to this is the argument that the Sunna explains the Qur'ān. Explaining is not abrogating. Besides, the Qur'ān is inimitable, the Sunna is not. What is not inimitable cannot supersede what is. God said, 'We shall bring one better than it, or like it.' The Sunna is created; what is created is not like what is uncreate. God also said, 'When We substitute one verse for another', and, 'Say, "It is not for me to alter it on my own initiative."' All these arguments indicate that the Qur'ān cannot be abrogated save by the Qur'ān.[11]

It is refreshing, if ironical, to see one of Šāfiʿī's regular Qur'ān evidences for fastening adherence to the Sunna around the necks of his opponents now in the hands of those who would argue the abrogation of the Qur'ān by the Sunna.

Q 59.7, in any case, has nothing to do with the Sunna. The verse occurs in a context regulating the distribution and division of spoils of battle.

The exploitation of irrelevant verses exposes the methods adopted in these uṣūl squabbles. But the report does show how dispute had encouraged the Šāfiʿites to sharpen up their tafsīr of the verses.

The development of the principle that the Sunna is inspired is illustrated in a comment of Ġazālī's:

There is no dispute concerning the view that the Prophet did not abrogate the Qur'ān on his own initiative [Q 10.15]. He did it in response to inspiration [Q 53.4]. The nāsikh in such cases was not worded in the Qur'ān style. Even if we consider him capable of abrogating the Qur'ān on the basis of his own ijtihād, the authority to exercise his discretion derived from God. Thus, God does the actual abrogating, operating through the medium of His Prophet. One ought thus to hold that the rulings of the Qur'ān may be abrogated by the Prophet, rather than solely by the Qur'ān. Although the inspiration [waḥy] in these cases is not Qur'ān inspiration, the Word of God is nevertheless one. The Word of God is both the nāsikh and the mansūkh. God does not have two words, one expressed in the Qur'ān style which we are bidden to recite publicly, and called the Qur'ān, while the other word is not Qur'ān. God has but one word which differs in the mode of its expression. On occasions, God indicates His Word by the Qur'ān, on others, by words in another style, not publicly recited, and called Sunna.

Both were mediated by the Prophet. In each case, the nāsikh is God alone Who indicates naskh by means of His Prophet at whose hands God instructs us of the abrogation of His Book. This none other than the Prophet is capable of manifesting; none other than God of initiating. Were God in this manner to abrogate a verse by the instrumentality of His Prophet, and subsequently to bring another verse similar to that which had been abrogated, He would have made good His promise [Q 2.106]. It is not necessary to consider only this second verse the actual nāsikh. God did not mean to say that He proposed to bring a verse superior to the first. No part of the Qur'ān is superior to another. He meant to state that He would bring a ruling superior to the first, in the sense of its being easier to perform, or richer in terms of reward.[12]

This statement marks the shaking off of Šāfiʿī's over-rigid doctrine that only the Qur'ān had abrogated the Qur'ān, as supposedly indicated by Q 2.106. Between the revelation of the first and second verses, Ġazālī invites us to suppose that Muḥammad might introduce a Sunna regulation. That sunna would be the nāsikh of the ruling of the earlier verse, while the second verse, in being revealed, redeems the divine promise to bring it.

Ġazālī asserts that the Qur'ān may be abrogated indifferently by the Qur'ān or by the Sunna, and that the Sunna may be abrogated by the Sunna or by the Qur'ān. Both alike come from God. He adds that if it be objected that Šāfiʿī held that the Qur'ān had never abrogated the Sunna, nor the Sunna the Qur'ān, and that Šāfiʿī was far too great a scholar not to have taken account of the various instances that had been cited, he, Ġazālī, suggests that Šāfiʿī might well have been arguing that one sunna superseded an earlier sunna, since the Prophet could set aside his own rulings. He was thus elucidator both of his own Sunna and of the Qur'ān.

The Qur'ān, in Šāfiʿī's view, could never act to elucidate the Sunna (invariably posterior to the Qur'ān which it elucidates). Only the second sunna abrogated the earlier sunna on the same topic; it elucidates the intervening Qur'ān verse on that topic. Whenever God revealed such a verse, at variance with the sunna which the Prophet had established, the Prophet immediately introduced his second sunna on the lines of the Qur'ān verse, to demonstrate that only like abrogates like.[13]

Šāfiʿī claims never to have come across an instance

of the Qur'ān's elucidating a sunna. For him, every sunna established to abrogate another sunna invariably survived in the transmitted Ḥadīth. His claim never to have found the Qur'ān elucidating a sunna may mean, either that such a thing had never been transmitted, or that it had never once occurred. If he meant the latter, his argument can be disposed of, in Ġazālī's opinion, by showing that it had occurred. Further, it can be documented from the Qur'ān itself. The Qur'ān imposed the Mecca qibla to replace the Jerusalem qibla which had been introduced in the Sunna. There is no necessity to postulate, as Šāfi'ī would have us do, in every such instance of abrogation, the existence at one time of a nāsikh sunna which has merely failed to reach us. Šāfi'ī's conclusion that the naskh of the Sunna by the Qur'ān had never occurred is mere pedantry.[14]

Baiḍāwī had an even shorter way with Šāfi'ī's theory:

> The majority concede that the Sunna abrogated the Qur'ān, as occurred in the case of the penalty of flogging [Q 24.2]. Šāfi'ī disputed the possibility and urged Q 2.106. He can be refuted by the consideration that the Sunna also was revealed.[15]

Since the occurrence of naskh can be demonstrated by appeal to the Qur'ān, and since the word naskh itself occurs in the Qur'ān, the theories of naskh were easily given the appearance of Qur'ānic sanction. The Sunna party could also claim, on the basis of the same reference, that the phenomenon had been of frequent occurrence during the Prophet's public ministry. Since God Himself had declared that He used naskh, there was no barrier to the claim that the Prophet had also used it. This had apparently been doubted, to judge by the circulation of ḥadīths stating that he had, on the analogy of naskh as it affected the texts of the Qur'ān. ʿUrwa alleges that his father told him that the Prophet would regulate some matter, then, after some time, replace his first ruling with a second regulation - just as the Qur'ān did.[16]

Clearly, by naskh the uṣūlīs meant replacement, a phenomenon the legitimacy of which none could question following these evidences from the two sources. naskh al ḥukm wa al tilāwa means, however, the suppression of the wording and the ruling. naskh al ḥukm dūna al tilāwa means the suppression of the earlier ruling alone. That can mean only its supersession.

The second formula had been constructed on the analogy of the first, and we have just encountered the allegation that the principle that naskh affects the Sunna had been constructed on the analogy of its having affected the Qur'ān. What, in fact, such procedures illustrate is the urgency felt by the uṣūlīs to find Qur'ānic support for a principle they desired to extend to rationalise every single instance of conflict of evidence or of conflict of sources.

The impression derived from a reading of the uṣūl works is that the analogy they alleged served to verify, rather than suggest, a principle. The naskh of one ḥadīth by another is a claim more frequently met in inter-madhab squabbles engendered by the simultaneous existence in the parallel schools of conflicting legal views. Šāfiʿī himself devoted his Ikhtilāf al Ḥadīth to exposing the errors in Fiqh documentation committed by his opponents.

The claim that one Qur'ān ruling had abrogated another tends rather to be encountered in the defence against the common enemy's minority objections of the legal views shared by the madāhib. One instance in point was the unanimity of the schools in the denial of the rights assigned to the widow in Q 2.240, on the ground that Q 2.234 (which deals with an entirely different subject) had been revealed later than verse 240. On this and similar topics, the conflict obtained, in fact, between the inherited Fiqh and the Qur'ān.

From our experience of Šāfi'ī's debating methods there arises the question of whether the claim that naskh had affected the Qur'ān by replacing some of its rulings, may not have been merely part of the response in defence of the Fiqh to the challenge offered by the Qur'ān party, who questioned the discrepancy between the Fiqh rulings and the rulings of the Book.

The quarrels over the question of whether the Qur'ān had abrogated the Sunna, judging by Šāfi'ī's reaction, point to a similar challenge. The Sunna must always be made to appear posterior to the Qur'ān, otherwise many Fiqh rulings would have to be abandoned. That is why Šāfi'ī asserted that the nāsikh sunna had always been handed down. He simply had not dared to claim that the Sunna had abrogated the Qur'ān. The entire drift of his method was to preserve and maintain the Sunna. This he sought to do by emphasising the Qur'ān's occasional ambiguity. Only thus could he hope to harmonise the Fiqh with the Book.

Those who argued, on the contrary, that the Sunna had

superseded the Qur'ān were simply in disagreement with Šāfiʿī's exegeses, hence with his Fiqh conclusions, or, if they agreed with his legal standpoint, merely indulging their differing uṣūl theories.[17]

The claim to find Qur'ānic sanction for the general theory of naskh (the substitution of one ruling for another) is diluted by the evident difficulty posed for the Muslims in their attempts to accommodate to their theory, and so justify their procedure, the Qur'ānic term naskh which, in both its Qur'ānic contexts, can mean only suppression, not the supersession of the uṣūlī.

If we look again at their principal Qur'ānic prop, Q 2.106: mā nansakh min āya aw nunsi hā na'ti bi khairin min hā aw mithli hā, we observe that if replacement is referred to in this verse, it can only be in the final clause: 'We shall bring something better than it, or something like it'; in which event, naskh refers to what necessitates the replacement, namely suppression. That is certainly the meaning of the word in its second context, Q 22.52, as the Muslims themselves unanimously insist.[18]

Their semantic difficulty is confirmed by the very clumsiness and artificiality of their naskh formulae.

1. When Muḥammad's forgetting became formalised, what was always intended to refer to suppression was cramped into the procrustean and absurdly inappropriate frame: naskh al ḥukm wa al tilāwa. Naskh al tilāwa would have sufficed, for if indeed there had originally been a ḥukm, it would normally now be unknown. Known or not, the ḥukm would have been of no interest to the Muslims. It certainly held no interest

for the legal specialists, and played no part in the extraction of the Law. This mode had been purely the invention of the exegetes who, acting from suspicion of words like 'forgetting' and under the influence of the technical jargon of the uṣūlīs, were attracted by a scientific-sounding phrase.

In all his writings, Šāfiʿī, for example, is supremely indifferent to exegeses that have no legal or jurisprudential application. Far from referring to omissions from the Qur'ān, Šāfiʿī was fully preoccupied with what is present in the Qur'ān. Central therefore to his interests was naskh al ḥukm dūna al tilāwa

On the basis of a variant consonantal reading of Q 2.106, which incidentally strengthens the suggestion that there was pressure to make the transition from mere forgetting to some conscious divine revelatory activity, such as either deliberate omission or replacement, Šāfiʿī interpreted the verse to mean: 'Whatsoever verse We replace and whatsoever revelation We postpone to a later time, We shall bring another like it, or better than it in the meantime.' This reading, nansa', like the reading adopted by the majority, nunsi, represents equally the flight from a reading of the script which provoked serious theological compunction for the Muslims, that is, nansa (we forget). God does not forget![19]

Ṭabarī, by contrast, was both a prominent uṣūlī, although his chief work in this field has not reached us,[20] and an outstanding, painstaking commentator on the Qur'ān, whose approach to exegesis was clearly influenced by his legal and jurisprudential interests. It is he who throws light on the connection dawning on the Muslim mind between the phenomena of forgetting and suppression or replacement denoted by the term naskh.

It appears that, with no fear of the implications, Saʿd b. abī Waqqāṣ recited Q 2.106: aw tansa hā. His reading was challenged, on the ground that Saʿīd b. al Musayyab read: aw tunsa hā. Saʿd countered with a reference to two further verses, Q 87.6-7: sa nuqri'uka fa lā tansā [illā mā šā'a allāh] and Q 18.24 uḏkur rabbaka iḏā nasīta.

Saʿd, a Meccan, in addition, challenged the isnād of the reading of Saʿīd, a Medinese.[21]

Both readings in question, here attributed to major figures of an earlier generation, had, as is clear, proceeded from clashing exegeses of Q 87, thence of Q 2. The technique of linking the two contexts is unmistakable.

Ṭabarī acquaints us with a further quarrel involving the technical implications of the Q 2 verse. Certain anonymous opponents had expressed the view that if Muḥammad be admitted to have merely forgotten parts of the revelation, the muṣḥaf and the Qur'ān would not be co-extensive. The muṣḥaf would not preserve a true and complete record of the revelations. As they hold this to be absurd, they cannot concede that the Prophet had ever forgotten a single syllable of the Qur'ān.[22] Arguments to the effect that Muḥammad had indeed forgotten parts of the Qur'ān, which appeal to Q 17.86, they reject on the reasonable grounds that that verse linguistically represents an unfulfilled hypothesis, and is thus rhetorical rather than affirmative.

The opponents betray, however, that their concern is less with the quality of Muḥammad's memory than with the present state of the Qur'ān texts, the muṣḥaf. This is shown by their further argument that the Prophet might be admitted to have forgotten part of the Qur'ān, but only for a moment. He recalled immediately what he had at first had difficulty in summoning to mind. Even if Muḥammad had forgotten some part of the revelation he was surrounded by the Companions who would not all simultaneously forget the very same passage.

Finally, it is their statement that Muḥammad could not forget some part of the Qur'ān unless it were mansūkh which enables us to realise that the argument concerned, not the question of the effect upon the present state of the Qur'ān texts of Muḥammad's human fallibility, but the implications for the present state of the Qur'ān texts both of (a) certain verses in the Qur'ān and of (b) certain ḥadīths in circulation, to the effect that on several occasions Muḥammad had admitted that he had forgotten, or was seen to have forgotten some part of the divine revelation. Those ḥadīths had originally been the product of earlier tafsīr quarrels about the meaning of those Qur'ān verses (sc. Q 2.106 and Q 87.6-7).

This can be seen from one ḥadīth in which forgetting has not yet been transmuted into naskh:

> The Prophet recited the Qur'ān and omitted an āya. When he had finished the prayer, he asked, 'Is Ubayy in the mosque?'

'Here I am, Messenger of God.'
'Then why didn't you prompt me?'
'I thought the āya had been withdrawn.'
'It hasn't been withdrawn, I forgot it.'[23]

The arguments on the exegesis of Q 87 and Q 2 can be summarised as dealing with the implications of the distinction between Muḥammad's forgetting (tansa) and Muḥammad's being caused to forget (tunsa/nunsi). The distinction was made between his human memory and his prophetic memory.

Unfortunately, the proviso added by Ṭabarī's opponents, unless it were mansūkh, is ambiguous. We have seen that the term naskh is defined now as to suppress, now as to replace, depending upon whether one is discussing the Qur'ān document or the Qur'ān source.

If Muḥammad forgot some part of the Qur'ān which God intended to remove from the muṣḥaf, or to replace in the muṣḥaf, Muḥammad's forgetting was of no material relevance. It was, in either case, divinely determined.

Ṭabarī, as we see from his argument, took the word in this context to mean replaced, since he urges two considerations: by Q 17.86, God did not mean that He would remove all the Qur'ān. He merely stated that He would remove such parts of it as His creatures did not need. Since we are in no need of Qur'ān materials which have been suppressed, these could well be removed and fail to come down to us in the muṣḥaf. Besides, there are traditions to the effect that this or that passage, mentioned by certain of the Companions as having once figured in the sacred texts, was removed. Anas reported on the verse revealed at the time of the Bi'r Ma'ūna massacre and Abū Mūsā al Aš'arī said they used to recite the ibn Ādam verse before its removal. Other similar reports are too numerous for Ṭabarī to quote.

Whether or not they were of interest to particular schools for the purposes of immediate exploitation, ḥadīths, of whatever provenance, flowed into the ageless stream of the Islamic Tradition. As nothing once called into existence in Islam ever quite perished, such reports having once been added to the general stock of Muslim learning were sooner or later used by Muslim scholars.

Thus it happened that the exegetical musings of one age generated ḥadīths which became the Tradition of a later age. The charm of this study lies in our observing how a later generation, in treating the Tradition that had come down to it and unaware that part of the Tradition had originated in older scholastic disputes, solemnly eyed the added material as part of the Fiqh and proceeded to construct its own new analyses, thus unconsciously in its turn contributing further additions to the fund of the general Tradition.

Theory passed through the thin membrane separating one Islamic science from another to become part of the data of the second science. Exegesis became sīra; sīra became Fiqh; and Fiqh must be traced back to an origin in either the Qur'ān or the Sunna.

Apparently we now have the Qur'ān's word for it: the muṣḥaf is incomplete and abrogation has occurred.

4 The background to the emergence of the third mode of *naskh*

1. THE EXEGESIS

A combination of *asbāb al nuzūl* and comment upon the verses themselves gave rise to two distinct strains of interpretation as to the meaning of Q 5.42-9:

> [Certain Jews] are very ready to listen to lies, prepared to incur divine wrath. If however they come to you, either judge between them or ignore them. If you ignore them, they cannot harm you. If you judge, judge between them impartially. God loves the impartial. (42) But how should they seek your judgment when they have the Torah in which is God's verdict, then turn their backs. They are not in fact believers. (43) We revealed the Torah in which is guidance and light; by which the prophets who submitted to God's will have judged the Jews, as also have the rabbis and the priest-scholars, by God's Book which they have preserved, whose witnesses they are. Fear not men. Me alone fear. Do not exchange My signs [*āyāt*] for a paltry gain. Whoso does not judge on the basis of what God has revealed is an unbeliever. (44) We imposed upon them [the rule]: a life for a life; an eye for an eye; a nose for a nose; an ear for an ear; a tooth for a tooth. Wounds may be repaid, but he who forgoes retaliation will have that counted as an expiation. Whoso does not judge in accordance with what God has revealed, is a wrongdoer. (45)...We have revealed the Book to you in truth and in confirmation of the foregoing revelations which it verifies.

> Judge therefore between them on the basis of what God has revealed. Do not listen to their views to the detriment of the truth that has come to you ... (48)

Only the minority exegetical tradition viewed this passage as having been revealed to regulate the laws governing the talio. The greater weight of exegetical judgment was thrown into the contrary assertion that the verses refer to the penalties for adultery.[1] Given the slight inducement of the statement that the prophets who had aslamū judged the Jews in accordance with the Law of the Torah, a massive haggada grew up as to the occasion of the revelation of Q 5. This body of comment is based partly on the interpretation of the Qur'ān's frequent admonition of the Jews for concealing part of what had been revealed to them, but it is also modelled on the story of the Christian prophet's confounding of the Jews in the case of the woman taken in adultery. Verses 46-7 of Q 5 continue:

> In the footsteps of the prophets We sent Jesus, son of Mary to confirm the Torah. To him We gave the Gospel in which is guidance and light and as a confirmation of the Torah which preceded him, and as a guidance and lesson to those who would avoid the wrath of God. Let therefore the people of the Gospel judge in accordance with what God revealed in it. Whoso does not judge on the basis of what God has revealed is in sin.

The Jews, it was alleged, had referred to Muḥammad for judgment when a man and woman of their community had committed adultery. Muḥammad enquired as to the penalty in the Torah. The scrolls were brought out for consultation, but one of the Jewish doctors covered over a particular passage with his hand. A supporter of Muḥammad, converted to Islam from Judaism, pointed this out and the man was made to remove his hand. The stoning verse was uncovered, and as a true prophet of the Lord, Muḥammad applied the verdict of God. Muḥammad stoned Jewish adulterers. The source of that penalty had been the stoning verse.

In time this became shortened. Muḥammad had stoned adulterers. The source of that penalty had been the stoning verse. This development can be traced without difficulty in Mālik's Muwaṭṭa', K. al Ḥudūd. There we find two strands: Muḥammad had stoned Jews; Muḥammad had stoned Muslims. The source was the stoning verse.

Already before Mālik the search had begun for the source of the Islamic Fiqh's stoning penalty. The old haggada narratives, having become halakha, had passed into the hands of the uṣūlīs and become part of their source-Tradition. Muḥammad had stoned on the basis of the Book of God.

It was now the uṣūlīs' task to relate the contents of the narratives to the conclusions of the Fiqh. These had derived, in this instance, not directly from the Qur'ān texts which we have before us in the muṣḥaf, but indirectly, from the intervening gossip about this or that implication of the Qur'ān verses, the occasion of their revelation, in connection with whom or what they had been revealed, and the traditional statements as to their meaning.

Stoning, as the attested practice of the Prophet, had next to be assigned to an origin in Sunna or Qur'ān, depending upon the source theory of the school.

At this point in our investigation it would be most

enlightening to discover what, if any, debt the Muslim _uṣūlīs_ owed to external influences in developing both their _Fiqh_ and their source theories. It is, for example, surely a striking coincidence that on this very topic of the penalty for adultery, the Islamic _ḥukm_, death by stoning, and its justification, the penalty laid down in the Book of God, exactly mirror both the Karā'ite penalty and its rationalisation.[2]

Unhappily, however, it is not possible in the present state of our knowledge to do more than merely draw attention to the coincidence. The basic research has not yet been done that might supply us with a clear picture of the contacts and relations between the first generations of the Muslim scholars and their Jewish counterparts, orthodox or schismatic.

Such relations were, in any case, in this instance, denied from the Muslim side.[3] They would not, in any event, have been indispensable to either the evolution of the actual penalty in the Islamic penal system or to the determination of thinking as to its source.

The stoning penalty of the Islamic _Fiqh_, in the view of the _uṣūlīs_, had derived from their Prophet. Muḥammad had stoned either to establish his Sunna, or to implement the rulings of the Book of God. If the former were the case, the Sunna had incontrovertibly abrogated the Qur'ān ruling, for all we find there is a flogging penalty introduced in Q 24.2. If the latter were the case, a very crucial question for _uṣūl al fiqh_ arises.

2. THE FIQH: THE PENALTY FOR ADULTERY

The discussion of this topic is exceedingly complex. Only those aspects of immediate relevance to our study will here be discussed.

The kernel of our problem is that the majority of the maḏāhib are unanimously of the view that in certain circumstances, the penalty for adultery is death by stoning. Now, we know that this penalty is not only nowhere mentioned in our texts of the Qur'ān, it is totally incompatible with the penalty that is mentioned: al zāniyatu wa al zānī fajlidū kulla wāḥidin minhumā mi'ata jaldatin (The adulteress and the adulterer, flog each one of them one hundred strokes) (Q 24.2).

Noting that this verse fails to distinguish between adultery and fornication, since the root employed, z n y, is interpreted rather in the sense of sexual misconduct, the scholars further assert that it apparently clashes with another verse of the Qur'ān which they also take to be a reference to the revealed penalty for the sexual misconduct of married women.

> Those of your women who commit acts of gross moral turpitude, seek against them the testimony of four of your number, and should these bear witness, confine the women in quarters until death release them or God appoint a way for them.

Q 4.15 was traditionally read as a reference to adultery. The immediately following verse 16: 'Those two of your number who commit like acts, punish them, but if they repent and amend, let them be', although phrased in the masculine dual, and thus possibly a reference to two males, has traditionally been read by most scholars as a reference to the male and female partners in the act of gross moral turpitude. The argument is that the dual is of common gender.

Various suggestions were mooted as to the nature of the punishment referred to, but as it has apparently been left to the Muslims to determine the penalty, and as the punishment laid down in the previous verse, imprisonment for life, is of greater severity, verse 15, it was thought, must refer to a sin of greater heinousness. It was for that reason concluded that the penalty for the female partner must be 'heavier' than that for the male.

Further, since the penalty of the second verse was presumed to be lighter and the sin envisaged thus less heinous, the dual could simultaneously be read as a reference to the two partners in some act of sexual misconduct of lesser gravity than that referred to in verse 15. Verse 16 was therefore construed as referring to fornication between unmarried partners.

Their penalty, whatever that was, had been overtaken and superseded by the flogging of Q 24.2.

In the Fiqh, Q 24.2's flogging penalty, in fact, applies exclusively to free unmarried persons guilty of sexual misconduct. Within these limits, Q 24.2 abrogated (i.e. replaced) Q 4.16. This is therefore an attested instance of naskh al ḥukm dūna al tilāwa.

In the wording of Q 4.15 'or God appoint a way', God had marked the penalty for married women as temporary. It is an example of what Šāfiʿī had called nasā' - the postponement of a revelation until a later time, with the revelation of an interim regulation in the meantime.

Now, we find in the Tradition a celebrated ḥadīth transmitted from ʿUbāda of which there are many very interesting variant versions. The 'basic form' of the report runs as follows:

> The Prophet said, 'Take it from me! God has now appointed a way for women: the virgin with the virgin, one hundred strokes and a year's banishment; the non-virgin with the non-virgin, one hundred strokes and stoning.'[4]

Stoning was established by the Sunna.

Among the interesting variants of this ḥadīth we find:

> The descent of inspiration [waḥy] was troublesome to the Prophet. His face would go ashen in colour. One day inspiration came down upon him and he showed the usual signs of distress. When he recovered, he said, 'Take it from me! God has appointed a way for the women: the non-virgin with the non-virgin and the virgin with the virgin. The non-virgin, one hundred strokes and death by stoning; the virgin, one hundred strokes and banishment for a year.'[5]

The stoning penalty had been established by God through the medium of that part of the Prophet's Sunna which was inspired.

This claim may be seen even more clearly in the other variant:

> We could tell when the inspiration descended upon the Prophet. When the words, 'or until God appoint a way', were revealed, and the inspiration ascended, the Prophet said, 'Take heed! God has now appointed the way: the virgin with the virgin, one hundred

> strokes and banishment for a year; the non-virgin with the non-virgin, one hundred strokes and death by stoning.'[6]

Some appeared concerned at the equity of imposing two penalties for a single misdemeanour and, without reference to ʿUbāda, make it certain that they were aware of a _Fiqh_-Qur'ān conflict. It is related that when a woman guilty of adultery was brought before ʿAlī, he flogged her and then had her stoned. Someone protested: 'but you have inflicted two penalties!' ʿAlī replied, 'I stoned her in accordance with the Sunna of the Prophet and flogged her in accordance with the Book of God.'[7] The expression Book of God here refers to Q 24.2. The equation in these contexts of the Book of God with the Qur'ān is crucial to the development of this discussion.

Others are reported as exclaiming, 'What is this stoning? The penalty in the Book of God is flogging.'[8]

ibn ʿAbbās reports a sermon by ʿUmar in the course of which he said, 'Men! stoning is a penalty laid down by God. Do not neglect it. It is in the Book of God and the Sunna of your Prophet. The Messenger of God stoned; Abū Bakr stoned, and I have stoned.'[9]

Mālik reports ibn ʿAbbās as declaring, 'I heard ʿUmar b. al Khaṭṭāb say, "Stoning in the Book of God is a just claim against the non-virgin, man or woman, who fornicates, when valid proof is adduced, or pregnancy ensues, or self-condemnation is volunteered."'[10]

What can here be meant by the Book of God?

Mālik reports also the celebrated _ḥadīth_ of the hired hand:

> Two men brought a case before the Prophet. One of them said, 'Messenger of God, judge between us in accordance with the Book of God.'
> The other, who was more familiar with litigation, said, 'Yes, Messenger of God, judge between us in accordance with the Book of God and let me speak first. My son served as a hired hand under this man, but he fornicated with his employer's wife. The man, informing me that my son had incurred the stoning penalty, I ransomed him from that penalty with 100 sheep and a slavegirl I had. Subsequently I enquired of the learned who informed me that the stoning penalty lay on the man's wife.'
> The Messenger of God said, 'By Him in Whose hand is my soul! I will judge between you in accordance with the Book of God. Your cattle and slavegirl are to be restored to you.'[11]

At this point, the direct speech ends, but the *ḥadīth* continues, 'He awarded the son 100 strokes and banished him for a year. He ordered Unais al Aslamī to go to the employer's wife, and in the event that she confess, imposed the stoning penalty. She confessed, and Unais stoned her.'

There are strong grounds for considering this continuation foreign and irrelevant to the *ḥadīth*. ibn Ḥajar, for example, comments,

> The Book of God might refer to the verdict of God. It has also been held that it refers to the Qur'ān. ibn Daqīq al ʿĪd suggested that the first explanation was preferable since neither stoning nor banishment is mentioned in the Qur'ān, apart from the general injunction to obey the Prophet's commands. One might also consider the possibility that the reference is to God's words, 'or until God appoint a way'. The Prophet showed that the way was the flogging and banishment of the virgin, and stoning

> the non-virgin. A further possibility, it may be, is that the Book of God is a reference to a verse whose wording alone has been withdrawn, that is, the stoning verse, although the verse also fails to mention banishment. Finally, the reference may be to the Qur'ān's prohibition of wasting another's property without legal title to it. The man had taken possession of the other's cattle and slavegirl, but the Prophet insisted that they be returned.[12]

The last suggestion may imply that the *ḥadīth* at one time terminated with the words 'Your cattle and slavegirl are to be restored to you.'

We have a report from ʿUmar that he said, 'The Messenger of God stoned, Abū Bakr stoned and I have stoned. I am not prepared to add to the Book of God, otherwise I would write it into the *muṣḥaf*, for I fear that there will come some people who, not finding it, will not accept it.'[13] Stoning must therefore be a sunna. ʿUmar admits that it had never figured in the Qur'ān. ʿUmar is credited with a further dictum,

> Do not complain about stoning. It is a just claim and I am minded to write it in the *muṣḥaf*. I fear that with the passage of time some will say, 'We do not find stoning in the Book of God', and on that pretext they will neglect a divine ruling which God revealed. Stoning is a just claim against the married person who fornicates, when there is adduced valid proof, or pregnancy ensues, or a confession is offered.[14]

ʿUmar appears in a further series of *ḥadīths* designed to inculcate an alternative view of the matter. He announced from the Prophet's pulpit,

> God sent Muḥammad with the truth and revealed to him the Book. Part of what God revealed was the stoning

> verse. We used to recite it and we memorised it. The Prophet stoned and we have stoned after him. I fear that with the passage of time some will say, 'We do not find stoning in the Book of God', and will therefore neglect a divine injunction which God revealed. Stoning is a just claim...[15]

In this hadīth the transition from the stoning penalty to the stoning verse has been made. What does the Book of God now mean?

In a variant version, ʿUmar fears that with the passage of time some will say, 'We do not find the stoning verse in the Book of God',[16] while in a further ʿUmar hadīth we are acquainted with the wording of the stoning verse. Mālik reports that when ʿUmar returned from the pilgrimage, he addressed the people of Medina,

> Men! the Sunna has been established, the obligatory duties imposed and you have been left in no uncertainty. Beware lest you neglect the stoning verse on account of those who say, 'We do not find two penalties in the Book of God.' The Prophet stoned, and we have stoned. By Him Who holds my soul in His hand! but that men would say, 'ʿUmar has added to the Book of God', I would write it in with my own hand, 'The šaikh and the šaikha, when they fornicate, stone them outright.'[17]

The version that occurs in the Hulya reads, 'I would write at the end of the Qur'ān.'

Abū Maʿšar has,

> But that men would say, 'ʿUmar has written what is not in the Book of God', I would write it in, for we used to recite it, 'The šaikh and the šaikha, when they fornicate, stone them outright, as an exemplary punishment from God. God is mighty, wise.'

In the Mabsūt, Sarakhsī reports,

> ʿUmar said from the pulpit, '...and part of what was revealed in the Qur'ān read, "the *šaikh* and the *šaikha*, when they fornicate, stone them outright". Some will repudiate this, and but that men would say, "ʿUmar has added to the Book of God," I would write it on the margin of the *muṣḥaf*.'[18]

ibn Ḥajar compares two versions of the ʿUmar *ḥadīth,* one related by ʿAlī b. ʿAbdullāh, teacher of Bukhārī, and the other related by Bukhārī himself. In ʿAlī's version we find

> ʿUmar declared, 'I fear that with the passage of time some will say, "We do not find stoning in the Book of God", and will neglect a divine injunction revealed by God. Stoning is a just claim against the non-virgin fornicator when valid proof is brought, or pregnancy occurs, or confession is made. We used to recite it, "the *šaikh* and the *šaikha*, when they fornicate, stone them outright." The Messenger of God stoned and we have stoned.'

Bukhārī's version stops at 'confession is made', and ibn Ḥajar suggests that Bukhārī deliberately ignored the remainder of the *ḥadīth*.

Nasā'ī stated that he knew of no transmitter who included the words of the 'verse' in this *ḥadīth*, apart from Sufyān who here transmits the report as from Zuhrī to ʿAlī b. ʿAbdullāh. Nasā'ī took Sufyān's version to be erroneous, as numerous transmitters relate the *ḥadīth* from Zuhrī without this addition.

But ibn Ḥajar reminds us that the report is transmitted by Mālik and by others in this form which he judges to be 'correct'.[19]

As a divine revelation, the stoning verse had been revealed as part of the Qur'ān. In which *sūra* did it originally appear?

> Ubayy asked Zirr b. Ḥubaiš, 'How many verses do you recite in sūrat al Aḥzāb?'
> Zirr replied, 'Seventy-three verses.'
> Ubayy asked if that was all. 'I have seen it,' he said, 'when it was the same length as Baqara. It contained the words "the šaikh and the šaikha, when they fornicate, stone them outright, as an exemplary punishment from God. God is mighty, wise."'[20]

This version of the stoning verse is a fair imitation of the Qur'ān style, drawing upon both Q 24.2, and Q 5.38, which is a penal verse, but Nöldeke observed that the terms šaikha and battata are alien to the vocabulary of the Qur'ān.[21]

An improved version had, 'as an exemplary punishment from God and His apostle'.[22]

> Ubayy said, 'It used to equal in length sūrat al Baqara and we used to recite in Aḥzāb the stoning verse.'
> Zirr asked, 'What is the stoning verse?'
> Ubayy recited, 'If the šaikh and the šaikha fornicate, stone them outright as an exemplary punishment from God. God is mighty, wise.'[23]

The stoning verse, therefore, once stood in the Qur'ān texts. Why is it now absent?

> Zaid b. Thābit and Sa'īd b. al 'Āṣ were writing out the muṣḥaf. When they came to this verse, Zaid said, 'I heard the Prophet say, "the šaikh and the šaikha."'
> 'Umar stated, 'When it was revealed, I went to the Messenger of God and said to him, "Shall I write it?" but he seemed to disapprove.' 'Umar added, 'Don't you see that the mature, if unwed, would only be flogged in the event of fornication, yet the youth, if wed, would be stoned?'[24]

In other words, the stoning verse is at variance with both

the ʿUbāda *ḥadīth* and the *Fiqh*. Doubtless that is why Ubayy was projected as having isolated three categories of unchaste: (a) virgins, (b) non-virgins and (c) the mature.[25]

The stoning verse involves an age criterion and is in conflict with the marital status criterion of ʿUbāda's *ḥadīth*. The name of Ubayy represents those who attempted to harmonise both documents. The source conflict is acknowledged by ibn Ḥajar, who comments that the reason for the withdrawal of the stoning verse was that the *Fiqh* was at variance with the apparently general wording of the verse.[26]

This observation may perhaps also explain why Mālik, who does not present the text of the ʿUbāda report, nevertheless glosses the terms *šaikh* and *šaikha* as *thayyib* and *thayyiba* (sc. non-virgin), reducing thereby the meaning of the stoning verse to coincide with the meaning of the ʿUbāda *ḥadīth*.

Further, ibn Ḥajar concluded that the reason for the withdrawal of the wording of the verse was conflict of opinion among the Companions. He reports that ʿUmar addressed the people, saying,

> Do not complain about stoning. It is a just claim and I was minded to write it into the *muṣḥaf*, so I consulted Ubayy. But he said, 'Didn't you come to me once before, when I was asking the Prophet for permission to recite the verse? You shoved me in the chest with the words, "Are you asking him to permit the recitation of the stoning verse when the people are as randy as donkeys?"'[27]

Marwān b. al Ḥakam asked Zaid why he would not write the verse in the *muṣḥaf*. Zaid replied,

> Don't you see that the youth if married is stoned? We raised this question with ʿUmar and he said, 'I'll see to it.' He went to the Prophet and asked his permission to record the verse. The Prophet said he could not permit that.[28]

The verse would have conflicted with the ʿUbāda ḥadīth which is the basis of the practice.

The Muslim exegetes concluded, on the basis of their reading of Q 87.6-7 that they must distinguish between the Qur'ān and the muṣḥaf. Relative to the first, the second is obviously incomplete.

We now consider a series of ḥadīths with one common theme: verses now absent from the muṣḥaf had once nonetheless been received direct from the Prophet. Common to the entire series is the use of the term aqra' (to teach to recite), derived from the verse in Q 87 with the reference to forgetting.

The aunt of Abū Usāma b. Sahl told him that the Prophet had instructed them in the reciting of the stoning verse.[29]

> Ubayy reports, 'The Messenger of God said to me, "God has commanded me to instruct you in the reciting of the Qur'ān." He then recited: "Did not those who rejected the Prophet among the people of the Book and the associators..." The verse continued, "Did ibn Ādam possess a wādī of property", or, "Were ibn Ādam to ask for a wādī of property and he received it, he would ask for a second, and if he received that, he would demand a third wādī. Only dust will fill the maw of ibn Ādam, but God relents to him who repents. The very faith in God's eyes is the Ḥanīfiya, not Judaism nor Christianity.

Whoso does good, it will never be denied him."'[30]

ibn ʿAbbās said, 'Did ibn Ādam possess two *wādīs* of pelf, he would desire a third. Only dust will fill the maw of ibn Ādam, but God relents to him who repents.' ʿUmar asked, 'What is this?' ibn ʿAbbās replied that Ubayy had instructed him to recite this. ʿUmar took ibn ʿAbbās to confront Ubayy. ʿUmar said, 'We don't say that.' Ubayy insisted that the Prophet had instructed him. ʿUmar asked him, 'Shall I write it into the *muṣḥaf*, in that case?' Ubayy said, 'Yes.' This was before the copying of the ʿUthmān *muṣḥafs* on the basis of which the practice now rests.[31]

Abū Mūsā al Ašʿarī reports, 'There was revealed a *sūra* the like of *Barā'a*, but it was later withdrawn.' He recalled of it, 'God will assist this polity with peoples who have no share in the Hereafter. Did ibn Ādam possess two *wādīs* of property, he would crave a third. Nothing will fill the maw of ibn Ādam but dust, but God will relent to him who repents.'[32]

Abū Wāqid al Laithī reports, 'When inspiration came upon the Prophet, we would go to him and he would instruct us in what had been revealed. I went to him once and he said, "God says, 'We sent down wealth for the upkeep of prayer and alms-giving. Were ibn Ādam to possess a *wādī* he would desire another like it, which, if he had, he would desire yet another. Nothing will fill the maw of ibn Ādam but dust, but God relents to him who repents.'"'[33]

Buraida claims to have heard the Prophet recite ibn Ādam at prayer. The *āya* was in *sūrat Yūsuf*.[34]

There can therefore be no doubt that it was Qur'ānic.

Abū Mūsā said, 'We used to recite *sūrat al Aḥzāb*, likening it for length and severity with *Barā'a.* But I have been caused to forget it, except that I recall the ibn Ādam verse.'[35]

Anas was unable to say whether ibn Ādam was a Qur'ān verse or not. He reports from Ubayy, 'We supposed that ibn Ādam was a Qur'ān verse until sūrat al Takāthur was revealed.'[36]

This report reduces ibn Ādam from ever having been a Qur'ān verse, to being merely a tafsīr of Takāthur.[37]

Aḥzāb was identified as the sūra originally containing the stoning verse, and, in addition to Ubayy and Abū Mūsā, ʿĀ'isha reports that Aḥzāb used to be recited, in the lifetime of the Prophet, as having 200 verses, but when ʿUthmān wrote out the muṣḥafs, all they could find was its present length.[38] A variant of this ḥadīth speaks of writing out the muṣḥaf with, however, no mention of date or of attribution. ibn al Anbārī concluded from ʿĀ'isha's report that God withdrew from the sūra everything in excess of its present length, and Mekkī reminds us that withdrawal is one of the modes of naskh.[39]

Aḥzāb has only seventy-three verses in today's muṣḥaf.

Mekkī grades the mansūkh of the Qur'ān into six categories, including that whose wording has been withdrawn from the muṣḥaf, although surviving in the memories. The consensus as to the contents of the muṣḥaf prevents that from being recited as part of the Qur'ān. The ruling remains valid, again on account of the consensus. His example of this category is the stoning verse.[40]

The contrast between the Qur'ān document and its relation with the valid Muslim prayer, and the Qur'ān source with its relation to the *šarīʿa* in the science of *Fiqh* could not be more explicitly drawn.

Mekkī's second category of *mansūkh* involves that whose ruling has been withdrawn and with it the memory of the wording. This class is known only from isolate reports. He instances the report from Abū Mūsā as to the *sūra* like *Barā'a* which was revealed, but later withdrawn. Abū Mūsā recalled something of it, but Mekkī resolutely refuses to go into further detail. The Qur'ān text cannot be established on the basis of reports. The many examples of this category he would therefore prefer to pass over in silence. God alone knows the truth of the matter.

A third category consists of that whose wording has been withdrawn from the *muṣḥaf*, whose ruling is void, but whose wording has not quite departed from the memories of men. The consensus as to the *muṣḥaf* has here again determined that this class may not be recited at prayer. Like the foregoing, this category is known solely through the medium of *ḥadīth* reports.

Only the Qur'ān texts, the document, is in view. The text of that document was not determined on the basis of stray reports. The text of the *muṣḥaf* was determined by *ijmāʿ*, the *muṣḥaf* is *mutawātir*.

Next are the verses whose rulings have been superseded by the rulings of other verses. In this category of *mansūkh*, the wording of both verses is extant in the *muṣḥaf*. One example would be Q 24.2, whose ruling superseded that of

Q 4.15-16.

In a further comment on the stoning verse, Mekkī informs us that that is one instance of something whose wording has been withdrawn from that which might be publicly recited (sc. at prayer). The wording had survived, but may not be recited as part of the Qur'ān. The ruling has persisted in the Fiqh on the grounds of the ijmā' or consensus that stoning is, in fact, the Law. The report is notorious that they used to recite: 'the šaikh and the šaikha'. The wording was later withdrawn from the unanimously settled wording of the muṣḥaf. The recital of the verse did not become established, yet the wording was never quite forgotten.

'Ā'iša explains how the wording came to be omitted from the muṣḥaf. The stoning verse and another verse were revealed and recorded on a sheet (ṣaḥīfa) which was placed for safe-keeping under her bedding. When the Prophet fell ill and the household were preoccupied with nursing him, a domestic animal got in from the yard and gobbled up the sheet.[41]

A SECOND INSTANCE OF THE THIRD MODE OF NASKH

Šāfi'ī was aware of a mode of naskh in which the original Qur'ān wording no longer appeared in the muṣḥaf although the ruling remained valid for the Fiqh.

He knew and used the ḥadīth about the stoning verse that had once figured in the Qur'ān before the collection of the texts into the muṣḥaf.[42] Yet we shall see that it played no part in his substantiation of the stoning penalty unanimously adopted by the fuqahā'.

On quite another legal topic, much debated, that of the minimum definition of the term riḍāʿ, or fosterage, Šāfiʿī showed a much more positive attitude.[43]

This was a question of some social importance since it defined the forbidden degrees and identified who might and who might not visit Muslim ladies.

> Riḍāʿ is a comprehensive term which might refer either to one suckling or to more than one, up to the complete course which takes two years [Q 2.233]. Indeed, the term could still apply after the two years. This being the case, it is incumbent on scholars to seek out some indication as to whether any bar to marriage is set up by the minimum that would constitute riḍāʿ. ʿĀʾiša reported, 'In what was revealed, ten attested sucklings were required to establish the ban. The ten were later replaced by five. The Prophet died and the five were still being recited in the Qurʾān.' She used to say, 'The Qurʾān was revealed with ten attested sucklings setting up the bar. These later became five.' No man ever called upon her who had not completed a course of five sucklings.
>
> ʿAbdullāh b. al Zubair reports, 'The Prophet said, "Not one and not two sucklings constitute the bar, nor one nor two sucks."'
>
> ʿUrwa reports that the Prophet commanded the wife of Abū Ḥudaifa to nurse Sālim five times to set up the bar. She did so and always considered Sālim a son.
>
> Sālim b. ʿAbdullāh reports that ʿĀʾiša sent him away and refused to see him. He was being suckled by her sister Umm Kulthum who had fallen ill after suckling him only three times. Sālim said, 'I could never visit ʿĀʾiša, since I had not completed the course of ten.'

Nor, Šāfiʻī points out, in the interests of his Fiqh, had Sālim completed the course of five. Šāfiʻī adopted the rule of five sucklings as coming from the Prophet on the strength of the ʻĀ'iša report that the five were Qur'ānic and constituted the ban. He was to enlarge on his views on the subject in his dispute with the Mālikīs.[44]

Here, he uses another ḥadīth: Ḥafṣa sent ʻĀṣim b. ʻAbdullāh b. Saʻd to her sister Fāṭima to be nursed ten times. This was to enable him to visit her.

The Mālikīs report the ʻĀ'iša ḥadīth that the five sucklings were being recited as part of the Qur'ān when the Prophet died; they report the Prophet's command to Sahla bint Suhail to nurse Sālim; they report from two widows of the Prophet; yet they choose to neglect all these reports in favour of the personal opinion of Saʻīd b. al Musayyab that a single suckling sets up the marriage bar. They ignore both the reports from ʻĀ'iša and her and Ḥafṣa's opinion in favour of the opinion of Saʻīd, although on other occasions they ignore Saʻīd's view in favour of their own opinions. They set aside what comes from the Prophet, from ʻĀ'iša, from Ḥafṣa, from ibn al Zubair and from Abū Huraira. They have shown themselves inconsistent.

Mekkī regards the ʻĀ'iša report on the ten and the five sucklings verses as one of the curiosities of this science:

> Neither the mansūkh nor the nāsikh [neither the ten nor the five] is today part of the Qur'ān text, yet the ruling derived from the nāsikh is upheld in some legal schools. Both the mansūkh and the nāsikh were regarded by Mālik and the Medinese as having been

> abrogated in respect of wording and ruling. They regarded the ultimate nāsikh on the subject as having been Q 4.23.[45]

In other words, as far as they were concerned, the minimum number, one suckling, sufficed to set up a marriage bar. 'This is sound doctrine, since the nāsikh is still recited, the mansūkh no longer recited.'[46]

That is just a roundabout way of telling us that on this topic, as far as the uṣūlī could judge, since the muṣḥaf adequately accounts for Mālik's view, he must have ignored all other statements. Saʿīd b. al Musayyab's opinion, so scathingly dismissed by Šāfiʿī as ra'y, would have been the expression of Saʿīd's view of the implications of Q 4.23, that is, it was tafsīr.

As far as we can judge, on this topic Šāfiʿī certainly deserves Mekkī's comment that he had upheld a Fiqh view based on the ruling of a verse whose wording does not appear in our muṣḥaf - it had been withdrawn.

In other words, Šāfiʿī acknowledged a third mode of naskh: naskh al tilāwa dūna al ḥukm. His ruling was based on a verse once revealed as part of the Qur'ān, which remained valid for Fiqh purposes despite the omission of the wording of the verse from the Qur'ān texts collected together in the muṣḥaf.

Mekkī's own example of this mode had been the stoning verse. It would therefore be instructive if, for completeness' sake, we enquired into Šāfiʿī's view of the source of the stoning penalty. His examination of this question is quite unrelated to his discussion of the problem of Qur'ān-Sunna abrogation, which we have seen he denied. Šāfiʿī discusses stoning under the heading of takhṣīṣ, part of the Sunna's elucidation of the Qur'ān.

Flogging, he argues, is mentioned in a Qur'ān statement couched in general terms, Q 24.2.[47] The meaning apparently is that flogging applies to all who engage in sexual misconduct. That this is not however the case is borne out by the Qur'ān itself which, in Q 4.25, excludes slave women from the full rigour of Q 24.2. Q 24.2's flogging is, therefore, not a general rule. While it may appear so, there are exceptions to it.

The scholar's business is to try and discover by an extensive study of the Sunna whether the Prophet had indicated further exceptions. Q 4.25 categorised the offenders according as they were free or slave. The ʿUbāda ḥadīth similarly categorised them according as they were virgin or non-virgin at the time of the offence.

Further, the Sunna, in the ʿUbāda ḥadīth, informed us of the abrogation of Q 4.15, since in the ḥadīth the Prophet declared, 'Now God has appointed the way', that is the way promised in Q 4. On the evidence of the same ḥadīth, the Sunna introduced a dual penalty: flogging and banishment for all virgin offenders; flogging and stoning for non-virgin offenders. The Sunna endorsed the Q 24.2 flogging penalty.

Yet another ḥadīth, that of the 'hired hand', shows that in his later period, the Prophet had abandoned the dual penalty established by his own Sunna. The penalty of the non-virgin was now stoning alone. ʿUbāda must be earlier than 'hired hand', as is indicated by this and by ʿUbāda's reference to the immediately foregoing punishment, that of

Q 4. ʿUbāda conveyed the first penalty to be revealed since the revelation of Q. 4.[48] It may also be deduced that 'hired hand' was later than ʿUbāda from its endorsing of the dual penalty for the virgin offender introduced in ʿUbāda.

The 'hired hand' report being later, leads to the conclusion that, in respect of the non-virgin, the flogging element of ʿUbāda's dual penalty had been abrogated.[49] The Sunna abrogated the Sunna. The penalty for non-virgins was stoning alone and that has remained the penalty of the Islamic Fiqh ever since.

Thus Šāfiʿī took the view that the source of the stoning penalty had been the Sunna of the Prophet. Other scholars fall into several classes.[50] We know of those who, finding no reference to the stoning penalty in the Qur'ān, simply rejected it. They insisted on acknowledging only the Qur'ān's flogging penalty.[51]

Others concluded that the fuqahā' had based the Fiqh in this instance on the Sunna. These uṣūlīs were then driven by simple logic to conclude that the Sunna had superseded the Qur'ān and adduced this example.

Those who denied that the Sunna had ever superseded the Qur'ān had no way to go but to argue that the source of the Fiqh's stoning penalty must have been the Qur'ān. They acknowledge that there is no reference in the texts of the muṣḥaf to a stoning penalty but insist that it must at one time have been mentioned in the Qur'ān. The Fiqh's stoning penalty indicates the Qur'ān's stoning verse. The wording had simply been omitted from the collected texts.

Šāfiʿī, obliged to accept the stoning penalty on

account of its presence in the Fiqh, yet denying a priori that the Sunna had ever superseded the Qur'ān, had endeavoured to argue that the stoning penalty had derived from the Sunna, not indeed as abrogating the Qur'ān, but as providing its ideal exegesis. This view breaks down on our observing that stoning is not the exegesis of flogging. Stoning represents in the ʿUbāda ḥadīth a blatant attempt to add to the Qur'ān ruling, and in the 'hired hand' ḥadīth, the frank substitution of a different ruling. The Qur'ān's corporal penalty was replaced by the Fiqh's capital penalty.

We investigated the circumstances that had prevented Šāfiʿī in his day from ever conceding that the Sunna had ever superseded the Qur'ān's rulings. His forensic skill was largely instrumental in rescuing the Sunna, and hence the Fiqh, from the propaganda of the Qur'ān party. As the threat to the Sunna receded, scholars in the post-Šāfiʿī period felt free to revert to the pre-Šāfiʿī position, that stoning had indeed represented an attested instance of the abrogation of the Qur'ān at the hands of the Sunna of the Prophet.

Only the members of the madhab set up in memory of Šāfiʿī continued to withstand the uṣūlīs' concession. Some of them had been deeply influenced by the compelling logic deployed by the imām in his several reviews of the origin and source of the stoning penalty. When they themselves came to tackle the problem, unable to accept that here was an undeniable instance of the abrogation of the Qur'ān by the Sunna - since it had been drummed into them that that had never happened, they concluded that it could only be an instance of the abrogation of the Qur'ān by the Qur'ān.

They reached a conclusion at variance with that achieved by Šāfiʿī himself who had been at pains to adopt a different approach. But we have noted that in his repeated investigations into the matter he had used uncharacteristically equivocal language: ʿUbāda he described as the first revelation since Q 4; stoning he described as remaining the sole penalty for the non-virgin when the flogging penalty had been abrogated. To be consistent, his admirers were forced to the conclusion that the stoning penalty had been the subject of a revelation. For some of them, this meant that it had been a Qur'ān revelation; for Šāfiʿī it meant a Sunna revelation.

That stoning had been a Qur'ān revelation was a conclusion that, for some, relieved the anxiety of their realisation that to abrogate the nāsikh must, in the jargon, be superior to the mansūkh, or at least its equal. This was a requirement derived by tendentious uṣūlī comments upon Q 2.106: na'ti bi khairin min hā aw mithli hā.

It incidentally placed their argument beyond the protests of those who pressed for the exclusive acknowledgment of the penalty that is mentioned in the Qur'ān texts.

The protests of those among the Khawārij and the Muʿtazila who would have none of the Fiqh's stoning penalty, on the ground that it nowhere appears in our texts of the Qur'ān, were now swept aside by the bald assertion that stoning had indeed been revealed as part of the Qur'ān. The stoning verse had merely been omitted from the collected texts of the revelation as preserved in the muṣḥaf.

Although this departs from the conclusion reached by Šāfiʿī, he too had arrived at the third mode of naskh, naskh al tilāwa dūna al ḥukm, in the course of his discussion of the riḍāʿ, or the Fiqh governing the fosterage of adults.

It was, therefore, solely on this topic of riḍāʿ that Šāfiʿī, although he does not use the terminology, had isolated naskh al tilāwa dūna al ḥukm. Indeed, he may even be said to have invented this third mode of naskh. On the question of stoning, he knew the wording of the so-called stoning verse. This he had learned from Mālik who used it in his K. al Ḥudūd, where it is to be found cheek by jowl with a reference to the Torah, and other materials suggesting that the source of the Islamic stoning penalty had been the Sunna. Mālik made no attempt to resolve his materials, and Šāfiʿī, as we have seen, does not emphasise the stoning verse ḥadīth, nor rely on it in his analysis.

Scholars long continued to raise arguments against the third mode of naskh and we have stated that it was never universally acknowledged.

Šāfiʿī adopted and defended the five sucklings' rule on the basis of the ʿĀ'iša ḥadīth. Mekkī (A.H. 437) knows a version of the ḥadīth related by Yaḥyā b. Saʿīd of Medina which does not contain the words, 'The Prophet died and they were still being recited as part of the Qur'ān.' The scholars and the uṣūlīs consider this version sound, since there can be no naskh after the death of the Prophet. It is not possible that there should be a part of the Qur'ān which the Muslims agreed to drop after the Prophet's death.[52]

Like many another ḥadīth document, the ʿĀ'iša report,

seeking to explain the loss of certain verses by asserting that the sheet on which they had been recorded had been gobbled up by a domestic animal, is a composite document representing the conflation of two originally separate and independent stories.

ibn Qutaiba (A.H. 276), patiently answering the objections of the Mu'tazila to ḥadīths which bring both Islam and learning into disrepute, addresses himself to the comparison between that ḥadīth as reported by Muḥammad b. Isḥāq and the 'sounder' version from Mālik.[53]

In the opinion of the Ḥadīth specialists, Mālik was by far the more reliable transmitter. He reported from 'Abdullāh b. abī Bakr from 'Amra from 'Ā'iša that she said,

> Among what had been revealed in the Qur'ān was the provision that ten attested sucklings set a bar to marriage. The ten were subsequently replaced by the rule that five attested sucklings set up the bar. The Prophet died and the five were still being recited as part of the Qur'ān.

Among the fuqahā' who adapted their Fiqh to this report were Šāfi'ī and Isḥāq (b. Rāhawaih), both of whom made five the minimum line of demarcation between what does and what does not establish a bar to marriage.

The wording of Mālik's version clearly differs from that of ibn Isḥāq's who mentioned both the 'suckling verse' and the 'stoning verse' in a single ḥadīth. Mālik's is the preferable version of the two.

ibn Qutaiba is inclined to an equal scepticism about the mention in the ibn Isḥāq report of the stoning verse and the supposed method of its withdrawal.

The attacks of such scholars on reports of this kind are directed, however, not at the central information conveyed in the reports, but at the peripheral details. What dismayed them was the low quality of rationalisation displayed in the reports which tended to bring the essential central information itself into disrepute in some quarters.

ibn Qutaiba resorts to logic. It is quite feasible that a ruling be revealed in the Qur'ān, yet the wording subsequently be annulled, leaving the ruling alone valid. ʿUmar reported this to have been the case in the instance of the stoning verse, and others have reported the like in connection with other revelations that had been part of the Qur'ān before the texts were brought together. If it is possible to abandon the ruling yet retain the wording in the muṣḥaf, it is equally possible to abandon the wording, yet retain the ruling in the Fiqh.

Similar is the tone of Zarkašī (A.H. 794) who reports that al Wāḥidī had given as an example of the abrogation of something whose wording was still in the muṣḥaf by something whose wording had not been endorsed for inclusion in the muṣḥaf, the abrogation of flogging by stoning, in the case of the non-virgin. Stoning is not publicly recited today, although it had been in the days of the Prophet. The ruling has remained valid, but the wording has not. Similarly, certain wordings have been endorsed as part of the muṣḥaf, whose rulings have ceased to be valid. If there can be a Qur'ān revelation which is recited, but not practised, there can be a Qur'ān regulation which is practised but not recited.[54]

The feature of the five sucklings report which least commended itself to the scholars was the claim that that verse was still being recited after the death of the Prophet. This detail conflicted head-on with another rule in the science of naskh: that abrogation occurs only at the hands of him who was responsible for the original ruling. Mekkī states it as follows: lā yajūz an yakūn al naskh illā qabla wafāt al nabī.[55] Sarakhsī (A.H. 490) states: inna al naskh lā yakūn illā ʿalā lisān man yunazzal ʿalaihi al waḥyu.[56]

Expressed in this fashion, the rule was always liable to misinterpretation owing to the mischance that the Qur'ān's term naskh had to do service for both withdrawal and replacement. Clearly, only replacement is intended by the rule, but in the interest of the rule as here expressed, Suyūṭī intervened to suggest one of two interpretations of ʿĀ'iša's report:

1. the Prophet's death approached and these words were still being recited as part of the revelation;
2. the Prophet died and it was some time before all the people came to hear of the abrogation of the verse.[57]

The confusion occasioned by the dual interpretation of the Qur'ānic term naskh at the hands of the uṣūlīs is clearly demonstrated in a statement by Zarkašī:

> The naskh [sic] of the wording and recital occurred by means of God's causing them to forget it. He withdrew it from their memories, while commanding them to neglect its public recital and its recording in the muṣḥaf. With the passage of time, it would quite disappear like the rest of God's revealed Books which He mentions in the Qur'ān, but nothing of which is known today. This can have happened either

> during the Prophet's life so that, when he died, the forgotten material was no longer being recited as part of the Qur'ān; or it might have happened after the death of the Prophet. It would still be extant in writing, but God would cause them to forget it. He would then remove it from their memories. But, of course, the naskh of any part of the revelation after the death of the Prophet is not possible.[58]

After Muḥammad's death the omission of a Qur'ān wording is conceivable; the alteration of a Qur'ān ruling is inconceivable.

Sarakhsī is prepared to concede that parts of the Qur'ān may have eluded the recording procedures during the Prophet's life, on account of the Qur'ān verses: mā nansakh min āya aw nunsi hā; 'If We wished, We could make away with what We have revealed to you'; 'We shall teach you to recite it and you will not forget - except what God wills.'

He will, however, have none of the suggestion that this is conceivable after the Prophet's death. The possibility, he claims, is not admitted by the Muslims.[59] The reports, allegedly from Abū Bakr, Anas, Ubayy and others, indicating the loss or the forgetting of this or that āya which 'they used to recite in the lifetime of the Prophet', he regards as circulated by the enemies of Islam bent upon its destruction.

Among such 'lies' he includes ʿUmar's report to the effect that the stoning verse had once been part of the Qur'ān, and he cannot explain how such a great scholar as Šāfiʿī should be represented by a similar view on the question of the suckling 'verses' as that alleged in the ʿĀ'iša report, which, incidentally, he words: 'and that was part of what was recited in the Qur'ān following the death of the Prophet'.

What guarantees for him the 'unsoundness' of the report is Q 15.9, 'We it is Who have revealed the Reminder, and We shall preserve it.' God clearly is not speaking of preserving it for His own benefit, since He is above and beyond all benefit. God cannot forget, nor grow heedless. It must therefore mean that He will preserve the Qur'ān for us men. We are all capable of forgetting revelation if God does not preserve it for us. Were we to insist upon a breach of that guarantee in respect of part of what was revealed, we might as well admit breach of the guarantee in respect of all of the Qur'ān. We could thus have no assurance that part of what is in our hands today, if not all of it, is not at variance with the <u>šarī'a</u> mediated by Muḥammad. But that would be the case if, by abrogating part of it after Muḥammad's death, God had caused men to adopt something different.

'Adopting something different' and 'forgetting' exhibit the ever-present confusion between the dual semantics imposed by the Muslims upon the term <u>naskh</u>.

It is Sarakhsī's view that Q 15.9 makes it certain that nothing can have been abrogated from the Qur'ān after Muḥammad's death, in the sense of fading away from men's memories. Reports to the effect that such had happened are mostly isolate. The story that stoning had once been part of the Book of God are to be interpreted: part of the verdict of God, in accordance with His Law. The story from 'Ā'iša is certainly not correct, for the destruction of her ṣaḥīfa would neither cause the allegeḍ verse to depart from the memories of all the Companions, nor prevent them from writing out the verse on a fresh ṣaḥīfa.

The author of the Mabānī considers both ʿUmar's and ʿĀ'iša's reports. Of the latter, he knows the form: kāna fī mā yuqra' min al qur'ān but makes a particular point of stressing that she did not say: kāna min al Qur'ān.[60] This enables him to argue that the root q r ' may be used of the Sunna.[61] The word Qur'ān he notes has two aspects in Arabic usage:

1. as the proper name of the book revealed to Muḥammad;
2. as the verbal noun of the root q r '.

ʿĀ'iša had used it in the latter sense.[62]

Naḥḥās, in his work on naskh, mentioned but rejected a mode of naskh in which

> a verse is revealed and recited, then abrogated and no longer recited, nor recorded in the muṣḥaf, although the ruling allegedly continued valid. Those who numbered this mode in their theory, adduced the ʿUmar ḥadīth: 'We recited, al šaikh wa al šaikha idā zanayā farjamūhumā al battata bi mā qaḍayā min al ladda.' The isnād is sound, but the wording is not to be regarded as Qur'ān handed down 'from the many to the many'. It is a sunna. One may say, 'I recited [q r '] x y or z' without meaning to imply that what one recited was necessarily once part of the Qur'ān.[63]

Similarly, the author of the Mabānī, in his comment on ʿUmar's ḥadīth, argues that the reports are isolate and cannot be set against that which is mutawātir. Rather a means ought to be established of reconciling isolate reports in order to make use of what information they convey. They might, for example, tell us that that was a sunna statement which they used to relate from the Prophet. The root q r ' may be used of the Sunna.[64]

ʿUmar is supposed to have been afraid of being accused of adding to the Book of God. One would not employ the term 'adding' when speaking of what is recognised as authentically Qur'ānic. Stoning was, in ʿUmar's view, an attested sunna, and hence an essential Islamic ruling, and an integral element in the Muhammadan revelation and Law. ʿUmar sought to exhort the Muslims to preserve it, to recite it and study it lest it be neglected. This is confirmed by his decision to summon a group of the Muhājirs and the Anṣār and inscribe their testimony on the margin of the muṣḥaf: 'The testimony of ʿUmar and of NN that the Messenger of God stoned adulterers.'

ʿUmar feared that there would come after him some who, aware that it is not to be found in the Qur'ān, would repudiate stoning. But, had it been Qur'ān, ʿUmar would have recorded it, without heed to what might be said, since he would have no excuse therein for leaving it out. Besides, if it really were Qur'ān, the people would not say that it wasn't. What ʿUmar feared was to record in the Qur'ān something that was not Qur'ān. He would then be justly accused of adding to the Qur'ān. His aim was to establish, not that stoning was Qur'ān, but that it was a divine imposition. That is shown by his speaking of entering it in the margin, as opposed to in the corpus of the text.

It was ʿUmar who urged Abū Bakr to assemble the texts of the Qur'ān in order to preserve them. How, then, should there have been omitted on that occasion just the thing that ʿUmar is supposed to have regarded as part of the Qur'ān? Presumably ʿUmar would not include something that Abū Bakr did not recognise as part of the Qur'ān. The other Companions who had collected the Qur'ān in the lifetime of the Prophet would surely have included the stoning verse in their personal codices, if they knew it. Had ʿUmar had any doubt, he needed only to have consulted them. If they did not know it, they would not enter it. It is absurd that Abū Bakr appears to have omitted the very verse that ʿUmar felt inclined to record.

Concluding that stoning had been a sunna, the author of the Mabānī finds excuse for the early Muslims who had spoken of it as a revelation, by reminding us that there are elements of the Sunna which were revealed.[65] They were not necessarily revealed as Qur'ān which must be recorded and which might be recited at prayer. Gabriel instructed Muḥammad in certain matters which, in that sense, were revelations. The Prophet would observe them, without recording them in the texts of the Qur'ān. Such rulings are attested as coming from God, but their wording was not recorded, since the mode of their revelation was not that of the revelation of the Qur'ān, now recited at prayer. That there was such a mode of revelation is indicated by the Prophet's words, 'I have been given the Qur'ān and along with it, its like [mithl].' That is a reference to the Sunna.

In the 'hired hand' ḥadīth, the Prophet said, 'I shall judge in accordance with the Book of God.' He thereupon inflicted the stoning penalty, of which there is no mention in the Book of God. He must have meant, therefore, by the expression the Book of God, the *ḥukm*, the verdict of God, revealed in the manner stated.

The Companions did not record the stoning verse despite the statement attributed to ʿUmar, and despite their certainty that the Prophet had stoned, and that stoning is one of God's injunctions upon the Muslims.

ʿUmar did not record it in spite of his certainty that it was an *āya* revealed by God, and in spite of his being Head of State and Church. ʿUmar knew perfectly well that it was not Qur'ān.

ibn Qutaiba had been familiar with the *ḥadīth*, 'I have been given the Qur'ān, and with it its like',[66] an undoubted calque on Q 2.106. He explained it as a reference to the Sunna which Gabriel brought to Muḥammad, as he brought him the Qur'ān. Thus, for ibn Qutaiba, as latterly also it had been for Šāfiʿī, the Sunna was part of revelation.

Šāfiʿī, in an exegetical dispute, had similarly asserted that the root *t l w* (cf. *tilāwa*) might be used equally of the Qur'ān and the Sunna.[67]

Like the anonymous author of the *Mabānī*, Zarkašī, after agonising long over the ʿUmar *ḥadīth*, at length concluded that this was an instance of the isolate report on the basis of which the text of the Qur'ān could not be established, although the relevant ruling might be ascertained.[68]

ibn Ẓufar in the *Yanbūʿ* considered that this case ought not to be included in the list of *āyas* withdrawn in respect of their wording alone. It was the subject of khabar al wāḥid which gives no basis for statements as to the text of the Qur'ān. In an undisguised reference to the parallel quarrels as to the wording of Q 2.106, and its interpretation, he argues that, in any event, stoning is not an instance of naskh. It is an example of rafʿ or of nasā' - deliberate omission from the muṣḥaf. The rulings of verses of this kind can be known from sources other than the original texts.[69]

Suyūṭī rejects Zarkašī's convenient solution. Stoning cannot be considered from the angle of khabar al wāḥid. ʿUmar had received his Qur'ān text direct from the Prophet. His own solution is merely apologetic: the reason for the withdrawal of this wording is the divine solicitude for the welfare of the Muslims. Non-recording of the verse means non-dissemination of the ruling. Where committed, the offence is best left undisclosed (a detail which has some measure of support in a source as distant in time as Mālik, K. al Ḥudūd).

Zurqānī improves even on Suyūṭī's banality by adding that the Qur'ān, the Word of God, is inimitable in, among other respects, its brevity - hence the omission of this verse![70] Besides, he argues, such things are unseemly, not merely to perform, but even to mention in so holy a book.[71]

5 The *muṣḥaf*: an incomplete record of the Qur'ān

It seems perfectly clear that in all this material - the formation of *ḥadīth* reports; the recognition of the inadequacy of the wording of this or that *ḥadīth* and the consequent improvement of the text; the commentary and criticism leading to 'interpretation' of the reports; appeal to the exegesis of this or that helpful Qur'ān verse - we are dealing with the attempt to provide the documentation of one of two allegations stemming from the ongoing theoretical discussion between two sets of *uṣūlīs*.

One group insisted, for methodological reasons, that the stoning or the suckling regulations had originally been revealed as part of the Qur'ān. The other group, appreciating that in this view lay serious hidden theoretical dangers for the creative role of the Sunna, argued that the stoning penalty had been introduced by the Prophet as an element in his Sunna.

Both groups are agreed on the common legal doctrine that stoning is indeed the Islamic penalty, and from the attempts of the *uṣūlīs* to document the unanimity of the *fuqahā'* there naturally developed the secondary dispute as to whether the Sunna might or might not supersede the Qur'ān.

Šāfi'ī had not invented the stoning penalty. It was in circulation before his day, as was also the stoning verse, in response to the challenge of those who rejected the Fiqh penalty on account of their inability to find any reference to it in the Qur'ān texts. Šāfiʿī, on the other hand, had espoused the ʿĀ'iša reports on the suckling verses and his argument clearly leads directly to naskh al tilāwa dūna al ḥukm.

Ṭabarī, the exegete, embraced and defended the view that there were omissions from the muṣḥaf which must therefore be distinct from the Qur'ān. By the latter, he would understand all that had ever been revealed to Muḥammad. By muṣḥaf, he would understand all of the Qur'ān which had been preserved in writing and passed down to posterity by the first generation of Muslims, the Companions. Ṭabari had reached this position solely on the basis of exegetical ḥadīths originally constructed to document one point of view as to the meaning of Q 87, and still in circulation in his day. Ṭabarī, the uṣūlī, found the source of the Islamic Law's stoning penalty in the Sunna. He therefore never had need of a principle of naskh al tilāwa dūna al ḥukm. As far as he was concerned, the Sunna in this instance undoubtedly had superseded the ruling of the Qur'ān.

Only those uṣūlīs who could never concede that the Sunna had abrogated the Qur'ān were responsible for the addition to the theory of this third mode of naskh.

> The wording al šaikh wa al šaikha has been withdrawn, but the ruling is still valid in Law. On this question, certain scholars advanced the view that the Qur'ān may be abrogated by the Sunna. They allege that Q 4.15 was abrogated by the ʿUbāda ḥadīth. This view is utterly unacceptable since even those

> who countenance the repeal of a Qur'ān ruling at the hands of the Sunna admit this only in the case of the mutawātir or mašhūr ḥadīth. Isolate reports may never in any circumstances supersede the Book. Further, all scholars are agreed that the wording of the Book could never be superseded, whatever the 'spread' of the report. Our opinion is that neither the ruling nor the wording of the Qur'ān can in any circumstances be superseded by the ḥadīth reports of the Sunna. Q 4 can be regarded as having been abrogated solely by the stoning verse.[1]

The Qur'ān, we are reminded by another scholar was established by the consensus. It is thus very different from that which is liable to provoke argument. The texts of the Qur'ān are securely recorded in the muṣḥaf, they are repeated on the tongues and preserved in the breasts of men. The Almighty has testified to its rulings, has promised to preserve it and has rendered His Prophet immune from errors, slips of the tongue or forgetfulness in respect of His revelations which He had taught him to recite.

The Sunna, on the contrary, has not come down from the whole body of the Muslims. It is transmitted by a mere one or two. The total number of the transmitters does not match that of the Qur'ān. How then could the Sunna replace the Qur'ān, when they are far from equal in terms of inimitability, textual preservation and transmission? Differences have afflicted the interpretation of the Sunna, somewhat reducing its probative force. The utmost that can be claimed on its behalf is that the Sunna serves to elucidate the Qur'ān, never to abrogate it.

Consider the case of Q 4.15. The text is mutawātir. It conveys the command to detain women in their quarters until death release them or God appoint a way. The Prophet said, 'Take it from me! God has now appointed the way', and he explained what that way was. It was the flogging penalty revealed in Q 24.2.[2]

> The Sunna - the Prophet's stoning the adulterer - has not been established by tawātur, but only by isolate reports. The most one might say is that the community unanimously accepts stoning and since ijmāʿ cannot abrogate a source (it merely serves to indicate the existence of a mutawātir source that did abrogate), to identify that source as having been a mutawātir sunna which, however, has not reached us, is no more satisfactory than to attribute the naskh in question to a mutawātir verse which also has failed to reach us owing to the withdrawal of the wording.[3]

Statements of this kind identify the methodological theories as the birthplace of the stoning verse.

> It cannot be argued, merely because ʿUmar said in his ḥadīth, 'But that I fear that men will accuse me of adding to the Qur'ān something that does not belong to it I would have recorded al šaikh wa al šaikha', or that, if recorded, it would have been written on the margin of the muṣḥaf, that that indicates that it was not really part of the Qur'ān. For we hold that it could have been a verse whose wording alone was withdrawn. Nor can it be held that āyat al šaikh wa al šaikha was never established by tawātur but depended solely upon ʿUmar's word; that the abrogation of the mutawātir [Q 24.2] by the isolate is never admitted by the scholars; and that, since stoning is documented solely in isolate reports, one is inevitably forced to the conclusion that stoning is derived from the consensus of the scholars. But the ijmāʿ cannot serve in its own right to abrogate a source - it merely indicates the

> fact of abrogation, and thus signals their awareness of the existence of a *mutawātir* source that did the abrogating. Thus, to postulate on this topic the existence at one time of a *mutawātir sunna*, which has not however reached us, is in no way preferable to postulating the existence at one time of a Qur'ān verse which has not reached us, owing to the withdrawal of the wording.[4]

The significant feature of the discussions is the central fact of the consensus among the *fuqahā'* that, in given circumstances, the Islamic penalty is in fact death by stoning. All that the discussions make clear is that what the Muslim who inherited the *Fiqh* rulings and then set out to review them in the light of the assumptions of *uṣūl al fiqh* sought to discover was, which of the two primary sources, conceived as underlying the *Fiqh*, had provided the document which led to the ruling and best served to verify it.

> ibn al Jawzī reports: 'The scholars are divided on the question of the documentation of the stoning penalty. One party argues that it was derived from a Qur'ān revelation whose wording alone, however, was withdrawn. The second party sees the source as having been the Sunna.'[5]

Only the first of the two groups interests us. It is surely undeniable, in the light of all that has been set out up to this point, that given that a sizeable number of the Muslim scholars - and those not among the least influential thinkers in the history of the development of the Islamic sciences - maintained that the Qur'ān had originally been of greater extent than is to be found in the texts as they have come down to us, the effect of such ideas upon the Muslim version of the history of the Qur'ān texts, and especially upon the history of their first collection, must be traceable in the collection *ḥadīths* as these begin to appear, and in their turn evolve in the light of the findings of *uṣūl al fiqh*.

The Muslims would naturally adopt that version of the history of the Qur'ān, and especially of its first collection, which was in conformity with their outlook. It was immaterial whether their theoretical views had derived from the implications of the *Fiqh*, or from the implications of exegetical *ḥadīths* relevant to the interpretation of certain Qur'ān verses.

Unlike Šāfiʿī, Ṭabarī was one of those scholars who accepted with equanimity the *uṣūl* proposition that the Sunna had superseded the Qur'ān. Ṭabarī had no theoretical need of any principle of *naskh al tilāwa dūna al ḥukm* - of a principle that is, that the *muṣḥaf* did not coincide with the Qur'ān. Ṭabarī found the source and the justification of the stoning penalty in the Sunna.[6] He did not require to posit the existence at one time of a stoning verse, present no longer in the *muṣḥaf*. But neither could he ignore the presence in the Tradition of *ḥadīths* reporting the absence of this or that *āya* of the Qur'ān from the texts which had been put together by the Companions. The verses had been forgotten either by the Prophet or by his Companions before the texts had been first assembled.

We have seen that such stories can be accounted for in terms of the exegesis of verses such as Q 87. But in the age of *taqlīd*, *ḥadīths* of sound *isnād* must be accepted. To that extent, therefore, Ṭabarī was obliged to suppose that Qur'ān and *muṣḥaf* were two distinct and separate entities.

Thus, scholars who for systematic reasons were driven to presume the presence in the Qur'ān at one time of certain legal rulings which are not referred to in the Qur'ān, were joined by scholars such as Ṭabarī who had no theoretical need to seek refuge in such an assumption. Both classes of scholar subscribed in common to the view that our present texts of the Qur'ān, that is, the *muṣḥaf*, must be incomplete.

The general view that the texts of the *muṣḥaf* are incomplete leads quite naturally to the exclusion of the Prophet from the history of their collection, but only as long as the Muslims are discussing the history of the Qur'ān document.

The Qur'ān, however, as we have already noted, was much more to the Muslims than merely a document. For them, the Qur'ān was both document and source. As document, it was referred to as the *muṣḥaf*. As source, it was known as *kitāb allāh*, the Book of God. Obviously the Muslims had to associate their Prophet with the Book of God, since only through him and by him was the Book of God knowable. The fact of the revelation to the Prophet is the sole sanction of *kitāb allāh* as source, both for those elements in which it happens to agree with the *muṣḥaf*, but even more particularly for those which *kitāb allāh* guarantees, despite their absence from the *muṣḥaf*. Instances met with were the stoning verse and the sucklings verse.

In brief, the term *kitāb allāh* represents a convenient concept of both a theoretical and an ideal pseudo-historical exegetically derived nature. The term *muṣḥaf*, by contrast, refers to a physical object.

The verbal distinction between *muṣḥaf* and *kitāb* was not always strictly observed and great care has to be exercised if one is to determine what, in any given context, is actually being discussed.

The Muslim argument on the collection of the Qur'ān texts is the reverse of the European. Since we 'know', but only by accepting at face value Muslim assertions to this effect, that the Qur'ān was not first collected until after the Prophet's death, we have on that account supposed that the likelihood is that it will be incomplete.[7] The Muslims, 'knowing' that it is incomplete, have on that account argued that it could not have been collected until after the Prophet's death.

Verses which remained valid for the *Fiqh* up to the moment of the Prophet's death, and were recognised as continuing valid after the Prophet's death, would not, one might suppose, have been omitted from the *muṣḥaf* if the texts of the revelation had been assembled, checked, edited and promulgated by the Prophet himself.

Unfortunately, as will also shortly be seen, the Muslims required simultaneously to hold certain other views touching the Qur'ān incompatible with this particular conclusion. One might instance their doctrine of the Qur'ān's *tawātur* alongside their acceptance and recognition of so-called Companion variant readings. The total evidence they have adduced in this sphere, and in that in confirmation of the sum of their attitudes, has led to confusion and serious contradiction within the Muslim accounts of the history of the collection of the texts of the Qur'ān. These confusions and contradictions will be of considerable assistance as we review and analyse their accounts.

PART II

The history of the collection of the Qur'ān texts

6 The first collection

The history of the collection of the Qur'ān texts was discussed by the Muslim under the aegis of three views:

1. the virtually unanimous opinion that our present Qur'ān texts (the muṣḥaf) are incomplete;
2. the virtually unanimous acceptance of the proposition that the first stage in the history of the Qur'ān texts was marked by the circulation of a number of not quite identical recensions privately assembled and independently organised by a number of Muḥammad's contemporaries;
3. the unanimous assertion that there obtains conflict between the sources of the Fiqh: Qur'ān and Sunna.

The major European work in this field is the magisterial Geschichte des Qorans (1860) by Th. Nöldeke, as revised by Fr. Schwally's second edition, part 2 (Leipzig 1919). Since the publication of this edition no new suggestions on the history of the Qur'ān texts have been advanced.

ʿAbdullāh b. ʿUmar reportedly said, 'Let none of you say, "I have got the whole of the Qur'ān." How does he know what all of it is? Much of the Qur'ān has gone [d h b]. Let him say instead, "I have got what has survived."'[1]

The intimate connection between this utterance and the classical ḥadīths on the collection of the Qur'ān texts is illustrated by a remark attributed to Zaid b. Thābit, 'The Prophet died and the Qur'ān had not been assembled into a single place.'[2] For it is this same Zaid who plays the central role in all the *ḥadīths* on the post-Muhammadan collection(s) of the revealed texts variously attributed to the Prophet's first, second and third successor.

In these reports, two motives are insistent: the failure by Muḥammad to collect and edit the texts; and the suggestion of the incompleteness, potential or actual which might have been expected to follow.

> Zaid reports, 'Abū Bakr sent for me on the occasion of the deaths of those killed in the Yemāma wars. I found ʿUmar b. al Khaṭṭāb with him. Abū Bakr said, "ʿUmar has just come to me and said, 'In the Yemāma fighting death has dealt most severely with the *qurrā'* and I fear it will deal with equal severity with them in other theatres of war and as a result much of the Qur'ān will perish [*d̲ h b*]. I am therefore of the opinion that you should command that the Qur'ān be collected.'" Abū Bakr added, "I said to ʿUmar, 'How can we do what the Prophet never did?' ʿUmar replied that it was nonetheless a good act. He did not cease replying to my scruples until God reconciled me to the undertaking." Abū Bakr continued, "Zaid, you are young and intelligent and we know nothing to your discredit. You used to record the revelations for the Prophet, so pursue the Qur'ān and collect it all together." By God! had they asked me to remove a mountain it could not have been more weighty than what they would now have me do in ordering me to collect the Qur'ān. I therefore asked them how they could do what the Prophet had not done but Abū Bakr insisted that it was permissible. He did not cease replying to my scruples until God reconciled me to the undertaking as He had already reconciled

> Abū Bakr and ʿUmar. I thereupon pursued the Qur'ān collecting it all together from palm-branches, flat stones and the memories of men. I found the last verse of sūrat al Tawba in the possession of Abū Khuzaima al Anṣārī, having found it with no one else, "There has now come to you..." to the end of the sūra.'
>
> The sheets [ṣuḥuf] that Zaid prepared in this manner remained in the keeping of Abū Bakr. On his death, they passed to ʿUmar who then bequeathed them on his death to his daughter Ḥafṣa.[3]

A number of points arising from this ḥadīth have been noted in the Muslim commentaries.

It reconciles a tradition that Abū Bakr was the first to collect the texts with variant traditions which ascribe the initiative to ʿUmar.[4]

The repetition of the motif that the Prophet had not collected the texts, together with the reference to the deaths of the qurrā' or Qur'ān memorisers, and ʿUmar's consequent fear that much of the Qur'ān would perish; the reference to the primitiveness of the materials on which the revelations had been recorded in the lifetime of the Prophet and upon which Zaid was partly dependent for the preparation of his recension - all these elements predispose one to an expectation that the edition prepared by Zaid might be incomplete. Yet such expectation is balanced by the assurance that our text is in actual fact complete.

Nöldeke exaggerated the role played by written documents in Zaid's activity, for we note here the emphasis placed upon the missing verse supplied by one man's memory. Zaid realised that a verse which he knew to be part of the revelation and which he recalled was not to be found among

Muḥammad's survivors. However he at last did discover it in one man's possession. The verse is therefore attested by two competent witnesses.

Reference is made explicitly to Zaid's youth. In addition, the information that Zaid had been employed to write down the revelations for the Prophet guarantees the isnād of Zaid's text. It is marfū', that is, received direct from the Prophet. Further, it dates from the Prophet's late period. As nothing to Zaid's discredit is known, his testimony is that of dū 'adlin.

But we also find in the Tradition the following:

> 'Umar b. al Khaṭṭāb enquired about a verse of the Book of God. On being informed that it had been in the possession of so-and-so who had been killed in the Yemāma wars, 'Umar exclaimed the formula expressing loss, 'We are God's and unto Him is our return.' 'Umar gave the command and the Qur'ān was collected. He was the first to collect the Qur'ān.[5]

The Qur'ān texts which come down to us from 'Umar's day are unquestionably incomplete.

Zuhrī reports that when slaughter befell the Muslims in the Yemāma it was Abū Bakr who feared that many of the qurrā' would perish.[6] Suggesting that nothing of the Qur'ān had been lost, this report concurs with the report from Zaid in indicating that our Qur'ān texts are in actual fact complete.

It is said that upward of 700 Companions fell in the Yemāma. Sufyān reports that when Sālim was slain 'Umar hastened to Abū Bakr.[7] But, as Sālim had already 'collected the Qur'ān into a single volume' - he was the first to collect the

Qur'ān, and gave it the name muṣḥaf, a word he had heard in Ethiopia[8] - his death would have had no damaging effect for the texts.

ʿAlī reported that the stoning verse had been revealed but those who bore it together with other verses in their memories perished in the Yemāma.[9]

Two questions have therefore been broached: 1. the completeness/incompleteness of the muṣḥaf; 2. the first to have collected it. This was either Abū Bakr, or ʿUmar or Sālim, or it might have been ʿAlī who 'on the death of the Prophet vowed that he would not don outdoor clothes until he had collected the Qur'ān into a single volume'.[10]

The task, whoever first accomplished it, was merely one of assembling the Qur'ān which 'already in the lifetime of the Prophet was recorded in writing. Abū Bakr's contribution was to arrange for the transfer of these sheets, then scattered about Medina, into a single volume.' God informs us that in Muḥammad's day the Qur'ān was written on 'pure sheets from which he recites'.[11] Q 98.2 may or may not refer to Muḥammad. In either event, the remark is exegetical rather than historical.

Only an appreciation that entirely independent needs, pulling in opposite directions and directing to differing conclusions, are operative here, will enable us to realise that several distinct Qur'ān's are envisaged in these apparently contradictory discussions.

Kitāb allāh is the source of the Islamic Law. The Qur'ān, Scripture and credentials of the polity of Islam, is ideally identical with that revealed to the Prophet and transmitted to our times without addition, without subtraction, a whole complete and true record of the divine revelations.[12] But the Qur'ān, the mutawātir document on the basis of whose texts alone the prayer of the Muslim is valid, nevertheless differs from both kitāb allāh and the muṣḥaf prepared by any of Muḥammad's Companions save only Abū Bakr or ʿUmar, or perhaps ʿUthmān.

The first to collect the Qur'ān between two covers was Abū Bakr. awwal man jamaʿa al Qur'ān baina lawḥain.[13]

ʿAlī said, 'God bless Abū Bakr! He was the first to collect the Qur'ān between two covers',[14] and again, 'the greatest reward in respect of the maṣāḥif will fall to Abū Bakr for he was the first to collect the text between two covers'.[15]

Hišām b. ʿUrwa reports his father as saying, 'Abū Bakr collected the Qur'ān after the death of the Prophet.'[16]

> ʿUmar was the first to collect the Qur'ān into a single volume [muṣḥaf]...ʿUmar desired to collect the Qur'ān. He addressed the people, 'Whoever among you received any part of the Qur'ān directly from the very mouth of the Prophet let him bring it here to us.'[17]

In one version of the report on ʿAlī's vow, we read, 'until I collected the Qur'ān between two covers'.

The commentators assure us that this version is erroneous. Only a single transmitter credits ʿAlī with a collection ab initio. The report is isolate.[18] Omitting the words, 'between two covers' or 'into a single volume', and supposing the transmission to be accurate, the meaning of jamaʿa al Qur'ān would be 'memorised the Qur'ān'.[19]

Similarly, where used of ʿUmar, the root j m ʿ signifies ašāra bi jamʿihi, 'advised its collection'.[20]

Schwally too readily swallowed the equation of j m ʿ with 'to get by heart'; but he dismissed the equation of j m ʿ with ašāra bi jamʿihi as arbitrary.[21]

Elsewhere we are assured that Zaid first wrote out the Qur'ān for Abū Bakr on scraps of leather and on palm-branches. On the death of Abū Bakr, ʿUmar appointed Zaid to transcribe his materials into the ṣaḥīfa which remained in ʿUmar's possession.[22] Zaid says that they had been accustomed to organising the Qur'ān from these scraps in the presence of the Prophet.[23]

> ʿUmar decided to collect the Qur'ān. He addressed the people, 'Let whoever received direct from the mouth of the Prophet any part of the Qur'ān now bring it here to us.' They had written what they had heard on sheets, tablets and palm-branches. ʿUmar would not accept anything from anyone until two witnesses bore testimony. He was assassinated while still engaged on his collection. His successor, ʿUthmān addressed the people, 'Let whoever has anything of the Book of God bring it here to us.' ʿUthmān would accept nothing from anyone until two witnesses bore testimony. Khuzaima b. Thābit said, 'I see that you have omitted two verses. You have not written them.' They asked what they were and he said, 'I had direct from the Prophet: "There has come to you...". ʿUthmān said, 'And I bear witness that these verses come from God.' He asked Khuzaima where they should enter them. He replied, 'Make them the close of the latest Qur'ānic revelation.' Thus was Barā'a sealed with these words.[24]

The report recalls not only the above Zaid ḥadīth. It is

also connected with the following:

> They collected the Qur'ān into a *muṣḥaf* in the reign of Abū Bakr, some men writing to the dictation of Ubayy. When they reached Q 9.127 some supposed that that was the last part of the Qur'ān to have been revealed. But Ubayy pointed out that the Prophet had taught him two verses more and, since they were the last of the Qur'ān to be revealed, the Book should close on the note on which it had begun.[25]

The concern with the *isnād* of the Qur'ān and its *tawātur* is patent. No part of the Qur'ān is *khabar wāḥid*, based on the word of a single guarantor. Nothing was accepted into the *muṣḥaf* until two witnesses bore testimony. Nothing was included unless it had been heard direct from the very mouth of the Prophet.

The concern with the dating of the collection is equally evident. In what concerns the *isnād*, the name of Ubayy has not yet finally been replaced by that of Zaid. Ubayy had served Muḥammad as amanuensis before Zaid's selection. Zaid is the later of two witnesses.[26] In a further *ḥadīth*, Ubayy's name had not yet been replaced by that of Ḥafṣa, 'They collected the Qur'ān from the codex prepared by Ubayy' (*Maṣāḥif*, p. 30).

Reference to the last verse of the Qur'ān to be revealed, and thus to be recorded, is in Suyūṭī's view a gratuitous allusion to matters other than collecting. There is nowhere any suggestion that the scraps of the revelations had been arranged chronologically. The date of revelation was ignored in arranging the Qur'ān texts. Dates are relevant only to *al nāsikh wa al mansūkh*.

The *ḥadīth* further represents an incomplete reaching

after fulfilment of a rule laid down in Q 2.282 for the correct action to be taken in recording a debt, 'Let the scribe write and let the borrower dictate.' Ubayy dictated and the others wrote. The ḥadīth however marks incomplete verification of the verses contributed by Ubayy, since he is their sole witness. ʿUmar and ʿUthmān had demanded two witnesses for acceptance into the muṣḥaf.

In the ʿUthmān ḥadīth, ʿUthmān himself volunteered corroboration of the testimony of Khuzaima b. Thābit. Earlier we noted Zaid b. Thābit's endorsement of the testimony of Abū Khuzaima on the very same verse. A further ḥadīth features one al Ḥārith b. Khuzaima who brought this very verse to ʿUmar.[27]

Q 2.282 carries the additional admonition, 'demand the testimony of two of your men'.

Abū Bakr ordered ʿUmar and Zaid to sit in the gate of the mosque and to include in the muṣḥaf only what was vouched for by the testimony of two men.[28]

ʿUthmān asked whose was the purest speech and whose the greatest acquaintance with the Qur'ān.[29] A variant might mean whose is the greatest acquaintance with the Book, alternatively, with the art of writing.[30] On their reply, he commanded, 'Let Saʿīd dictate and let Zaid write.'

This proper solicitude of the Muslims to find, consistently throughout every phase of the first moves to record the Qur'ān texts, two witnesses to authenticate verses to be included in the muṣḥaf, a motif undeniably derived from Q 2.282, led to a remarkable status being conferred upon the individual from whom Zaid, in the reign of Abū Bakr, had recovered the verse from Q 9 which he had failed to find with anyone else. Unhappily, however, the elegance of this rationalisation is marred by uncertainty as to the man's identity.

'Khuzaima was known as dū al šahādatain. The Prophet had declared his testimony equal to that of two men.'[31]

The verse was volunteered by Abū Khuzaima. 'The Prophet had declared his evidence the equal of that of two men.'[32]

In default of this item of information, Q 2.282's two witnesses might refer to abstract testimonies. Zaid's words, 'I did not find it with anyone else', were interpreted to mean that he had not found the verse in writing with anyone else.[33] That indicates that Zaid had not been satisfied with mere remembrance to the exclusion of written evidence, nor had he been satisfied with mere written records until that which was found in writing was endorsed by the memories of other witnesses.[34] The memories and the written records together thus afford two classes of testimony: receipt of the revelations direct from the Prophet - samā'; recording - kitāba (i.e. recording during the Prophet's lifetime).

Two principal tendencies are detectable throughout the confusions of the ḥadīths:

1. The muṣḥaf is incomplete. Its collection was not undertaken until some time after the death of the Prophet.

> Zuhrī reports, 'We have heard that many Qur'ān passages were revealed but that those who had memorised them fell in the Yemāma fighting. Those passages had not been written down and, following the deaths of those who knew them, were no longer

> known; nor had Abū Bakr, nor ʿUmar nor ʿUthmān as yet collected the texts of the Qur'ān.[35] Those lost passages were not to be found with anyone after the deaths of those who had memorised them. This, I understand, was one of the considerations which impelled them to pursue the Qur'ān during the reign of Abū Bakr, committing it to sheets for fear that there should perish in further theatres of war men who bore much of the Qur'ān which they would take to the grave with them on their fall, and which, with their passing, would not be found with any other.[36]

The motif of the Qur'ān's incompleteness collides head-on with the Qur'ān's tawātur.

2. The Qur'ān texts in the hands of the Muslims represent the universal Qur'ān Tradition of the text as preserved by the countless number of Muḥammad's Companions living on at and around Medina after the Prophet's death.

The device of the two witnesses, borrowed as we see from the Qur'ān source, was intended to rebut any suggestion arising from the oldest accounts of the collection of the Qur'ān texts that the muṣḥaf represented that class of dubious information from the Apostolic age dubbed in the jargon of the Ḥadīth specialists khabar al wāḥid, the isolate report.

> It does not follow from Zaid's saying that he had failed to find the āya from sūrat al Tawba in the possession of anyone else, that at that time it was not mutawātira among those who had learnt their Qur'ān from the Companions, but had not heard it direct from the Prophet. What Zaid was seeking was the evidence of those who had had their Qur'ān texts direct from the Prophet. Besides, it is probable that when Zaid found it with Abū Khuzaima the other Companions recalled having heard it. Zaid himself certainly recalled that he had heard it...

> al Da'ūdī commented that Abū Khuzaima was not the sole witness. Zaid knew the verse. It was thus attested by two men. Da'ūdī was under the misapprehension that the rule that the Qur'ān text cannot be established on the basis of the isolate report refers to reports from single individuals. That is not the case. By isolate is meant all reports which do not satisfy all the conditions of tawātur. The number of transmitters might be considerable and yet, should one of the conditions of tawātur be lacking, the report would be regarded as isolate. The correct interpretation of Zaid's remark that he had failed to find the āya with anyone else is that he had failed to find it in writing, not that he had failed to find those who bore it in their memories.[37]
>
> The reports that ʿUmar would not accept anything into the muṣḥaf until two witnesses had borne testimony indicate that Zaid did not satisfy himself with merely finding something in writing. He further required in his extremely cautious approach that those who had received the Qur'ān direct from the Prophet should also give their testimony, although Zaid himself knew that the verse was an authentic part of the Qur'ān.[38]

The technical desirability of furnishing the Qur'ān texts with the tawātur now demanded by the scholars is adequately reflected in the various techniques which have been worked into the texts or into the interpretation of the available collection ḥadīths.

A significant and troublesome breach of this rule of tawātur will shortly occupy our attention.

The extreme caution exercised by Zaid in his work of pursuing and collecting the Qur'ān texts was a sufficient guarantee that what the Muslims found in their copies of the muṣḥaf consisted solely of texts that properly belonged there, and that nothing that did not belong there had found its way into the text.

There was no similar guarantee that all that did belong there had been included and that nothing that belonged to the Qur'ān had been excluded.

Zaid's test, it will be seen, was negative.

Nöldeke expressed the commonsense view that it may be doubted whether in the very earliest days, when he had next to no following, Muḥammad had already begun to have his revelations recorded. If he had not, then it is always possible that some of the earliest Qur'ān revelations have not survived.[39] The suggestion is inherently probable. It is not of course the view that the Muslims have formed.

We have already considered what for convenience I called the exegetes' concern for the distinction between Muḥammad's human and his prophetic memory. It is of the utmost import that we bear in mind constantly when reviewing the Muslim accounts of the history of the texts of the Qur'ān that Muḥammad, the Prophet, could never merely forget any of the Qur'ān, even if Muḥammad, the man, might occasionally fail to recall this or that verse in ordinary everyday life, as when, for example, he went into the mosque to pray. 'The Messenger of God heard a man recite by night and said, "May God have mercy on that man! He has just reminded me of verse so-and-so that I had forgotten from sūra such-and-such."'[40]

More than once already we have traced such reports to the disputes on the exegesis of verses containing functions of the root n s y.

Bukhārī preserves a ḥadīth to the effect that some men waited upon ibn ʿAbbās, cousin and supporter of ʿAlī, and later upon Muḥammad b. al Ḥanafiya, son of ʿAlī and himself a figurehead in the Šīʿa's claims on behalf of the Holy Family. To the question whether Muḥammad had 'left anything' each of these notables in turn replied that Muḥammad had left no more than may be found between the 'two covers'. ibn Ḥajar comments, 'Muḥammad did not omit from the muṣḥaf any part of the Qur'ān which ought to be publicly recited [at prayer].'[41]

That implies that there is Qur'ān material missing from the muṣḥaf that need not be publicly recited. For ibn Ḥajar, the ḥadīth denies the existence outside the muṣḥaf of verses which ought to have been included.

That implies that there are verses that ought not to be included in the muṣḥaf. He finds this reading of the tafsīr of the ḥadīth confirmed by other reports from Companions mentioning Qur'ān materials revealed, but subsequently withdrawn in respect of their wording. That had not prejudiced the continuing legal validity of their rulings. The wording had simply been omitted from the muṣḥaf. An instance of the kind is ʿUmar's report on the omission of the stoning verse.

Other verses had been withdrawn in respect of both their wording and ruling. An example in the Tradition is Anas' ḥadīth on the Qur'ān's reference to the Bi'r Maʿūna martyrs. Further cases include Ubayy's remark that Aḥzāb had originally been as long as Baqara; Ḥudaifa's remark, 'They don't recite a quarter of al Barā'a today.'

These are all sound ḥadīths and represent instances
of naskh al ḥukm wa al tilāwa and naskh al tilāwa dūna al ḥukm.
Both are types of Qur'ān omission from the muṣḥaf.

Omissions fall into two classes: revelations withdrawn in respect of their wording and ruling - withdrawn from
both document and source; and, secondly, revelations
withdrawn in respect of their wording alone - withdrawn from
the document alone.

> The Qāḍī Abū Bakr al Bāqillānī states, 'The entire
> Qur'ān revealed by God and commanded by Him to be
> recorded in writing, except what He suppressed,
> wording and ruling together, or wording only, although
> He may also have suppressed the ruling, is this which
> is between the two covers. Not one jot is missing
> and not one tittle has been added.'[42]

The Qāḍī has defined the muṣḥaf, not the Qur'ān. Only Qur'ān
verses whose wording has been unaffected by the two modes of
withdrawal have been included in the muṣḥaf. Excluded,
therefore, were all passages whose wording and ruling had
been nullified and all passages whose wording alone had been
nullified. In the latter case, the ruling may well have
continued valid as in the case of the stoning verse.

Insofar, therefore, as the formal contents of the Qur'ān are
concerned, we cannot afford not to take into account the
Islamic theories of nāsikh and mansūkh. As already
indicated, the theories have influenced the Muslim accounts
of the history and collection of the Qur'ān texts to the
extent of consciously, deliberately and systematically
excluding Muḥammad from all stages of the preparation and
promulgation of the Qur'ān texts which we have before us

today. In short, there are no Muslim accounts of the collection of the Qur'ān. There are only accounts of the history of the collection of the muṣḥaf. These are the children of the history of the Muslim concept 'Qur'ān'.

The Prophet's removal from the history of the collection of our texts of the Qur'ān was rationalised into the virtual impossibility of his participation. On Zaid's remark that the Prophet had died before the Qur'ān had been brought together, Khaṭṭābī reflected,

> It is likely that the reason the Prophet did not collect the Qur'ān into a single volume was his expectation that naskh would affect either some of its legal provisions, or some of the wording. But once the revelation of the Qur'ān ceased on the Prophet's death, God inspired his successors to the task of collecting the texts of the Qur'ān in fulfilment of the divine promise to preserve it.[43]

Zarkašī saw the danger of Muḥammad's playing his part in the collection of the texts for

> with naskh a regular event, had Muḥammad brought the Qur'ān into a single volume and then some part of the wording were withdrawn, the seeds of the corruption of Islam might well have been sown. God preserved the texts of the revelation in the memories of the Muslims until the time when naskh was possible had come to an end.[44]

Naskh in both these statements visibly refers only to the withdrawal of wording.

Taking ḥadīths about Muḥammad's forgetting, or a verse being withdrawn at their face value, European scholars have all missed the point.

ʿAbdullāh b. Masʿūd reported that the Prophet had

taught him to recite a particular Qur'ān verse which he learned by heart and copied out in his personal muṣḥaf. When night came, and ʿAbdullāh rose to pray, he desired to recite that āya but could not recall a syllable. In the morning he consulted his muṣḥaf, only to find the page blank! He mentioned this to the Prophet who told him that that verse had been withdrawn that very night.

Nöldeke argued,

> Eine vollständige Sammlung des ganzen Qorāns war schon seinem Verfasser selbst kaum möglich. Denn nicht nur hatte er auch nach der Überlieferung der Muslime und sogar dem Zeugnisse des Qorāns manche Stücke schon selbst vergessen, manche wurden auch absichtlich von ihm verändert.[45]

The Qur'ān whose testimony is here invoked is Q 2.106 and Q 87.6-7!

The Muslim accounts we have just considered, and which Nöldeke has just oversimplified, are rather more subtle than he or Schwally realised.

The commentators spoke of the withdrawal of either the ruling or the wording of Qur'ān verses, and we have learnt that the latter phenomenon had in the theory of the uṣūlīs two aspects: withdrawal of both wording and ruling; withdrawal of the wording alone. In the latter case, the withdrawal of the wording was held to have had no effect upon the validity of the ruling. Naturally, it had no significance whatsoever for the contents of the muṣḥaf.

In the classical stage of the development of the new sub-science of naskh three phenomena were isolated.

1. Naskh al ḥukm wa al tilāwa, the suppression of both

the wording and the ruling of an alleged revealed Qur'ān statement.

2. Naskh al ḥukm dūna al tilāwa, the suppression of one Qur'ān ruling, replaced by another Qur'ān ruling or by a Sunna ruling; the suppression of a Sunna ruling, replaced by another Sunna ruling, or by a Qur'ān ruling.

3. Naskh al tilāwa dūna al ḥukm, the suppression of a Qur'ān wording without prejudice, however, to the continuing validity of its own ruling for legal purposes (i.e. for Fiqh-validation purposes in uṣūl al fiqh).

The commentators spoke above of both 1 and 2 and both are presented also in Nöldeke's statement. But neither Nöldeke nor any other European writer on the history of the collection of the Qur'ān texts has, although using the Muslim accounts, taken the measure of the pressure exerted upon the shaping of the reports on Zaid's activities by the third category of naskh.

Without a detailed analysis of the invention and development of this third mode of naskh, such as we have attempted to provide in this study, it is impossible to make sense of the entire body of Muslim utterances on the history of the collection(s) of the Qur'ān texts, or to expose the compromise character of the Muslim accounts of the several stages through which the Qur'ān texts were envisaged as having passed.

The three naskh formulae can themselves be shown to have evolved as compromise statements following a lengthy period of anxiety caused by the apparent conflicts both within the texts of the Tradition and between the Fiqh and a Tradition seen as consisting of both Qur'ān and Sunna.

In the discussions on the Qur'ānic component of that Tradition, two of the formulae, which can have relevance only for the Qur'ān, presuppose omissions from the texts of the Qur'ān document. Omissions, in the nature of things, can be documented solely on the basis of ḥadīth reports.

The third formula, naskh al ḥukm dūna al tilāwa, refers impartially either to the Qur'ān or the Sunna source. Its wording indicates the embarrassment caused by the presence in our Qur'ān texts of verses thought by the uṣūlī to have become inoperative since the fuqahā' had ignored them. The Qur'ān document was not always a source.

The formula naskh al ḥukm wa al tilāwa represents the final formalisation of the exegetically derived notion that Muḥammad had forgotten/been caused to forget unspecified parts of the Qur'ān revelation.

Naskh al tilāwa dūna al ḥukm represents the claim of a Qur'ānic origin for certain Fiqh rulings nowhere mentioned in the transmitted texts of the Qur'ān document, the muṣḥaf, and even, as in the case of the stoning penalty, flying in the face of the ruling which is there mentioned. In brief, the formula represents an attempt at notional interpolation in an ideal text. Naskh al tilāwa dūna al ḥukm faced difficulties peculiar to itself. Had the wording really been suppressed, the ruling derived from the wording would have been left without the support of any existing documentary source. This mode of naskh has never been universally acknowledged.[46] It was the creation of only some _uṣūlīs_ who, in naming it, would appear to have hit upon the expedient of placing it, in terms of nomenclature, under the aegis of the analogy that could be drawn from the formula _naskh al ḥukm wa al tilāwa_, by exploitation of the middle term, that is, _naskh al ḥukm dūna al tilāwa_.

This last formula is the _naskh_ of the _uṣūlīs_ par excellence. The term _naskh_ here means replacement or supersession. In the other formulae alone does the term _naskh_ respect both Qur'ānic and Arabic usage in carrying its true meaning of suppression.

The origin of all the semantic difficulties was the anxiety to rationalise the visible interplay between the three factors of _Fiqh_, Sunna and Qur'ān.

Given this kind of theoretical treatment of the Qur'ān source, we shall have to conclude that the Muslims simply could not afford to be seen in possession of a Qur'ān that had come down to them in writing from the Prophet.

This explains why the classical _ḥadīths_ had to place the collection of the Qur'ān texts into the time following the death of Muḥammad. The connection between the Qur'ān document and the Prophet to whom it had been revealed had at all costs to be broken.

This need is indicated by the emphatic repetition of the motif that the collectors among the Prophet's successors were conscious that they proposed to do something that the Prophet personally had never either undertaken, nor, indeed, apparently recommended.

Care is also taken to convey the gratuitous

information that only the dread of the loss of Qur'ān materials or the shocked recognition of actual loss had enabled them to quieten their scruples and to embark on what they unanimously acknowledged to be an innovation, for Abū Bakr's hesitation was that of one who preferred to follow the Sunna of the Prophet in all things avoiding innovation (bidʿa). ʿUmar had had to reassure him by pointing out that certain bidaʿ may be not merely unavoidable, but even positively commendable.

7 The ʿUthmān collection

Here, once again, as we have now grown accustomed to expect, a multitude of factors are at play in the shaping of the hadīths.

In terms of hadīth materials, this might be called the major collection. The reports on the motives which impelled ʿUthmān to undertake his collection of the Qur'ān are again conflicting. Some envisage his contribution as merely the piety of completing a task already taken in hand, but interrupted on the untimely death of his great predecessor, ʿUmar.

Other reports entirely alter the placing of the ʿUthmān initiative on behalf of the Book of God in the historical perspective of the development of the texts. They do not conceive it to have been concerned with the extent of the revelations surviving to his day. Rather, his aim was to select from amid a welter of rival Qur'ān texts, each claiming to be the uniquely authentic record of what had been revealed to Muḥammad, a single text to be officially promulgated as the textus receptus of the Muslims. No deviation from this text would henceforward be tolerated, or indeed possible, for it is also reported that ʿUthmān required the destruction of all other recorded Qur'ān texts.

It is apparent that these are not only alternative

statements on the motives guiding ʿUthmān's initiative. They are totally incompatible judgments on the history of the book. The basic contradiction between these two views has hitherto not been appreciated.

'Abū Bakr collected the scattered fragments of the Qur'ān on sheets. ʿUthmān collected the sheets into a single volume.'[1] This is not quite the same as: 'Abū Bakr collected the Qur'ān into volumes on the deaths of those killed at Yemāma. ʿUthmān later derived from these volumes a single text.'

'Abū Bakr collected the Qur'ān between two covers' differs from 'ʿUthmān formed but a single text': ʿUthmān alladī jamaʿa al maṣāḥif ʿalā muṣḥaf wāḥid.

'ʿUthmān united the Muslims on a single text'[2]: Jamaʿa ʿUthmān al nās ʿalā hāḏa al muṣḥaf, is not what Abū Bakr did when he jamaʿa al Qur'ān.[3]

The collection of the Qur'ān ab initio (jamʿ al Qur'ān fī ṣaḥīfa, fī ṣuḥuf, fī muṣḥaf, baina lawḥain) is a distinctive activity and has, we have seen, been ascribed to numerous individuals among the Companion generation, including each of Muḥammad's four immediate successors as Head of State, Abū Bakr, ʿUmar, ʿUthmān, ʿAlī.

The provision of a textus receptus (jamʿ al maṣāḥif ʿalā muṣḥaf wāḥid, jamʿ al nās ʿalā muṣḥaf) in which the root j m ʿ abandons the meaning 'to collect' to take on the force of 'collating', 'reconciling', is a different activity and has been attributed to only one of Muḥammad's successors, ʿUthmān b. ʿAffān (A.D. 644-56).

According to the jamʿ al Qur'ān tradition, the Qur'ān

fragments were not first collected into one place until some twelve years after the death of Muḥammad. That would represent a considerable delay when the difficulties of the enterprise would have been aggravated by the diaspora of Muḥammad's major lieutenants into the conquered territories, and by the deaths of many of the first-generation Muslims. The preservation of the texts of the Qur'ān had been assured and their authenticity guaranteed by appeal to the mechanical, formal Islamic requirement of two qualified witnesses to a written document.

The alternative _jamʿ al maṣāḥif_ view requires our assent to the contrary proposition. Not only had the Qur'ān texts been organised, preserved and collected at a much earlier date, but this had been done on innumerable occasions and by innumerable persons. On the accession of the Prophet's third successor there existed such an unwieldy body of materials that it was not only possible but essential to establish a _textus receptus ne varietur_ while many of those best qualified to bring this vital undertaking to a successful conclusion were still happily alive.

This second view, a mature sophistication of the first, was the product of considerations quite distinct from those which underlie the earlier version out of which it grew. Here, the doctrine of the _tawātur_, which guarantees the contents of a revealed Book transmitted with the endorsement of an entire generation, is uppermost.

The unspoken corollary of this representation of Qur'ānic affairs should be that the chances of authentic Qur'ān material failing to gain admittance to the officially promulgated canon must have been immeasurably reduced. Like Zaid's test, this test is negative and must have been aimed at some target. The extent of the Qur'ān is no longer the issue. The reports envisage, rather, tolerable agreement on the contents, with such disagreements as are highlighted concentrated almost exclusively on the 'correct' reading of what appears to be conceived of as a commonly accepted and generally agreed textual base. This tradition is aimed at what are known as variant Qur'ān readings. It derives from a generation familiar with the ijmāʿ concept.

> 'Ḥuḏaifa b. al Yemān came to ʿUthmān direct from the Aḏarbaijān and Armenian frontier where, uniting the forces from Iraq with those from Syria, he had had an opportunity to observe regional differences over the Qur'ān. "Commander of the faithful," he advised, "take this umma in hand before they differ about the Book like Christians and Jews." ʿUthmān sent asking Ḥafṣa to lend him the sheets [inherited by her father, ʿUmar, from Abū Bakr, and now in her possession] "so that we can copy them into other volumes and then return them." She sent her ṣuḥuf to ʿUthmān who summoned Zaid, Saʿīd b. al ʿĀṣ, ʿAbdul Raḥmān b. al Ḥārith b. Hišām and ʿAbdullāh b. al Zubair and commanded them to copy the sheets into several volumes. Addressing the group from Qurais̆, he added, "Wherever you differ from Zaid, write the word in the dialect of Qurais̆ for it was revealed in that tongue."
>
> When they had copied the sheets, ʿUthmān sent a copy to each of the main centres of the empire with the command that all other Qur'ān materials, whether in single sheet form, or in whole volumes, were to be burned.'
>
> Zuhrī adds, 'Khārija b. Zaid informed me that Zaid said, "I noticed that a verse of sūrat al Aḥzāb,

> which I had been used to hear the Prophet recite, was missing. I found it in the keeping of Khuzaima b. Thābit and entered it in the appropriate place."'[4]

Ṭabarī mentions only two commissioners, Zaid and Abān b. Saʿīd b. al ʿĀṣ,[5] but according to the isnād critics, Abān had already died in the reign of ʿUmar.

Ḥuḏaifa figures in a second ḥadīth series which reports textual differences, not only between Iraq and Syria, but also between rival groups of Iraqis.

> We were sitting in the mosque and ʿAbdullāh was reciting the Qur'ān when Ḥuḏaifa came in and said, 'The reading of ibn Umm ʿAbd! [i.e. ʿAbdullāh] The reading of Abū Mūsā! By God! if I am spared to reach the Commander of the Faithful, I will recommend that he impose a single Qur'ān reading!' ʿAbdullāh became very angry and spoke sharply to Ḥuḏaifa who fell silent.[6]

> 'Yazīd b. Muʿāwiya was in the mosque in the time of al Walīd b. ʿUqba, sitting in a group among whom was Ḥuḏaifa. An official called out, 'Those who follow the reading of Abū Mūsā, go to the corner nearest the Kinda door. Those who follow ʿAbdullāh's reading, go to the corner nearest ʿAbdullāh's house.' Their reading of Q 2.196 did not agree. One group read, 'Perform the pilgrimage to God.' The others read it, 'Perform the pilgrimage to the Kaʿba.' Ḥuḏaifa became very angry, his eyes reddened and he rose, parting his qamīṣ at the waist, although in the mosque. This was during the reign of ʿUthmān. Ḥuḏaifa exclaimed, 'Will someone go to the Commander of the Faithful, or shall I go myself? This is what happened in the previous dispensations.' He came over and sat down, saying, 'God sent Muḥammad who, with those who went forward, fought those who went back until God gave victory to His religion. God

> took Muḥammad and Islam made strides. To succeed him, God chose Abū Bakr who reigned as long as God chose. God then took him and Islam made rapid strides. God appointed ʿUmar who sat in the midst of Islam. God then took him also. Islam spread rapidly. God next chose ʿUthmān. God's oath! Islam is on the point of such expansion that soon you will replace all other religions.'[7]

The conclusion which such reports invite us to draw is that there was genuine fear that Islam, like the religions before it, would be fragmented into warring sects as a result of the differences arising in the reading of the sacred texts. ʿUthmān's purpose and his achievement was to unite the Muslims on the basis of a single agreed Qur'ān reading.[8]

> During the reign of ʿUthmān, teachers were teaching this or that reading to their students. When the students met and disagreed about the reading, they reported the differences to their teachers. They would defend their readings, condemning the others as heretical. News of this came to ʿUthmān's ears and he addressed the people, 'You who are here around me are disputing as to the Qur'ān, and pronouncing it differently. It follows that those who are distant in the various regional centres of Islam are even more widely divided. Companions of Muḥammad! act in unison; come together and write out an imām for the Muslims.'[9]

The reading disputes were apparently not restricted to the provinces. They appear to have prevailed also at Medina. We are unfortunately given no information on the nature of these differences, nor any explanation as to how they might have arisen.

The unification of the Muslims on the basis of a single text is envisaged as having been due to the corporate efforts of the Companions resident at Medina.

The piety of the objective aimed at by ʿUthmān had commended itself to the šūrā of Muḥammad's senior adherents.

This note of unanimity was further endorsed by appeal to the authority of ʿAlī who is projected as averring that what ʿUthmān had done in respect of the muṣḥaf, and especially in respect of the most sensitive issue of all, the alleged destruction of all Qur'ānic records other than the textus receptus achieved as the result of his initiative, he had done only after the fullest consultation with the Companions. Far from protesting at his highhandedness, they had applauded and blessed his decisiveness.

> By God! he did not act on the muṣḥaf except in the fullest consultation with us, for he said, 'What is your view in this matter of reading? I have heard that some even say, "My reading is superior to yours.' That is tantamount to heresy.' We asked him, 'What are you thinking to do?' He replied, 'My view is that we should unite the Muslims on the basis of a single muṣḥaf. That way, there will be no disagreement, no segmentation.' We replied, 'An excellent idea!' Someone then asked, 'Whose is the purest Arabic? and whose the greatest acquaintance with the recitation [alt. Qur'ān]?' They said that the purest Arabic was that of Saʿīd b. al ʿĀṣ and that the one most acquainted with the recitation [Qur'ān] was Zaid b. Thābit.
>
> ʿUthmān said, 'Let the one write and the other dictate.' The two then set to work and in this way ʿUthmān united the Muslims on the basis of a single text.

ʿAlī concludes his report with the declaration, 'Had I been in power, I should have done just what ʿUthmān did.'[10]

The extreme Šīʿa, the Rāfiḍīs, alleged that the impious rulers had expunged from the muṣḥaf some 500 verses including those which most unambiguously marked out ʿAlī as the appointed successor to the Prophet.

We have already seen the reply to this accusation ascribed to two of the great leaders of the Šīʿa, ibn ʿAbbās and ibn al Ḥanafiya. The ready endorsement of ʿUthmān's action by ʿAlī is directed precisely at this sort of Šīʿī complaint. The rebels against ʿUthmān, justifying their revolt, enumerated amongst their grievances their resentment at his 'having expunged the muṣḥafs'.[11] Besides, it is reasonably argued on the other side, ʿAlī succeeded ʿUthmān and if he had had any reservations about the Qur'ān text, he could easily have reinstated what he regarded as the authentic revelations.[12]

Compromise ḥadīths are known which conflate the two ideas of a collation of extant texts and their collection.

> Muṣʿab b. Saʿd reports, 'ʿUthmān addressed the people, "It is now thirteen years since your Prophet left you and you are not unanimous on the Qur'ān. You talk about the reading of Ubayy and the reading of ʿAbdullāh. Some even say, 'By God! my reading is right and yours is wrong.' I now summon you all to bring here whatever part of the Book of God you possess." One would come with a parchment or a scrap of leather with a Qur'ān verse on it [fīhi al Qur'ān] until there was gathered great store of such. ʿUthmān adjured them one by one, "You heard the Prophet recite this?" They would answer that that was so. After this ʿUthmān asked, "Whose acquaintance with the Book is greatest?" They replied, "His who wrote it out for the Prophet." He asked, "Whose Arabic is best?" They said, "Saʿīd's."

> ʿUthmān said, "Let Saʿīd dictate and Zaid write."'... Muṣʿab adds, 'I heard some Companions of the Prophet say, "ʿUthmān did well to undertake it."'[13]

A second version places the event fifteen years after the Prophet's death and mentions the bringing of tablets, shoulder-blades and stripped palm-fronds all bearing writing (fīhi al kitāb) or parts of the Book. There is no allusion to any earlier collection and, as the celebrated ṣuḥuf of Ḥafṣa are quite unmentioned, no backward link is intended between ʿUthmān's and ʿUmar's or Abū Bakr's collection. ʿUthmān's is envisaged as the earliest collection since the revelation of the Qur'ān to the Prophet.

The two witnesses motif is once more prominent. The ḥadīth is thus concerned chiefly with the isnād of the Qur'ān and its reference back to the Prophet. ʿUthmān concerned himself with certifying that the texts he had collected had been received direct from the Prophet. Simultaneously, he was concerned to put an end to the disunity created by variant readings and to provide the basis for a universal reading. The existence of the variant readings is rationalised by reference to the Companions, some of whom are identified. That is the isnād of the readings varying from ʿUthmān's. The elimination of variants was ʿUthmān's chief aim.

> Ḥuḏaifa said to ʿUthmān, 'Whatever you would do if you heard someone talking of the reading of so-and-so, and the reading of another, as the non-Muslims do, then do it now.'[14]

> Ḥuḏaifa said, 'The Kufans say, "the text of ʿAbdullāh"; the Basrans say, "the text of Abū Mūsā".

By God! if I reach the Commander of the faithful, I will recommend that he drown these readings.'[15] ʿAbdullāh said, 'Do and God will drown you, but not in water!'[16]

ʿAbdullāh, Ḥudaifa and Abū Mūsā were on the roof of Abū Mūsā's house. ʿAbdullāh said, 'I hear you say such-and-such.' Ḥudaifa said, 'Yes, I deplore folk talking about this one's reading and that one's reading. They are differing like non-Muslims.' Ḥudaifa continued, 'ʿAbdullāh b. Qais, you were sent to the Basrans as governor and teacher. They have adopted your adab, your dialect and your text.'

To b. Masʿūd he said, 'You were sent to the Kūfans as their teacher and they have adopted your adab, your dialect and your reading.'

'In that case,' retorted b. Masʿūd, 'I have not misled them. There is no verse in the Book of God but that I know where and in what connection it was revealed. Did I know of anyone more learned than myself on the subject I should go to him.'[17]

This allusion to asbāb al nuzūl, the dates and circumstances of the individual revelations, indicates that we are dealing with more than the text. Where and in what connection a text was revealed bears directly upon the aḥkām of the Qur'ān. By adab is meant Fiqh. The term 'dialect' refers to ʿAbdullāh's speech habits (i.e. to his text). By reading is meant his exegesis, or the exegesis which has been attached to ʿAbdullāh's name. ʿAbdullāh's text, exegesis and Fiqh represent those sciences as developed and cultivated at Kūfa. Abū Mūsā represents the sciences of the Basran centre.

Q 2.187 reads, 'seek what God permits you' - wabtaġū mā kataba allāh lakum. By mā kataba, b. ʿAbbās is reported to have understood lailat al qadr. Abū Hišām al Rifāʿī said, 'kaḏā qara'ahā Muʿāḏ'. That cannot be a reference to Muʿāḏ's text, but only to his exegesis.[18]

Variant readings, although transmitted from Companions, claim to derive from the Prophet himself.

> A man recited in the presence of ʿUmar who corrected him. The man, incensed, claimed to have recited for the Prophet and he had not corrected him. They carried their dispute to Muḥammad. When the Prophet endorsed the man's claim that Muḥammad had personally instructed him, doubts sprang up in ʿUmar's mind. Reading ʿUmar's expression, the Prophet struck him on the chest, exclaiming, 'Out devil!' Muḥammad then explained, 'All the modes of reciting are correct so long as you don't turn a statement on mercy into one on wrath and vice-versa.'[19]

There may be different readings (texts). The wording of the Qur'ān is not its most relevant feature. The meaning matters above all. Differing readings were known to the Prophet and he lacked the pedantry to object.

> Ubayy entered the mosque and, hearing a man recite, asked him who had instructed him. The man replied that he had been taught by the Prophet. Ubayy went in search of the Prophet. When the man recited, Muḥammad said, 'That is correct.' Ubayy protested, 'But you taught me to recite so-and-so.'
>
> The Prophet said that Ubayy was right too. 'Right? right?' burst out Ubayy in perplexity. The Prophet struck him on the chest and prayed, 'Oh God! cause doubt to depart.' Ubayy broke into a sweat as his heart filled with terror. Muḥammad disclosed that two angels had come to him. One said, 'Recite the Qur'ān in one form.' The other advised Muḥammad to ask for more than this. That was repeated several times until finally the first angel said, 'Very well. Recite it in seven forms.' The

> Prophet said, 'Each of the forms is grace-giving, protecting, so long as you don't terminate a punishment verse with an expression of mercy, or vice-versa - as you might for example say, Let's go; or, let's be off.'[20]

The different readings have the Prophet's (and Heaven's) approval. Differences in utterance are not material. The meaning is paramount. The differing readings are all equally valid, having been revealed in parallel. The difference appears to consist simply in the use of this as opposed to that synonym. That ought to occasion neither wonder nor alarm, neither squabbling nor scandal. All readings are correct. All readings come down from the days of the Prophet. All readings carry the seal of his approbation.

But differences reported from the Companions on Qur'ān matters, which divided them already in the days of the Prophet, concerned more than merely verbal matters.

> ʿAbdullāh reports, 'We differed about a sūra, as to whether it consisted of thirty-five or thirty-six verses, so we went to the Prophet who was engaged in conversation with ʿAlī. When we told him we disagreed over the reading, his face reddened as he replied, "Those before you perished through their disagreements." He whispered something to ʿAlī who said, "The Prophet commands you to recite as you were taught."'[21]

Concern with the punctuation of the Qur'ān masks more than merely reading differences. Q 4.101 apparently indicates that travellers may abbreviate the ritual prayer if threatened with attack. That the restriction is absolute, in the sense that the prayer might be cut short only if the Muslims had reason to fear attack, was a view attributed by some of the fuqahāʾ to ʿĀʾiša. ʿAlī is the authority for the contrary view that the ritual prayer may be shortened by travellers. Appealing to asbāb al nuzūl, ʿAlī claimed that the first half of the verse had been revealed to the Prophet in reply to a question put to him on the subject. The answer, as revealed, read 'No blame is incurred if, when travelling, you shorten the prayer.' Only a year later, on the occasion of a fresh revelation, was the context extended to include the reference to fear of attack. The addition, however, bears only upon the second half of the verse.[22]

The main burden of our ḥadīths was that reading differences are much less grave than disagreement. Tolerance must be exercised on all sides and the right to differ mutually recognised if disunity is to be avoided.

> Zaid b. Arqam reports that a man went to the Prophet and said, 'ʿAbdullāh b. Masʿūd taught me to recite a particular sūra; Zaid b. Thābit taught me the same sūra, and so did Ubayy. The readings of all three are different. Whose reading ought I to adopt?' The Prophet remained silent. ʿAlī, who was by his side, said, 'Every man ought to recite it as he was taught. Each of the modes is acceptable and equally valid.'[23]

This reply would have been of little help to our man, but the general message is clear. The faithful should not find scandal in the circulation of the several Qurʾān recensions attributed to the Companions. Muḥammad himself had been aware of their existence and had not insisted on imposing a universal reading. He had urged understanding and mutual forbearance upon his followers, exhorting them by his example to lay aside petty, narrow chauvinism and pedantry. All the Companion versions of the Qur'ān (to which we must now add Zaid's) are correct and equally valid.

> ʿUmar said, 'I heard Hišām b. Ḥukaim reciting _sūrat al Furqān_ and listened to his recital. On observing that he was reading many forms which the Prophet had not taught me, I all but rushed upon him as he prayed. But I waited patiently as he continued, and, collaring him when he had finished, I asked him, 'Who taught you to recite this _sūra_?' He claimed that the Prophet had taught him. I said, 'By God! you're lying!' I dragged him to the Prophet telling him that I had heard Hišām recite many forms he had not taught me. The Prophet said, 'Let him go. Recite, Hišām.' He recited the reading I had already heard from him. The Prophet said, 'That is how it was revealed.' He then said, 'Recite, ʿUmar', and I recited what he had taught me. He said, 'That's right. That is how it was revealed. This Qur'ān was revealed in seven forms, so recite what is easiest.'[24]

The scholars were to disapprove of the use by the Muslims of the post-Apostolic ages of isolate Qur'ān readings at prayer. That is not, however, the point of the report. The earliest rationalisation of reading variants was that, as all had been revealed, all were equally legitimate. Abū Huraira reports the Prophet as saying, 'The Qur'ān was revealed in seven forms and contention about the Qur'ān is disbelief.'[25]

Both Abū Huraira, who became a Muslim only in the year A.H. 7, and Ubayy, who was Medinese, localise this dictum in Muslim eyes in the Prophet's late period.

That the Qur'ān was revealed in seven versions reinforces, or is reinforced by, the idea that it had been revealed piecemeal. It would otherwise have been very difficult to keep the seven different forms apart in Muḥammad's mind.[26]

This *ḥadīth* on the seven forms gave rise to an extensive comment literature, as the Muslims endeavoured to identify the different readings which were all equally correct and valid.

Many attempted to relate the different forms to the linguistic situation. It was therefore alleged that the Qur'ān had been revealed in each of the seven dialects of Muḍar, the great branch of the Arab nation from which the Prophet sprang.[27] These dialects were listed as: Huḏail, Kināna, Qais, Ḍabba, Taim al Rabbāb, Asad b. Khuzaima and Qurais̆.

ibn ʿAbbās is credited with the distribution: five Hawāzin-type dialects, Qurais̆ and Khuzāʿa.[28]

ʿAbdullāh b. Masʿūd had reportedly permitted a non-Arab to substitute another word for one he was incapable of pronouncing correctly, owing to the strange Arabic phoneme. ʿAbdullāh explained that error would consist solely in reading a mercy verse as a punishment verse, or vice-versa, or in adding to the Book of God something that did not belong there.[29]

In one version of Muḥammad's encounter with the revealing angel, the Prophet pleaded that he had been sent to a nation of illiterates and was granted the concession of multiple readings.[30] The concession, in Ṭaḥāwī's view, allowed for their inability to keep to the exact wording of a single reading, unaccustomed as they were to reading, writing and accuracy in verbatim memorising. The concession was later withdrawn when, with their growing acquaintance with writing and with accuracy in reproduction, the necessity originally justifying it was removed.[31]

In Ṭabarī's view, the recitation of the Qur'ān in all of the seven forms had never been obligatory. It had merely been a concession in the early days. Once the Companions observed that the Muslims were splitting into bickering factions in the absence of a single text, they reached a consensus on the desirability of providing an agreed form. In the undertaking, the Companions were infallible, and they agreed that they should copy out that which they were satisfied had been endorsed on the occasion of the Prophet's final meeting with Gabriel and that all else besides be abandoned.[32]

Whether it was ʿUmar or ʿUthmān who had collected the Qur'ān, the suggestion that linguistic considerations were present to the mind of the Head of State provided a convenient means of harmonising the attribution of such a collection with reports on parallel variant readings. These had been ascribed to Companions and, as we have seen, each reading claimed to be marfūʿ, to have been known to and approved by the Prophet. That was the function of the story about the seven forms. The ḥadīth was most easily understood to refer to the varying dialects.

When ʿUmar determined to write out the imām, he ordered a group of the Companions to set to work and advised them that, if they disagreed linguistically, they should write it in the language of Muḍar, since it had been revealed to a man of Muḍar.[33]

ʿUmar is said to have admonished ʿAbdullāh for teaching the Qur'ān in the language of Huḏail. It had been revealed in the language of Qurais̆ and ought to be taught in that language.[34]

The ḥadīth, and the one above on the resolution of any differences among the Qur'ān commissioners, were designed to explain how a divine Book revealed to a man of Mecca came to be preserved in the recension prepared by a man of Medina.

But, as the Qur'ān text features usages thought to be other than those of the Qurais̆ dialect, al Bāqillānī was constrained to add that ʿUthmān's advice to the commissioners is to be interpreted in the sense that the bulk, not necessarily the whole, had been revealed in the dialect of Qurais̆.[35]

A further modification was imposed upon the scholars. ʿAbdullāh, in the case of the non-Arab had permitted the substitution of one word for another. ʿAbdullāh was a non-Meccan. The substitution would have been presumably a synonym in his dialect for a word in the Meccan dialect. Then there was the story of ʿUmar's quarrel with His̆ām. Not only were ʿUmar and His̆ām fellow tribesmen. Both were fellow tribesmen of the Prophet.[36] The reference to dialects was thus watered down to a reference to synonyms. The aim was to rationalise the claim that there had existed variant readings transmitted from several Companions of the Prophet.

Another question sprang naturally to minds receptive to the notion that variant readings, or even variant muṣḥafs, had been transmitted from the several Companions. ʿUthmān is supposed to have imposed a single reading. By definition, that would have imposed a fixed sūra order. The question provided a convenient basis for improving the plausibility of the claims on behalf of the variant readings. The Companions had taught variant readings in the various regions. The variant readings were taught from the variant muṣḥafs prepared for their personal use. In addition to these variant readings, the variant muṣḥafs had been arranged in a variant sūra order.

Some distinction ought to be made between Abū Bakr's collection and that of ʿUthmān. Since Abū Bakr had collected his muṣḥaf on separate sheets (ṣuḥuf) no particular sūra order need have been fixed on that occasion. This has enabled the Muslims to argue, in a manner not fully appreciated by European writers on this question, that there were, in fact, two distinct caliphal collections of the Qur'ān texts, and not merely two conflicting attributions of its first collection. These two collections, by Abū Bakr and by ʿUthmān, were not, in the eyes of later scholars, competitive attributions. They were complementary operations, the later completing what the earlier had made possible. The distinction at any rate enabled the Muslims to provide a motive for and an effect of ʿUthmān's action.

> ʿUthmān organised the sūras in the order we are now familiar with. In addition, he restricted the reading to a single dialect - that of Quraiš in which it had been revealed. Hitherto, there had been a concession permitting the reciting of the Qur'ān in dialects other than that of Mecca so that the burden of scruple imposed upon converts at the outset of the new revelation should be minimal. Those days were now recognised by ʿUthmān to be gone, not least since much danger was to be feared from the continuation of

> that freedom and especially since some overliteralness in the local attachment to a particular reading might give the impression of, or even lead to, the fragmentation of the Islamic unity.[37]

> ʿUthmān's collection occurred when differences had become frequent. They were reciting in all the rich multiplicity of their Arab dialects. He copied out the sheets into a single muṣḥaf, arranged the sūras and restricted the text to a single dialect - that of Qurais̆ on the plea that it had been revealed in the tongue of Mecca.[38]

The variant readings had arisen from the Qur'ān's having originally been revealed in umpteen dialects. ibn ʿAbbās stated, 'The Qur'ān was revealed in seven dialects [luġāt]' - not aḥruf![39]

There had originally been no restriction on how it might be recited. Some had employed the synonyms of their own dialect, or as dictated by their own speech habits; others had used synonyms of the same dialect. The most important thing had been to achieve the precise spirit of what had been revealed to Muḥammad.

Some dozen years after the death of the Prophet, ʿUthmān, sensing the dangers both present and future that inhered in such liberty, took steps to provide a single text for the entire empire by the simple expedient of restricting the reading henceforward to a single text drawn up in the Qurais̆ dialect, the most obvious choice since that had been the language of the Prophet.

Sending out copies of his work to the main centres in the provinces, ʿUthmān commanded that all other texts of the Qur'ān be expunged, shredded or consigned to the flames.

From that day forward, it would be quite inconceivable that variant Qur'ān readings could be reported from any quarter. The readings of the Prophet's Companions, all of which bore Muḥammad's seal of approval as 'correct renderings' of the divine Book, had served their purpose as the instruments of the initial transmission of the revelations to the Muslims of the outlying regions of the expanding Muslim empire. With increasing prosperity and growing educational opportunity, it would now be a matter of comparative ease to disseminate, as the unique Qur'ān text for use by the Muslims everywhere, the text which commended itself to the consensus of the Companions.

This text had been arrived at only after the most rigorous enquiries by the commission appointed for the purpose by the Head of State. We have seen something of the scholarly caution with which the commission had approached its sacred task, including in the completed draft only what it had no human reason to doubt had come down from the direct instruction of the Prophet via the most veracious witnesses. The text of the Book of God has thus been traceable, since ʿUthmān's day, back to the Prophet and from him to Gabriel, the angel of the revelation, by means of an absolutely reliable and unshakable *isnād*.

We have seen that to the questions, when and by whom was the Qur'ān first collected, a variety of answers had been proposed which it was the business of successive generations of Muslim scholars to resolve. This they attempted to do by assuming that there had been not one but several collections. But this attitude itself was merely an attempt to harmonise the conflicting attributions. For some obviously held that the Qur'ān had first been collected by Abū Bakr.

Others thought that this had been the work of ʿUmar, while yet others believed that it had been accomplished by ʿUthmān. These two views were reconcilable by joining them together on the supposition that ʿUthmān had seen through to completion the pious work embarked on by his predecessor. Nöldeke perceived that this leaves no means to carry the process back to Abū Bakr.[40]

If, as was also done, ʿUmar's role were reduced to that of merely advising the collection, he could have advised only Abū Bakr, which leaves no means of carrying the process forward to ʿUthmān.

A device was needed to knit the various phases together. This is the role played by the ṣuḥuf of Ḥafṣa, who, besides being the daughter of ʿUmar, was also a widow of the Prophet. The solution was not always consistently applied, for we found versions of the report on ʿUthmān's Qur'ān initiative which portrayed that too as a collection ab initio. Modern European writers have greatly exaggerated the part played in the story by the ṣuḥuf of Ḥafṣa. They are not in the literature on the collection of the Qur'ān 'die sicherste Tatsache des ganzen Berichtes', as Schwally claimed.[41] Bell argued: 'That Ḥafṣa had a copy of the Qur'ān on ṣuḥuf seems certain',[42] and of that fact, he alleged, 'there is no doubt'.[43]

Failing to delve beneath the surface of the Muslim reports, they would have the ʿUthmān text nothing more than a mere copy of the codex of Ḥafṣa.[44] That is certainly erroneous.

The one constant and unvarying factor throughout all versions of the ḥadīths on the collection of the Qur'ān texts - whether that allegedly undertaken as early as the reign of Abū Bakr, within little more than a year of the Prophet's death, or that completed as late as a dozen years after the death of Muḥammad, in the reign of ʿUthmān, or even later still in the time of Marwān b. al Ḥakam - was the central part played, both as the amanuensis of the Prophet himself and as the rapporteur of the various caliphal initiatives on Qur'ān matters, by Zaid b. Thābit.

8 The Qur'ān collections: a review

European scholars have analysed the *ḥadīths* on the collection of the Qur'ān on the assumption that in the end only one could be accepted as true. In a sense this is erroneous. The Muslim reports are not in fact in disagreement; they are in perfect agreement, for common to all of them is the constant and unvarying allegation that, whoever may have been the first to collect the Qur'ān texts, it was certainly not the Prophet to whom they had been revealed. No scholar has hitherto suspected that perhaps all the *ḥadīths* are equally untrue.

The exclusion of the Prophet from the collection of the Qur'ān was a prime desideratum of the *uṣūlīs* wrestling with the serious problems generated by some of their own theoretical positions.

We must therefore never lose sight of the part played in shaping the Muslim versions of the history of the Qur'ān texts by *uṣūl* theories of *naskh*, and especially by the two theories which posit the absence from the *muṣḥaf* of verses which it was firmly believed had nevertheless been part of the Qur'ān.

In all discussions on the collection of the *muṣḥaf*, we are primarily concerned with two issues:

1. the *isnād* of the *muṣḥaf* (i.e. the actual reading),

2. the textual incompleteness of the <u>muṣḥaf</u>.

> Abū Bakr's aim had been to collect the Qur'ān between two covers. ʿUthmān's was to collect those readings attested as coming from the Prophet and to reject all non-canonical readings. He aimed to unite the Muslims on the basis of a single text, containing no interpolations and no Qur'ān provisions whose wording had been withdrawn but which still appeared in the written text with verses whose inclusion in the final version of the text had been endorsed and thus preserved as required to be publicly recited [at prayer].[1]

Sarakhsī, we recall, informed us that the preservation of the interpolations was the function of the Companion readings.[2]

The Qur'ān provisions whose wording had been withdrawn related to <u>Fiqh</u> rulings and were of the type: <u>naskh al tilāwa dūna al ḥukm</u>.

All Sunnī Muslim discussions on the history of the Qur'ān text presuppose the operations of <u>naskh</u>. When a generation of Muslims had first been driven by a noisy minority to take the Qur'ān source into more serious consideration, the texts of the <u>muṣḥaf</u>, the Qur'ān document, were found occasionally to be unrelated to the <u>Fiqh</u> that had already evolved.

Certain elements of that Law could not be fitted to the existing document, but no insuperable problem need arise if the Law could now be attributed to the Sunna source, documented by reference to the <u>Ḥadīth</u>. Certain counter-doctrines had also adopted Sunna form. Where the <u>muṣḥaf</u> contained a statement on the legal topic at variance with a statement of the Sunna, the solution was to be sought in the theory of abrogation. Only in its light could the <u>fuqahā'</u>

be shown to have preferred the Sunna statement, as apparently on other topics they had preferred one Qur'ān statement to another, or one Sunna statement to another.

The *maḏāhib* no longer granted the widow the right to one year's accommodation and maintenance following the husband's death. ʿAbdullāh b. al Zubair therefore asked ʿUthmān what had possessed him to include Q 2.240 in the *muṣḥaf*, when he knew it to have been abrogated by Q 2.234. 'Because,' replied ʿUthmān, 'I know it to be part of the Qur'ān text.'[3]

Once the view that the Qur'ān, like the Sunna, had been from the first the root of the *Fiqh* became itself part of the *uṣūl al fiqh* axiom, scholars, assisted by the general lack of information on the history of the earliest period, persuaded themselves that the lacunae in their Qur'ān texts could be accounted for rationally only on the assumption that the Prophet had not collected and checked the revelations. For in no other way could they explain a verse which ought to be of the Qur'ān, but which is not in the *muṣḥaf*. Theoretical positions adopted in *uṣūl al fiqh* worked against the free and easy assumption that the Sunna had abrogated the Qur'ān. Only the Qur'ān might abrogate the Qur'ān. This technical view was reinforced by an exegetical view derived from Q 87 which pointed to the incompleteness of the *muṣḥaf*. The distinction now felt between Qur'ān and *muṣḥaf* led first to the third mode of *naskh*, *naskh al tilāwa dūna al ḥukm*, and thence to the Qur'ān collection *ḥadīths*.

Several motives thus lay behind the drive to exclude the Prophet from the history of the collection of the *muṣḥaf*, but two motives outweighed all others:

1. the desire to facilitate reference to the Qur'ān source of matters agreed in the Fiqh but unmentioned in the Qur'ān document;
2. the need to justify regional attitudes on certain questions by referring them to locally recognised Qur'ān variants, when the opposition referred to the Qur'ān source and to the presently existing Qur'ān document, the muṣḥaf (one of the myriad examples had concerned the ṭawāf between Ṣafā and Marwa).

The Muslims themselves acknowledged the pressure of the naskh theories upon the collection ḥadīths. We are familiar with the explicit second-level argument that the Prophet forbore to collect, edit and publish the texts of the revelation since, so long as he lived, abrogation remained a possible hazard. Any collection made before his death, when revelation ceased absolutely, must have led to confusion and uncertainty. Even the collection made soon after his death led to confusion and uncertainty when later compared with the Fiqh. But in ʿUthmān's reply to ibn al Zubair, we see that the attempt to use the muṣḥaf to throw doubts on the naskh theories had been of no avail.

That the rationalisation of the placing of the collection of the Qur'ān into the period following the Prophet's death, on the plea that abrogation was a daily possibility while Muḥammad lived, is itself absurd, is clear from the consideration that the 'classic instances of abrogation' - the phrase is Ḥāzimī's[4] - consist in the simultaneous presence in the muṣḥaf of statements held to be mutually exclusive, naskh al ḥukm dūna al tilāwa.

We have also pointed out, however, that the term naskh means more to the Muslim than merely abrogation. It carries the further connotation of omission. That etymology was forced upon certain uṣūlīs by the exegetes. The Qur'ān texts were, thus, already incomplete in the Prophet's lifetime. Alternatively, it had this meaning for other uṣūlīs for whom the Sunna had never abrogated the Qur'ān. This had the interesting consequence that, whereas their opposite number in another uṣūl school could with equanimity speak of the abrogation of this or that verse by this or that ḥadīth, these men had doomed themselves to posit the existence of an abrogating verse. Their scientific certainty could not be shaken by failure to locate that verse in the muṣḥaf. It must have been omitted when the muṣḥaf was collected. No verse still legally valid when the Prophet died would have been omitted if the Prophet had collected the Qur'ān. The omission, and hence the collection, had occurred only after his death.

> ibn ʿAbbās asked ʿUthmān what possessed him to place sūrat al Anfāl, one of the mathānī, with Barā'a, one of the mi'īn, join them with no bismillāh between them and place them among the seven lengthy sūras. ʿUthmān replied that often the Prophet received quite long revelations. He would call for one of the scribes and say, 'Put these verses in the sūra in which so-and-so occurs.' Anfāl was among the first of the Medina revelations and Barā'a among the last. Since its contents resembled those of Anfāl, ʿUthmān took it to belong with it, for the Prophet had died without explaining that it was part of it.[5]

Mālik had a shorter explanation for the absence of this

bismillāh. The beginning of *Barā'a* fell out and its *bismillāh* fell out with it.[6]

If Muḥammad is not to be permitted to have collected the Qur'ān, then, in order to guarantee that the *muṣḥaf* is nevertheless complete, authentic and involves neither deficiency nor unwarranted addition, its collection must be attributed to a senior Companion. With certain reservations, it would be immaterial which Companion was chosen. Some were obviously disposed to attribute the enterprise to a Head of State and Church. Hence the attributions to Abū Bakr, ʿUmar, ʿUthmān and ʿAlī. Other attributions include the Prophet's widows: ʿĀ'iša, Ḥafṣa and Umm Salama.[7] Among the Companions were named: Miqdād (or Muʿāḏ),[8] Abū Mūsā, ʿAbdullāh, ʿUbāda and Zaid b. Thābit.

The attribution to Ubayy has proved unhappy since he is elsewhere alleged to have entirely repudiated the theory of *naskh*, with interesting consequences.[9]

The Qur'ān text, in short, like any other sunna in the *Ḥadīth* canon, as a component of the Islamic Tradition has been equipped with an *isnād*.

A useful by-product of this procedure is that those who still cannot bring themselves to concede that in any circumstances a divinely guided Prophet could forget any of his revelations, but who yet held that the Qur'ān document, the *muṣḥaf*, is incomplete, by transferring its preservation to the Companions, could likewise transfer to them any omissions. That was the line taken by Ṭūsī among the exegetes.[10] Besides *āyat al naskh*, Q 2.106 contains two terms: *mā nansakh* and *aw nunsi*. Those who read the second to mean 'cause to forget' applied that to the Companions.

Once equipped with its *isnād*, the Qur'ān would become a *sunna mutawātira* to which would be attached the highest degree of probative force. It would thus be accorded in certain schools of *uṣūl* the same consideration and treatment extended to any other sunna of the same degree of 'spread'. It would have the capacity to abrogate any other *ḥadīth* or to be abrogated by another *sunna mutawātira*.

The Ḥuḏaifa *ḥadīths* had pointed to local and rival canons of the Qur'ān, reminiscent of the rest of the *ḥadīth* weaponry with which the scholars fought to support or to rebut this or that local legal opinion. Like the *ḥadīths*, their Qur'ān was authenticated by appeal to the authority of this or that Companion called upon to serve as the eponym of the local *Fiqh*.

The same Ḥuḏaifa *ḥadīths* induced the assumption that the Companion-*muṣḥafs* were pre-ʿUthmānic. They were presumably given their quietus on the completion of Zaid's work on behalf of ʿUthmān. But ibn Masʿūd, the eponym of the Qur'ān of the Kufans, is reported to have burst out, 'I recited from the very mouth of the Prophet some seventy *sūras* while Zaid still had his ringlets and was playing with his companions.'[11] In a second version, 'The Prophet taught me to recite seventy *sūras* which I had mastered before Zaid had even become a Muslim.'[12] Or, again, 'Am I to be debarred from copying the *muṣḥafs* and the job given to a man who was an infidel in his father's reins when I first became a Muslim?'[13] ʿAbdullāh is supposed to have enjoined his followers, 'Lay up your Qur'ān's! How can you order me to recite the reading of Zaid, when I recited from the very mouth of the Prophet some seventy sūras?'

'Am I,' asks ʿAbdullāh, 'to abandon what I acquired from the very lips of the Prophet?'[14]

> I went to Abū Mūsā's house and saw there ʿAbdullāh and Ḥudaifa. I sat with them. They had a muṣḥaf that ʿUthmān had sent ordering them to make their Qur'ān's conform with it. Abū Mūsā declared that anything in his muṣḥaf and lacking in ʿUthmān's was not to be omitted. Anything in ʿUthmān's and lacking in his own was to be added. Ḥudaifa asked, 'What is the point of all our work? Nobody in this region will give up the reading of this šaikh, meaning ʿAbdullāh, and nobody of Yemenī origin will give up the reading of Abū Mūsā.' Ḥudaifa it was who had advised ʿUthmān to unite the muṣḥafs on the basis of a single muṣḥaf.[15]

ʿUthmān's initiative to provide a single universal reading would appear to have failed in the face of the determination of the regions to abide by the interpolations which they traced to the Companions.

We shall now expect to find references not only to alleged pre-ʿUthmānic codices but also to occasional post-ʿUthmānic readings at variance with the muṣḥaf.

It would therefore surely be hazardous to continue to doubt that what lies behind the attribution to this or that Companion of a codex is identical with what lies behind the attribution to the Companion of a reading at variance with 'the single text'. Attribution of a codex was intended to lend colour to attribution of a variant reading.

The attribution to a Companion of a codex was, in turn, identical with the attribution to the Companion of a store of information on the Sunna documented in the *ḥadīths* circulated and 'supported' in his name. The Qur'ān itself is a *sunna mutawātira* and variant readings are variant *ḥadīths*. There is no more reason for a willing suspension of disbelief in respect of the reading of ʿAbdullāh, of Abū Mūsā, of Ubayy, or of any other Companion than there is in relation to *ḥaddathanā* ʿAbdullāh, Abū Mūsā, Ubayy, or any other Companion.

If we accept the readings of the Companions because we accept that they had private codices, we ought in logic to accept also their *ḥadīths*. Both are transmitted in precisely the same way, and with the same *isnāds*. One set of traditions conveys their information for the Qur'ān, the other set their information for the Sunna. The two sets are identical in shape and format. If we are inclined to reject one set, we ought by the same logic to reject the other equally.

One would be immeasurably more impressed by that achievement which the *ḥadīths* on the collection of the *muṣḥaf* seek to ascribe to ʿUthmān - namely, his having thereby at a stroke united the Muslims on the basis of a single reading - if in fact variations on textual matters were seen to have become impossible after his reign. That his initiative in this direction was a total failure is, however, admitted in further *ḥadīths* which show ʿUthmān either resignedly permitting, or himself using, readings at variance with those enshrined in the *muṣḥaf* associated with his name.[16]

ʿUthmān sent to ʿAlī for information on the grievances of the rebels. Among these was resentment at his having 'expunged the *muṣḥafs*'. ʿUthmān replied, 'The Qur'ān came from God. I prohibited the variant readings since I feared dissension. But now, read it as you please.'[17]

It is said that when ʿUthmān received the completed *muṣḥaf*, he noticed certain linguistic irregularities. 'Had he who dictated it been of Huḏail and the scribe of Thaqīf,' he said, 'this would never have happened.'[18]

ʿAbdullāh b. Masʿūd, we recall, was of Huḏail. The report looks uncommonly like a pro-ʿAbdullāh, that is, a pro-Kūfa, propaganda vehicle.

ʿAbdullāh is supposed to have said, 'Hide your Qur'ān's! How can you order me to use the reading of Zaid when I recited from the very lips of the Prophet seventy-odd *sūras*?'

Not only is there no evidence that reading uniformity prevailed after ʿUthmān's day, there is, on the contrary, ample indication in the *Fiqh* works, and especially in the *tafsīr* works, that the exact opposite was increasingly the case. ʿUthmān was assassinated and laid in his grave and the heyday of *ikhtilāf* was yet to come.

What, then, if any, is that great achievement with which the memory of ʿUthmān is to be glorified? To understand the Muslim traditions it will be necessary to reconsider the background against which the initiative ascribed to ʿUthmān was thought to have occurred.

The Iraqis and the Syrians, the Kufans and the Basrans were all said to have indulged in mutual recrimination, exchanging accusations of error, even of heresy in respect of their readings of the Qur'ān. This runs exactly parallel with their mutual indictment of their respective sunnas. Any mention of the dialect rationalisation of the reading differences is merely the acknowledgement that in ʿUthmān's day the linguistic sciences had not yet evolved - the _varia lingua_ rather than the _varia lectio_. Besides, some _ḥadīths_ had distinguished dialect from reading.

The dialect problem had apparently not been overcome by the very work ascribed to ʿUthmān, as we have just seen. Nor had the reading problem been settled by his supposed provision of a uniform consonantal matrix. Goldziher has signalled a disputed vocalic reading for the very _Tawba_ verse which Zaid is said to have reinstated: There has now come to you a prophet from amongst your own number (_anfusikum_); from amongst the most precious among you (_anfasikum_). The variant has been ascribed, not merely to Companions, but even to the Prophet himself![19]

Scholars could explain the creation of the Muslim linguistic sciences after the death of ʿUthmān as centring upon solicitude for the avoidance of incorrect theology occasioned by incorrect reading of the sacred texts.[20] The consonantal base of the text was envisaged as having been fixed, but not the vocalic values. Were this the case, liberty would be little affected. There would yet remain to the scholars such scope for variant readings that it is simply not possible to understand why ʿAbdullāh was projected as so violently opposed to ʿUthmān's obvious good sense.

When, however, we consider the variant readings attributed to the ancient authorities, to whom appeal is constantly made by the rival groupings in the course of their undignified squabbles over the details of the Qur'ān texts, our surprise increases. It is exceedingly difficult for us to comprehend what might have given rise to such widespread fuss. For no major differences of doctrine can be constructed on the basis of the parallel readings based on the ʿUthmānic consonantal outline, yet ascribed to muṣḥafs other than his. All the rival readings unquestionably represent one and the same text. They are substantially agreed in what they transmit, varying from one another only to the extent of the occasional preference for one of a number of possible inflections and the use or non-use of certain minor conjunctives. Here and there the variants depart from ʿUthmān to the extent of employing this or that synonym. None of these variants is of great import.

We have, however, seen that the variant codices are further differentiated from ʿUthmān by a limited number of attempted interpolations. A detailed study of the use made of appeal to the ʿAbdullāh or Ubayy readings against ʿUthmān leads to the conclusion that the traditional accounts of the act and motive of ʿUthmān cannot possibly be correct. A single reminder will suffice to make the point:

> The fast in expiation of breach of an oath need not be consecutive, even if ʿAbdullāh did read: 'three [consecutive] days', since this addition is not mutawātir. It is therefore not part of the Qur'ān. Perhaps ʿAbdullāh adduced this reading to clarify what he considered a justifiable exegesis. Perhaps he attracted to this verse, by analogy, the restriction that is found in the verse on the ẓihār.[21] Abū Ḥanīfa, who conceded that this interpolation is not Qur'ānic, accepted ʿAbdullāh's view on this topic,

> but as a *ḥadīth*. But the practice ought to be based exclusively on what is explicitly attributed to the Prophet.'[22]

This can only mean that the scholars who adduced the variant readings ascribed to ʿAbdullāh did so in exactly the spirit in which they adduced *ḥadīths* attributed to ʿAbdullāh. Sarakhsī argued that God had caused the other Companions to forget this reading, but permitted ʿAbdullāh to transmit it so that the ruling might be preserved.

The post-Šāfiʿī practice of regarding the *ḥadīths* traced from the Prophet as having absolute priority over the *ḥadīths* from all others did not affect the variant Qur'ān readings. All our information on the Qur'ān derives solely from Companions, since no codex or *muṣḥaf* has been explicitly ascribed to Muḥammad.

A new way therefore had to be discovered of resolving the conflicts between reading-*ḥadīths*.

Bergsträsser discusses the Qur'ān variants:

> Goldziher treated the variants in the readings of ʿAbdullāh on the same footing as other versions of the readings, that is in general from the viewpoint of regarding them as departures from the 'authentic text'. Certainly, in the variants ascribed to him are instances enough in which the ʿUthmānic text has been wrongly altered, or in which a motive for the variation from the ʿUthmānic text is discernible, and hence the ibn Masʿūd text is to this extent secondary. The most important although not the most frequent of such motives is certainly the sort which Goldziher placed in the foreground: the side-stepping of possible stumbling blocks; the provision of pertinent elucidations; the linguistic clarification of obscure texts; the avoidance of unusual or faulty

expressions and stylistic infelicities; together with a general disposition to smoothe and simplify the utterance. Yet the ibn Masʿūd text need not always be treated as simply 'corrected' wherever it chances to read more smoothly than the ʿUthmānic text. Examination of synonyms which replace the individual words of the ʿUthmānic text, and Goldziher had already noted the frequency of synonyms in the non-ʿUthmānic texts, indicates that often the word occurring in the ibn Masʿūd text is the more familiar and the more suitable, but not always. This is explicable by supposing that in such cases either it is the ʿUthmānic that is secondary to the ibn Masʿūd, or more properly that many Qur'ān verses were in circulation in variant oral versions differentiated one from another by the selection made from a number of synonyms and that the ibn Masʿūd, or both texts directly and independently of each other drew upon this oral tradition. Such direct adoption from an oral store of Tradition is the more likely explanation in the majority of those cases where the ibn Masʿūd text offers an unambiguous form or orthography as against the ambiguous ʿUthmānic reading. In such cases, the relation between the two is clearly not one in which the author of the ibn Masʿūd variants had the ʿUthmānic text before him and, recognising the ambiguity of his 'Vorlage', prepared to select a positive reading. Rather, for him, the meaning of the verse was still alive and this is what he sought to express in the clearest possible manner. He differs from the author of the ʿUthmānic texts in that he makes even greater efforts to achieve a clear expression insofar as the deficiencies of the script will permit this. Finally, it is necessary to posit the existence of a parallel tradition independent of the ʿUthmānic text to account for those innumerable variants which are too trivial and insignificant to be regarded as deliberate alterations, or such as

> those which bear the stamp of the original readings, or at the very least, as in the case of several greater variations occurring in the last sūras, the mark of total independence from the ʿUthmānic text.[23]

This is a fair sample of European investigation by intuition. Several issues are raised: the reported synonyms; the deficiencies of the script and the effect that might have had on men who had memorised the Qur'ān; the greater differences in the last sūras with their 'stamp' and 'mark' of independence.

To attribute not merely variant readings but whole variant muṣḥafs to the Companions, and achieve a degree of credibility in doing so, it was necessary to attribute to them greater or lesser differences from the ʿUthmānic text. It was also necessary to ascribe to the Companion codices several features not mentioned here, such as a different ordering of the sūras, some attempted interpolations, and even the omission of one or more chapters of the Qur'ān.

In common with the Muslims, Bergsträsser in acknowledging the existence of such an entity as the ʿUthmānic text has no difficulty in identifying which text it is. Whether compiled by ʿUthmān or another is for the moment irrelevant, just as the question of whether the ʿAbdullāh text had any historical connection with the generation of the Companions may also be set aside for the present. The important thing is the fact of their difference. The nature of their difference is the crucial point of our enquiry.

In common with the European scholars, Bergsträsser approached the problem by considering the Qur'ān as exclusively a literary monument. To the Muslims also, the

Qur'ān is of course a document, recognised by what may or may not traditionally be recited in the ritual prayer. However, to the Muslims, the Qur'ān is primarily a source. If we consider it in this light, we shall be led to conclusions different from those we have just noted.

That the motive behind the promulgation of the Qur'ān texts in the form in which we now have them was an attempt (as the Muslims see it) to narrow down the range of documents available for the derivation of the Law is, on first hearing, inherently plausible on the pattern of the narrowing down of the range of materials available in the extra-Qur'ānic Tradition. That, we saw, followed the work of Šāfi'ī in the definition of the Sunna as the Sunna of the Prophet which had resulted in improvements in methodology. This analogy between the history of the Qur'ān source and that of the Sunna source was the work of Muslim scholars.

Their view would be acceptable likewise on historical grounds were it the case, which it emphatically is not, that the promulgated Qur'ān text reflects the _Fiqh_ as faithfully as does the Sunna. To extend the analogy, we ought now to possess, alongside the _muṣḥafs_ of the Companions, the _muṣḥaf_ transmitted from the Prophet. That would presumably, in the post-Šāfi'ī ages, gradually have dislodged the Companion texts as thoroughly as the Sunna of the Prophet dislodged the Companion-_ḥadīths_. As it is, we see that all our information on the Qur'ān derives wholly and exclusively from the Companions, since even the officially promulgated _muṣḥaf_, on the basis of which alone the prayers of the Muslims are valid, did not succeed in driving out the habit of referring to Companion codices or variant readings, and since this _textus receptus_ is still known as the _muṣḥaf_ of ʿUthmān.

How little the admirable aim of narrowing down the source materials was in fact realised in the Qur'ān field, even where we view its use as merely documenting as opposed to deriving the Law, becomes clearer upon consideration of the use which could still be made, generations after ʿUthmān's death, of the Qur'ān in support of the local _Fiqh_, especially but not solely in view of the deficiencies of the script, which long continued to permit the schools that degree of freedom which the imposition of a single text was supposed to have limited.

Here is the very crux of the Qur'ān problem. The freedom of the schools had not been at all circumscribed. On the contrary, _ikhtilāf_, far from withering away on the provision of a single text, appears to be only beginning. The most likely explanation of this clear contradiction is precisely that, for the schools, the ʿUthmānic and the non-ʿUthmānic Qur'ān traditions were regarded as parallel and equally sovereign. The one interacted upon the other, as they developed to play out their function as the Tradition-based documentation from the Qur'ān source, to which this or that _madhab_ appealed for support on this or that topic of the local _Fiqh_.

We have seen examples of just such appeals to the ʿAbdullāh or Ubayy readings. Those were not of course variant Qur'ān readings. They were attempted additions to the text. That is what the disputes were really about.

The use of non-ʿUthmānic readings at prayer was

banned since they were not universally recognised. The validity of the prayer was conditional upon use of the *mutawātir* Qur'ān document. The appeals we mention were to the ʿAbdullāh or Ubayy Qur'ān sources, for they concerned the *Fiqh* of the Qur'ān. This is the area in which we find appeals to the Companion *muṣḥafs*, as we noted above in Sarakhsī's appeal (p. 171).

In response to the fundamentalist challenge, based on the view that only the Qur'ān was adequate to serve as source, the Qur'ān entered the methodological debate. This was at that stage in the discussion when the appeal to the sunna of the Companions was on the point of being replaced by appeal to the Sunna of the Prophet. The Companion *muṣḥafs* failed to make a complete transition.

Although they now began to speak of and to adduce the texts of the Sunna of the Prophet, the legal scholars did not advance to the point of adducing in addition the *muṣḥaf* of the Prophet. Qur'ān variants, in other words, concern only Companions - variant readings vary from the text now attributed to ʿUthmān.

The difference between the Qur'ān source and the Sunna source is quite simply that behind the appeal to either lay the tacit assumption that the text derived from the Prophet. In the case of the Sunna alone, the claim had to become explicit and had to be set out explicitly in the *isnād* prefaced to each *ḥadīth*.

That the variant readings appealed to continued to be associated with individuals among the Companions suggests that they had always been recognised as varying from the generally accepted Qur'ān texts.

The suggestion by Bergsträsser that the ʻUthmānic and the non-ʻUthmānic Qur'ān traditions were independently and directly drawing upon an underlying store of oral tradition is complicated by the fact that, so far as they have been examined to date, all Qur'ān MSS exhibit throughout the ʻUthmānic text.

One might have expected, as so often happens in literary history, that some evidence of the existence of non-ʻUthmānic, not to speak of pre-ʻUthmānic codices would have survived in some remote corner of the Islamic world, especially since ibn Masʻūd ordered his followers to lay up their Qur'ān's in hiding and withhold them from the government agents charged with their destruction.

A solution to these problems is to be sought in distinguishing those variants which are 'too trivial and insignificant to be regarded as deliberate alterations' from those whose motivation in the projection back to the revealed Book of the disputed details of the Fiqh is unmistakable. In other words, we too must learn to distinguish between the Qur'ān text and the Qur'ān source.

We argued that it was irrelevant to the revealed status of the Qur'ān document whether one read: aṣwabu, aqwamu or ahya'u (Q 73.6); ṣaiḥa or zaqya (Q 36.29).

On the other hand, it was of the highest significance for the history of the development of Islamic Law and to the attendant school polemic whether one read fa mā stamtaʻtum bihi minhunna (Q 4.24) with or without the attempted interpolation ilā ajalin musamman.[24] The sole purpose of the attempt was to provide a Qur'ānic basis (aṣl) for the doctrine of temporary marriage, mutʿa, whose rejection by other scholars was currently based upon evidence circulating in the Sunna.

As one element in the Tradition, the Qur'ān was here being used in the role of counter-sunna, less open to ready rejection because 'stronger' than a ḥadīth.

It was this role of the Qur'ān that gave rise to the extensive disputes on the reading in which variants are never either trivial or insignificant.

The subtlety of ascribing variant readings to Ubayy lies in the existence of a series of ḥadīths of an originally exegetical origin in which we are informed that Ubayy stoutly refused to abandon any part of the Qur'ān wording he had received direct from the Prophet. Ubayy, we are told, would have none of the doctrine of the withdrawal of any part of the Qur'ān text.[25] ʿUmar, on the other hand, who is credited in the Ḥadīth with the prohibition of the very usage not merely adumbrated but specifically documented in the supposed Ubayy text, figures in the ḥadīths attempting to convince Ubayy from the Qur'ān itself (Q 2.106) of the reality of all the naskh phenomena.[26]

This representation of Ubayy's insistence on the quranicity of the words for the sake of establishing the quranicity of the practice, is the reverse of the classical uṣūl's insistence on the quranicity of the ruling on account of the quranicity of the wording. This betrays the very raison d'être of Ubayy's 'reading'.

The mutʿa doctrine had been embraced by an

insufficient number of Sunnī Muslims to acquire probative roots in all the recognised sources. In view of the contents of certain ḥadīths, temporary marriage was admitted by some to have once been permitted; it was however alleged to have been suppressed by statements in both Qur'ān and Sunna.

Other doctrines, more widely acquiesced in, had had no difficulty in acquiring satisfactory bases in both Qur'ān and Sunna. Nowhere explicitly mentioned in the ʿUthmānic text of the Qur'ān, mutʿa rested solely on the evidence of the Sunna. When challenged, it advanced its documentation to the Qur'ān, appealing to the reported, and, for some, convenient refusal of Ubayy's to abandon once revealed matter.

Rejection techniques available to the uṣūlīs thus included, for both Qur'ān and Sunna, isnād critique (i.e. acceptance of both conflicting documents accompanied by the assertion that one chanced to be later than the other). In the case of the Qur'ān only, abrogation might have affected the wording alone, or both wording and ruling. This last was to be the ground for the rejection of mutʿa, Ubayy's reading notwithstanding. Designed as a Qur'ān evidence, the Ubayy reading might have been expected to overcome the weaker ḥadīth evidence, but it was seen to be at odds with the universal text of Q 4.24.

A reading promoted by the proponents of a particular practice, urging a particular exegesis of Q 4.24, was ignored or rejected by those who did not care for the practice. The reading was attributed to a Companion.

The variations in the information provided by the

Companions for the Qur'ān thus correspond exactly to the variations in the information they provide for the Sunna for which, as for the Qur'ān, they are the common eponyms.

Yet there is a degree of difference between the Sunna-variations and the Qur'ān-variations, reflected in their respective developments. From the quarrels over the _ḥadīths_ of ʿAbdullāh and the _ḥadīths_ of another, there had emerged the _ḥadīths_ of the Prophet conveying the Sunna of the Prophet. That development provided one solution to the problem of the conflict of _ḥadīths_. The Sunna of the Prophet never again yielded after Šāfiʿī to _ḥadīths_ from the Companions.

The same development had also provoked improvement in the _isnāds_ which in turn raised the fresh problem of the evident conflict between _ḥadīths_ now reported as coming from the Prophet. A _ḥadīth_ from the Prophet reported by a later Companion, it was decided, indicated the abrogation of the conflicting _ḥadīth_ from the Prophet transmitted by the earlier Companion. In this procedure, we witness the birth of the theories of _naskh_.

Individual variant readings reported from the senior Companions developed into the _muṣḥafs_ of those Companions, there being no better rationalisation of the reported variants. From the codex of ʿAbdullāh, Ubayy, Abū Mūsā, ʿĀ'iša, Umm Salama, Ḥafṣa and others, there did not, however, evolve the codex of the Prophet.

That there are inauthentic _ḥadīths_ from the Companions, and hence from the Prophet, designed to document some particular element of local _Fiqh_, is not difficult to demonstrate. That there are inauthentic elements in the

Qur'ān information reported from the Companions is no more difficult to demonstrate. Indeed, more than one learned Muslim has been seen in the foregoing to be perfectly aware that the variants reported were in fact nothing more than exegetical comments, as opposed to actual 'readings'.

What is certain is that such variants never gained acceptance into the text. At best, they were obliged to remain the variant of the Companion sponsor.

Certain of these variants, in this case undisguised attempted interpolations, were reported collectively from several senior Companions. They too were forced to remain qur'ān's outside the Qur'ān since again they failed to achieve admittance into the text between the two covers. It is because they adumbrated (documented) legal doctrines of more than merely local interest that they were attributed to a collective, and not simply described as the variant of some individual Companion and entrusted to his personal codex.

This adds for the Qur'ān an element additional to the suggestion that the ʿUthmānic and the non-ʿUthmānic Qur'ān texts were drawing upon an underlying common Qur'ān tradition, whether oral or otherwise.

That suggestion in itself tends to direct one's thinking towards an ancient Qur'ān tradition, flowing upwards since the days of Muḥammad and ultimately breaking surface (as the *ḥadīth* had earlier done) at a point in time when some imperious necessity was being felt to call upon the Qur'ān to provide documentary evidence to buttress specific positions in the intense competition between the regional practices and legal viewpoints. When this occurred, it occurred in separate phases.

In the case of the rivalry between the local legal views, certain developments occurring in the Sunna field failed to occur in the Qur'ān field. In the light of the uṣūl doctrine on the Sunna source, the Sunna documents proved extremely malleable in the hands of the schools. With the Qur'ān, on the contrary, any departure from the transmitted text universally acknowledged and traditionally employed at prayer is never referred to as 'Qur'ān' in that loose fashion in which the word Sunna is bandied about. Qur'ān variants have always been identified as the 'reading' of some individual Companion.

Even more striking is the case of those items of Qur'ān information which are referred neither to the ʿUthmānic nor to the individual Companion Qur'ān texts. These are the 'readings' of the Qur'ān intended to document legal views upheld over a large part of the Muslim world, and not merely advanced and defended by the scholars of a particular regional grouping. These were 'readings' held to date from the time of the Prophet, but from before the time of the collection of the Qur'ān texts (i.e. naskh al tilāwa dūna al ḥukm).

A Qur'ān text, in other words, associated with a Head of State and Church, ʿUthmān, is always set apart from the variant Qur'ān readings or even texts attributed to individual Companions, while itself always being likewise distinguished from another Qur'ān text associated with another Head of State and Church, the Prophet.

A Qur'ān text, the ʿUthmānic, distinguishable from the variant Companion texts, has always retained an objective historical identity, and there is no sign in the literature of any ambiguity as to precisely what that text was. It is the text that looks in two opposite directions. It differs from the texts ascribed to the other Companions; and it differs from the text revealed to Muḥammad. Relative to the Companion texts, ʿUthmān is the text without interpolations. Relative to the revealed Qur'ān, ʿUthmān is incomplete. Its collection could not but be placed in the period after Muḥammad.

The Companion readings and the Companion-muṣḥafs played a role parallel to that played by the Companion-ḥadīths. They were therefore the creation of the regional rivalries.

The concept of the total original Qur'ān revelation is met with only in the documentation of legal attitudes shared by all or by the majority of the regions. Appeal to the Qur'ān in cases such as the stoning penalty had been forced upon the scholars by one of two compelling factors: either by the challenge thrown down by the fundamentalist groups who did not admit that the Sunna had a role to play as a source for the Law, or who insisted that the Qur'ān be seen to be the primary source; or by the belief of the scholars that stoning did in fact derive from the Qur'ān.

We attempted earlier to enquire into the origins of that belief and, if the analysis offered in our discussion of the Q 5 passages were thought to have merit, several conclusions follow. It is possible that the older generation of Muslim scholars stoutly maintaining that the Fiqh's stoning penalty had been derived from the Qur'ān were justified in their claims if, that is, by assigning the stoning penalty to the Qur'ān they meant the Qur'ān in the general sense, that is, the muṣḥaf plus its exegesis.

It is not difficult to see how stoning could have come to be mentioned in the course of wide-ranging gossip about the meanings and implications of the Q 5 verses. One must bear in mind the essentially narrative (haggada) nature of tafsīr and asbāb al nuzūl and the tafsīr nature (halakha) of much of the sīra, or biography of the Prophet.

The entry of stoning in some such manner into the discussions could also very easily and early become obscured for the succeeding generation. One may perhaps be justified in pointing again to the unanimity of the schools on this question in the widely separated regions. This unanimity might tend to indicate the antiquity of the belief that stoning is indeed the Islamic penalty.

The irony of the suggestion increases when we recall the anguish felt by some uṣūlīs who had been taught never to concede that the Sunna had ever abrogated a Qur'ān ruling. It was their participation in this discussion that had reinforced the allegation that the stoning penalty had derived from the Qur'ān.

If stoning did commend itself to the ancient fuqahā' in the manner suggested, by passing over from the exegesis into the Fiqh, the standpoint of those who argued that stoning had originated in the Sunna becomes even more ironic.

What passes for the Sunna of the Companions contains a considerable degree of material of undoubted exegetical origin. Viewed in this light, the tension between the Qur'ān and the Sunna can be almost totally eliminated, and the necessity to formulate a special theory of abrogation to solve the problem shown to be illusory.

Once the demand for Islamic documentation had arisen in the atmosphere of incessant school rivalry, the function of the ḥadīth in documenting the Sunna was significant. It has been amply demonstrated that this had important effects for the flexibility of the individual ḥadīth document. Indeed, it was this very flexibility that provided Goldziher with his clue to the inauthenticity of much of the Ḥadīth in general.

We have seen that the Qur'ān, on the contrary, in taking its place alongside the Ḥadīth for the purposes of documentation, proved considerably more intractable material. The Qur'ān was flexible only within very exiguous limits. Local variation was possible solely within the range demonstrated by readings based on the consonantal framework of the universally agreed text.

The scholars were in consequence driven to seek the liberties they craved in varying the vocalic data (arjulakum/arjulikum), or the diacritical pointing (yaṭhurna/yaṭṭahirna), or by questioning the punctuation of the individual verses, that is, the syntax of the individual utterances. Otherwise they could only resort to attempted interpolation.

All readings and variants required to be documented by reference to one or more of the Prophet's generation. Beyond this, linguistic considerations could be urged in favour of certain views the Muslims sought to establish, not on the basis of the inherited text, but in despite of the text, in the ingenious ta'wīl to which on occasion they had recourse.

These determined, if obvious, efforts reflected the need they felt to circumvent a basically unyielding Book. Both the very unhelpfulness of the Qur'ān document when called upon to behave as the Qur'ān source, and the frequent embarrassment it caused the Muslim scholars speak very strongly for its authenticity as a document, in the sense that it does not have any of the appearance of having been concocted after the evolution of the legal doctrine with the aim of supplying its documentation. Indeed, the Qur'ān texts frequently contradict the Fiqh, 'und da ist es Sache der spitzfindigen Theologen und Harmonistiker sich zurecht zu finden'.[27]

We encountered in the Ḥadīth materials treating of the earliest collection of the Qur'ān indications of the concern of the Companions for the extent of the Qur'ān heritage. Ḥadīths of that kind can be detached from another type of ḥadīths, which reflected awareness of the sense of scandal which must result if the community of the faithful were seen not to be united on the reading of their sacred Book.

The reading variants that were identified had been rationalised by attribution to the several Companions, an attribution sustainable solely on the premise that the Qur'ān had not been given definitive form by the Prophet to whom it had been revealed. The attribution did nothing to lessen the sense of scandal. Hence the further assertion was made that the Prophet had for reasons of policy sanctioned recitation in the various Arab dialects.

This explanation broke down on the consideration that ʿUmar and a fellow Meccan had disputed the reading. The further explanation was provided that the differing readings had involved synonyms drawn from one and the same dialect. The paramount factor was apparently the common meaning which all codices or readings shared.

None of these successive rationalisations suffices to elucidate the problem of the class of variants which consist in interpolations relative to the ʿUthmān text. None of them takes account either of yet another Muslim doctrine which, in its implications, is hostile to any suggestion that the Qur'ān at any stage in its history had ever been transmitted according to the sense alone.

The doctrine of the *iʿjāz* of the Qur'ān (its miraculous nature) - a central element in *dalā'il al nubuwwa*, a central element in the 'proofs' of Muḥammad's claims and now advanced on its own behalf as a 'proof' of the claims of Islam - developed in the course of the external polemic and was directed at non-Muslims. It could not, however, be left out of account in the internal polemics among the Muslims.

The report that ʿUmar had quarrelled with a fellow Meccan, inexplicable on the ground of dialect difference, and therefore explained on the grounds of choice of synonyms, sins in its turn against the *iʿjāz* doctrine in the eyes of those who interpreted the term, erroneously, to mean the inimitability of the Qur'ān in strict literary terms. That which is verbally inimitable can scarcely have passed through a phase of multiple wordings when the individual Companions had the Prophet's permission to substitute whichever word chanced to correspond with the meaning revealed by God. ibn al Jazarī exclaims, 'Whoever alleges that any of the Companions thought it legitimate to transmit the Qur'ān according to the sense alone is a liar!'[28]

The scholars therefore had to supply a further rationalisation of ʿUmar's reported quarrel with a fellow Meccan. The function of the report had been merely to make the point that the different readings had been countenanced by the Prophet, and were thus still legitimate. But we have seen the difficulties that ambush so many of the ḥadīth reports, leading to ever more subtle interpretations and harmonisations.

The origin of the reported difference was simply that ʿUmar had memorised the sūra at an early date. Hišām had learned it in its later form. Hišām became a Muslim only at the time of the conquest of Mecca. ʿUmar was unaware of the later additions to the sūra.[29]

This explanation shows neatly the application of the theory of the isnād to the Qur'ān information reaching us from the Companions of the Prophet.

We now arrive at the core of the vast corpus of traditions on all aspects of the reading and of the collecting of the Qur'ān texts. The principal considerations were the isnād and the relating of all available reports, from whatever quarter, to the yardstick of the theories of abrogation. The later supersedes the earlier if they disagree.

9 The *isnād* of the Qur'ān

Statements which assert that the Qur'ān already existed in collected form in the days of the Prophet confront not the question: when precisely was the Qur'ān first collected in the form we now know as the *muṣḥaf*? but the quite different question: is the *muṣḥaf* a complete record of the divine revelations to Muḥammad?

The ʿUthmān collection tradition corresponds to another question: which Qur'ān tradition is the more authentic, the Ḥijāzī tradition represented in the universally acknowledged text; or the Kufan tradition claiming descent from ibn Masʿūd; or the Basran stemming from Abū Mūsā; or the Syrian from Ubayy (or from Miqdād/? Muʿāḏ)?

The Abū Bakr – ʿUmar tradition could very well be, as Schwally suggested, an attempt to project the credit and priority of merit to the first and most revered of Muḥammad's successors.[1]

It could as well represent for the Medinese tradition the conscious effort to pre-date the rival non-Arabian traditions by projecting ʿUthmān's initiative further back into the pre-diaspora Islam of Medina, and thus nearer to the Prophet under the aegis of the *isnād*: Zaid b. Thābit – ʿUmar – Abū Bakr.

Ṭayālisī draws our attention to an interesting rule-of-thumb: 'He shall be *imām* [at prayer] whose knowledge of the Book of God is most extensive and whose acquaintance with it is most ancient. If two men be alike in this respect, he shall be *imām* whose adherence to Islam was the earlier.'[2]

This recalls the dispute as to which of Muḥammad's followers had been converted to Islam earliest and thus enjoyed the longest association with the Prophet. His acquaintance with the Prophet's views and conduct would presumably have been the most extensive. We might now relate this to the disputes about the first to collect the Qur'ān: Abū Bakr, or ʿUmar, or ʿUthmān, or ʿAlī.

In the legal sciences, where *ḥadīth* reports clash, a brilliant and elegantly simple technique was deployed to resolve the problem. This involved employment of *isnād* theory in terms of *ta'akhkhur*, the later abrogates the earlier if they differ.[3]

This resulted, however, in earliness of conversion being driven out in favour of lateness of conversion. The change occurred in the time of Šāfiʿī, much of whose work was directed at the systematisation of the appeals to abrogation. For traces of the older rule appear to have affected his reasoning on the question of the prayer in times of peril. Faced with conflict of *ḥadīths*, Šāfiʿī's preference for the report from Khawwāt b. Jubair is explicitly determined by his awareness that Khawwāt was older than ibn ʿUmar and had associated longer with the Prophet.[4]

Indeed the very frequency with which Šāfiʿī must insist in his polemic with representatives of the other schools that, in the event of a clash of *ḥadīths*, it is the later that invariably is to be adopted, suggests that that principle was in his day something novel.

In the light of this technical development, the traditions on ʿUthmān's collection of the Qur'ān would, since they clash with traditions reporting earlier collections, be seen to post-date the collections attributed both to Abū Bakr and to ʿUmar, but also, much more importantly, they report events later than the formation of the codices of the other contemporaries of Muḥammad.

Confirmation that the Qur'ān collection *ḥadīths* were influenced by the theories of *naskh* is provided by a study of the *isnād* attributed to the *muṣḥaf*, that is, of the prominent role assigned at each stage in the history of its collection and promulgation to the figure of Zaid b. Thābit.

It might now be more profitable, therefore, to begin to think in terms of the Zaid b. Thābit codex of the Qur'ān being placed in conscious and polemic opposition to the codices of ʿAbdullāh, Ubayy, Abū Mūsā and any other first generation Muslim.

The attachment of Zaid's name to the ʿUthmān *muṣḥaf*, to the ʿUmar recension and to the Abū Bakr recension undoubtedly occurred later than the attribution of variant readings or variant recensions to the other adherents of the Prophet.

It is extremely interesting to note in addition that, apart from allegedly having collected the Qur'ān, neither ʿUmar nor Abū Bakr was credited with a personal codex, that is, with a variant reading analogous to that attributed to the others. ʿUthmān is occasionally mentioned in connection with variants, but to a very much lesser extent than ʿAbdullāh or Ubayy.

When ʿAbdullāh was made to assert that he had learned his Qur'ān from the Prophet before Zaid had reached puberty; or that he had become a Muslim before Zaid was even conceived, this had without doubt been intended, under the older rule governing *isnāds*, to pre-empt the primacy in codex matters in favour of ʿAbdullāh's readings. That was also the aim of the following utterances placed in the mouth of the Prophet: 'Whoever wishes to recite the Qur'ān in the purest form, that in which it was revealed, let him recite the reading of ibn Umm ʿAbd [ʿAbdullāh].'[5] 'Whatsoever ʿAbdullāh teaches you to recite, follow it.'[6]

That there was rivalry on the question of the *isnād* of the Qur'ān, and that the question was to be solved by reference to the principle of abrogation, is clear from a series of *ḥadīths*, the first of which endorses incidentally our suggestion of attributing a codex to Zaid b. Thābit.

> A man complained to the Prophet, 'ʿAbdullāh taught me to recite a *sūra* of the Qur'ān. Zaid taught me the same *sūra* and so too did Ubayy. The readings of all three differ. Whose reading ought I to adopt?' The Prophet remained silent. ʿAlī who was at his side replied, 'Every man should recite as he was taught. Each of the readings is acceptable, valid.'[7]

Bukhārī quotes from Muḥammad's daughter, Fāṭima, a report to the effect that the Prophet one day informed her that Gabriel was in the habit of checking the revelations with him annually. On this occasion, Gabriel had just checked them twice, from which the Prophet surmised that his death was imminent.[8]

Since the Qur'ān had been revealed in seven forms, had Gabriel checked all seven, or only one, and, if so, which one?[9] Aḥmad, ibn abī Da'ūd and Ṭabarī are all credited with the view that the ʿUthmān text was based on the reading reviewed by Gabriel in his final meeting with Muḥammad. In an ibn Sīrīn version of the ḥadīth, it is reported that 'the Muslims are of the view that our present text is the latest of all the texts, having been reviewed on the occasion of the final check'.[10]

Mujāhid reports ibn ʿAbbās as asking, 'Which of the two texts do you consider the later?' They replied that the Zaid text was the later, which ibn ʿAbbās repudiated. 'The Prophet,' he argued, 'reviewed the Qur'ān annually with Gabriel and twice in the year he died. The reading of ʿAbdullāh represents the later of the two final reviews.'[11] By Zaid's text is meant the ʿUthmān muṣḥaf.

> Ibrāhīm reports that ibn ʿAbbās heard some man refer to 'the former Qur'ān text'. He asked him what he meant. The man explained, 'ʿUmar sent ʿAbdullāh to Kūfa as instructor and the people there adopted his reading. ʿUthmān altered the text, and so they refer to ʿAbdullāh's reading as "the former text".' ibn ʿAbbās rejected this. 'ʿAbdullāh's is the later, based on the final review.'
>
> ibn ʿAbbās also reports that ʿAbdullāh attended the final review and learned what had been withdrawn and what had been abrogated.[12]

Zaid is also said to have attended the final review and to have learned what was withdrawn and what remained.[13]

> al Bag̈awī in Šarḥ al Sunna, concluded, 'The muṣḥaf which has been traditionally accepted represents the final review text. ʿUthmān ordered it to be copied into the muṣḥafs he despatched throughout the empire, simultaneously making away with all other Qur'ān materials with the aim of preventing differences. Whatever is at variance with the written text is now to be regarded in the same light as that which has been abrogated and withdrawn. It is no longer competent for any man to go beyond the text.'[14]

Ṭabarī taught that the Companions agreed to write out that which they were certain represented the text as checked on the occasion of the final review. They were unanimous that all other Qur'ān materials must be abandoned.[15]

> The Qāḍī Abū Bakr holds 'that the entirety of the Qur'ān, as God revealed it, and as He commanded that it be recorded, such as He did not abrogate, nor withdraw in respect of the wording alone, is represented in the muṣḥaf of ʿUthmān.'[16]

In Bāqillānī's view, therefore, the ʿUthmān muṣḥaf, as collected by Zaid, equals the Qur'ān minus two classes of verses: naskh al ḥukm wa al tilāwa and naskh al tilāwa dūna al ḥukm.

ibn Ẓibyān reports that ibn ʿAbbās asked him which of the two texts he recited. He replied the former reading, that of ibn Umm ʿAbd (i.e. ʿAbdullāh's). 'But,' said ibn ʿAbbās, 'it is the later of the two.'[17]

ʿAbdullāh is himself reported as declaring, 'Did I know of anyone whom camels could reach who had later information on the final review than I have, I should go to him.'

The 'annual review' and especially the 'final review' is transparently a motif deliberately framed to overcome the recognised difficulty that everyone knew that Zaid was much younger than ʿAbdullāh and a much later adherent of the Prophet. Zaid thus represented a threat to the ʿAbdullāh text of the Qur'ān.

Zaid's youth and late conversion had, under the aegis of naskh, become precisely Zaid's strength. His selection as the guarantor of what was now known as the ʿUthmān muṣḥaf, must have represented the conscious implication that Zaid's reading was younger than and therefore superseded all other older codices of the text.

One thrills to the elegance of the reasoning by which the Muslims extricate themselves from problems of their own creation, nothing lost, and nothing even risked. 'Sālim died at Yemāma; Muʿāḏ in ʿUmar's reign; both Ubayy and ʿAbdullāh in ʿUthmān's reign. Zaid died much later than them all and thus attained to leadership in respect of the Qur'ān reading.'[18]

The attempts noted earlier to make ʿAbdullāh's earliness of conversion pre-empt the primacy in codex matters in his favour, rebounded in the later isnād theory to the disadvantage of ʿAbdullāh and in favour of Zaid. Considerably younger than ʿAbdullāh, and surviving all the major Companions who had an interest in Qur'ān affairs, Zaid serves as the guarantor of the latest Qur'ān Tradition, and that recension to which his name was attached was seen to have abrogated all earlier recensions, codices and readings.

The ʿUthmān collection tradition thus stands opposed not to the Abū Bakr – ʿUmar collection tradition, but to the variant reading, variant codex traditions. These could be used to counter the Sunna in disputes where the Sunna was seen to be at variance with the 'Qur'ān'. They might also be seen in that stage of the development of the legal sciences in which the Qur'ān had come to be seen as a stronger source, superior to the Sunna, to be used to counter some view making appeal to the 'Qur'ān'.

Borrowing the techniques of the Sunna, the 'Qur'ān' now counter-attacked as the ʿUthmān *muṣḥaf*, co-opting Zaid precisely on account of his youth and the lateness of his conversion in combination with the lateness of the caliphate of ʿUthmān. The *isnād* Zaid - ʿUthmān is doubly late, representing Islam's last link with the city of the Prophet of God.

The masses of *ḥadīth* materials which surround the various differing versions of the collection of the Qur'ān texts, only some of which we have reviewed, are but the consequence of the central and really significant assertion which all the reports share in common.

The *ḥadīths* agree in holding that Muḥammad had not left an edited Qur'ān text to his followers.

The assertion is, of course, contradictory, since, given all the work that had gone into the principle that God would cause His Prophet to forget only what it suited God to have him forget, it not being part of the divine plan that it should form part of the *muṣḥaf* and on that account operate upon the post-Muhammadan legal praxis, God could still have permitted Muḥammad in the final stages of his life to promulgate a complete record of the divine revelations in their divinely intended final form. This could have reflected the final review text and would have reconciled that *Ḥadīth* motif with the exegetically derived 'forgetting' motif.

The contradiction was, however, inescapable. The reports had been designed to account for two incompatible principles of faith. The agreed *Fiqh* opinions were derived from the Qur'ān and from the Prophet to whom the Qur'ān had been revealed. There was, however, a demonstrable break between the Islamic legal doctrines on the one hand and the historical Muḥammad and the contents of the Qur'ān on the other. Neither of the two articles of faith could be abandoned.

The final review text would have sufficed to explain the absence from our Qur'ān texts of once revealed matter in conformity with the divine author's intention that all such matter should not form part of the final promulgated text. The absent matter was a number of verses of type: *naskh al ḥukm wa al tilāwa*.

The final review text would, however, fail to explain, indeed it would render impossible, the omission from the officially promulgated *muṣḥaf* of Qur'ān matter which it was not part of the divine intention to omit. Yet such omission had, it is alleged, occurred. For certain elements of the *Fiqh* doctrine, for example, for all the legal schools, the stoning 'verse', and for some of the schools only, the five sucklings 'verse', both verified by reference to the 'Qur'ān' as having been revealed, are quite unmentioned in the *muṣḥaf*. These are verses of the type: *naskh al tilāwa dūna al ḥukm*. The justification of this class of Qur'ān omissions is quite impossible save on the hypothesis that our Qur'ān texts are post-Muhammadan.

Where legal views of a type not referred to in the 'Qur'ān' are agreed in the Fiqh, one might have expected appeal to the Companion muṣḥafs. That should have served the lawyers' purpose, on the analogy of their regular appeal to the Companions for information on the Sunna. That that was not, however, the technique adopted, suggests that such appeal would not have served. That in turn suggests that appeal to the Companion muṣḥafs served a more specialised need.

On the question of omission from Qur'ān records, ʿAbdullāh reported that the Prophet had taught him an āya or a sūra. He got it by heart and copied it into his muṣḥaf. When night came, ʿAbdullāh attempted to recite the passage in his prayers, but could not recall a single syllable. In the morning he checked his muṣḥaf, only to find the page blank! He reported immediately to the Prophet who told him that that passage had been withdrawn overnight.

Nöldeke exploited this story to conclude that it provided evidence that Muḥammad had struck out Qur'ān passages with his own hand.[19] The story is certainly no more than exegetically inspired pseudo-sīra adduced to reinforce one side of the disputed tafsīr of the Qur'ān references to naskh and nunsi (insā').[20]

It is surely a curious circumstance that the personalities called upon in the Tradition to testify to historical occurrences of the phenomena of Qur'ān omissions, whether by the normal processes of human forgetting or by the supernormal intervention of the deity, coincide with those personalities engaged in one or other of the various stages in the history of the formation of the Qur'ān texts.

It is the self-same personalities that reappear in the guise of the eponyms of the rival local legal opinions. Furthermore, the local statements of the Law were held to have been derived either from their respective sponsors' store of Sunna materials, or from their variant Qur'ān readings.

It is likewise a curious fact that none of the great first generation Readers is a representative of the Prophet's tribe of Quraiš, although there has been an effort to insist that the Qur'ān had been revealed in the dialect of Mecca. It is doubtless this consideration which lies behind the various suggestions of Qur'ān commissions appointed by ʿUthmān and comprising a majority of Qurašī members. It undoubtedly also accounts for the appearance of the Qurašī caliphs, Abū Bakr, ʿUmar, ʿUthmān or ʿAlī, in the various stages of the preparation of the Qur'ān texts. The task of the commissioners had been to control the text arrived at by the Medinese Zaid. But, as the caliphs are all of Quraiš, the commissioners are redundant. Besides, as we have seen, the dialect hypothesis survived even the ʿUthmān collection. When the completed muṣḥaf was delivered, ʿUthmān, observing certain irregular usages, said, 'Had it been dictated by a man from Huḏail and recorded by a man from Thaqīf, this would not have happened.'[21]

ʿUmar is reported to have insisted, 'Let none dictate the texts of our muṣḥafs save men of Quraiš and Thaqīf.[22]

The reference to Huḏail reminds us that ʿAbdullāh was a Huḏalī. ʿUmar is said to have written to him, admonishing him to instruct the people in Qurašī, not in Huḏalī readings, for the Qur'ān had been revealed in the dialect of Mecca.[23]

This dialect theory had presumably arisen from and thriven upon the heterogeneous tribal affiliations of the prominent Readers. ʿAbdullāh was of Huḏail, Ubayy and Zaid were both Medinese and Abū Mūsā was Yemenī.

Zaid, however, alone of all these personalities, appears consistently in all phases of Qur'ān text development, from the Medina period of the revelation to the Prophet whom he served as scribe, through each of the reported Abū Bakr, ʿUmar and ʿUthmān initiatives on behalf of the Book of God.

In the light provided by such a striking series of coincidences, a coherent pattern underlying all the traditions on Qur'ān codices and Qur'ān collections begins finally to emerge.

The variant muṣḥafs of the senior Companions represent the Qur'ānic pole of the symbolic part they play in the Sunna. Qur'ānic evidences are adduced in their names by the rival schools in their disputes. Their variant codices correspond exactly to their variant ḥadīths. Readings and codices, as well as ḥadīths were ascribed to them in the same way and to the same end. Both Qur'ān and Sunna ascriptions were the device to furnish the documents from the Tradition that would speak in favour of the local school view.

That the readings adduced in the course of disputes between the lawyers are not to be found in our texts of the Qur'ān is an objection most easily dealt with by assigning them to the personal muṣḥafs prepared for their own use and that of their followers by the several Companion school-

patrons.

That their personal muṣḥafs are not available for scientific scrutiny is best answered by alleging their destruction at the hands of ʿUthmān on the occasion of his 'uniting the Muslims on the basis of a single text'. ʿUthmān can be portrayed as prudent or highhanded, depending on the point of view.

The major difficulty in the way of our accepting this presentation of the matter is that for some reason this act of ʿUthmān's has never prevented those readings from being adduced in abundance in inter-school quarrels, for centuries after they were supposed to have been rooted out. Not that this objection has been overlooked. ʿAbdullāh allegedly bade his pupils and followers to lay up their Qur'ān's in hiding and to withhold them from ʿUthmān's agents charged with their destruction. Unfortunately for the ḥadīth, this report can easily be shown to be derived from an indifferent exegesis of Q 3.161, a verse quite unrelated to the issue. Besides, ʿAbdullāh's words are reported as addressed, not to his faithful followers, but to the government agents sent to confiscate ʿAbdullāh's text of the Qur'ān.

The Companions furnished evidence for the Qur'ān as they furnished evidence for the Sunna. In the latter sphere, technical improvements in methodology were reflected in the evolution of Companion-ḥadīths into Prophet-ḥadīths, as the maḏāhib learned how to advance their evidence in step with the theoretical developments which had resulted in the emergence of the Sunna of the Prophet. The maḏāhib hoped thereby to preserve the local body of legal materials intact, in the face of the threat posed by this novel insistence on appeal to the Prophet, rather than to the Companions. Their legal differences continued to be exposed by the still visible conflicts in a body of materials all of which was now attributed to the Prophet. But their temporary dismay was dealt with by considering the *isnāds* of this body of *ḥadīths*. Reports could be preserved if they could be shown to come down from the Prophet via Companions of later and later date of conversion. These later reports could be proclaimed to have abrogated reports coming down from the Prophet via Companions of earlier conversion or death-dates.

In the Qur'ān sphere, on the other hand, we noted a very striking difference. The information from the Companion generation similarly carries its *isnād*, yet here there had been no necessity to improve the *isnāds* to the same degree required in the Sunna. Attributions did not pass beyond the Companion generation to seek out the Prophet himself.

Developments in the *isnād* science in the field of Qur'ān studies lagged far behind parallel developments in the Sunna science. The reason for this comparative backwardness is not far to seek. Quite simply, the situation in the Qur'ān field was the reverse of that obtaining in the Sunna. As a document, the Qur'ān had existed and was universally known, having been universally employed for ritual purposes for ages before it became the Qur'ān source of the *uṣūlīs*.

Thus, three principal factors worked on the Muslim discussion of the Qur'ān:

1. The exegesis of certain verses indicating that as the Prophet had forgotten/been caused to forget, the Qur'ān was

not fully represented in the *muṣḥaf*.

2. Conflict between the *Fiqh* and the contents of the *muṣḥaf*. The *uṣūlīs* who rejected the principle of the abrogation of the Qur'ān by the Sunna argued that certain legal rulings of Islam had derived from the Qur'ān, even if no corresponding wording could be shown to be present in the *muṣḥaf*. For these scholars also the Qur'ān was not fully represented in the *muṣḥaf*.

Theological and exegetical arguments operated against any suggestion that the wording of, for example, the stoning verse had been merely lost or mislaid, or just forgotten by the Prophet or by his Companions. Besides, the stoning verse had always remained valid for legal purposes, since stoning had remained the Islamic penalty. The ruling had been in force during the Prophet's lifetime, remained in force until the Prophet's death, was in force during the reigns of his successors and remained in force until the age of the *fuqahā'*, since when it has been handed down from generation to generation of the Muslims.

No Islamic legal provision could conceivably have been based on something that had been abrogated during the Prophet's lifetime, and there certainly can be no abrogation after the Prophet's death.

No Qur'ānic revelation continuing without interruption to apply to the *Fiqh* could conceivably have been omitted from the *muṣḥaf*, if the *muṣḥaf* had been prepared and promulgated by the Prophet. The Prophet for that reason could not conceivably have been responsible for the formation of the *muṣḥaf*.

Like the Muslims, the non-Muslim scholar must recognise and respect this difference introduced between the Qur'ān as text and the Qur'ān as source.

3. The third and final factor was the *isnād* of the Qur'ān text, the *muṣḥaf*.

Zaid's youth and the lateness of his conversion together imply the lateness of his information for both the Sunna and the Qur'ān, in each of which fields he is a prominent and distinguished personality.

As in the Sunna, so also in the Qur'ān field, Zaid is the hallmark of the last-period information from the Prophet. His *muṣḥaf*, that is, the *muṣḥaf* placed under the aegis of his name, is the *nāsikh* of all other known *muṣḥafs* and any readings they may contain.

Two quite disparate attitudes to reported Qur'ān variants were reflected in the Islamic literature. There is firstly an expression of reprobation and reprehension. This was instanced in the *hadīths* featuring Ḥuḏaifa and his quarrels with ʿAbdullāh and Abū Mūsā, leading to the advice he offered to ʿUthmān.

Secondly, however, there is a preference for harmony achieved by rationalising and justifying the reported variants, representative of the later catholicity of the Muslim attitudes.

The Muslims never developed a technique for judging the truth of the contents of their *ḥadīths*. Except in the case of the most blatant forgeries, offensive to faith and to reason alike, the utmost their concentration upon the *isnād* of the *ḥadīths* enabled them to do was to pass judgment on the likelihood of whether A had met B and could therefore have received information from him. No ḥadīth of sound isnād could be ignored, far less set aside, without even more compelling evidence to indicate a greater probability (r j ḥ).

The analytical approach failing to evolve, subtle minds, in thrall to traditional Islamic knowledge, had to be content with ever more ingenious interpretation and harmonisation. Some examples of this we have already met, and others we shall shortly meet in detail.

The attitude to the ḥadīths on the history of the Qur'ān texts was expressed variously. The reported Qur'ān variants led to the postulation of an ancient indifference to the details of the reading of the texts, providing only that the meaning remained unaffected. A matured explanation of the reported variants was to assume an ancient indifference to the dialect employed to convey the meaning. That view derived from and rationalised the first explanation.

Thirdly, since the dialect hypothesis broke down under scrutiny, there next emerged the 'seven acceptable readings' theory which postulated that the number of acceptable readings represented the number of parallel revelations made to the Prophet. Among some forty varying interpretations of that ḥadīth canvassed, one view was that the reference is to the seven Qur'ān codices compiled by Abū Bakr, ʿUmar, ʿUthmān, ʿAlī, ʿAbdullāh, Ubayy and ibn ʿAbbās.[24] The suggestion is irregular, since we have already noted that we nowhere else meet with the attribution to several of these personalities of a private Qur'ān codex. The ḥadīth is noteworthy insofar as it makes ʿUthmān one among other muṣḥafs.

Ḥuḏaifa and ʿUthmān were projected as alarmed at the reading disputes which threatened the Muslims of Iraq and Syria (and of Medina) with the sort of squabbles and divisions which had afflicted Jews and Christians, and in which each of these communities had squandered the social and political advantages which flow from the possession of a divine revelation. The solution urged by the party lurking behind this attitude was that the Muslims be seen to be united on the basis of a single *muṣḥaf* before the unity of Islam was similarly shattered.

Others took a much less alarmist view. Abū Huraira's authority was borrowed for the report that the Prophet himself had stated that the Qur'ān had been revealed in seven versions and that only contention over the Qur'ān was unbelief.[25] This view would license school *ikhtilāf* while prohibiting only public contention. Such dangers as might be apprehended for Islam lay not in the fact of local differences, but in making these differences the occasion of quarrels and exaggerated mutual accusations of error, or of attributing to one's opponents the possession and use of incorrect texts. This is the plea of minorities against majorities. The Muslims must respect one another's right to differ even on such sensitive matters as Qur'ān text. The primary consideration in the recitation of the Qur'ān was that it should always faithfully reflect the meaning of the revealed texts. Provided there was no distortion of the divine intention the vocabulary used to clothe God's meaning was quite immaterial. 'All the readings are correct and equally valid, so long as you do not terminate a mercy verse with a reference to punishment or vice versa.'[26]

This view was intended to be confirmed by a conciliatory remark reported from Zuhrī, 'I have heard that these are the seven forms, and that they express but one meaning with no disagreement as to what is permitted and what forbidden.'[27] The remark refers only to consonantal/vocalic variations from ʿUthmān and quite ignores the most significant feature of reported variants, namely, the attempt to document differing local approaches to certain legal questions. In all cases of that kind, what was in view was the use of the Qur'ān source to which the Qur'ān document was being made to conform.

The synonyms/dialects and other rationalisations are in this area of Qur'ān use totally irrelevant.

ʿAlqama al Nakhaʿī reports ʿAbdullāh's departure from Kūfa.

> He took leave, saying, 'Do not contend about the Qur'ān. It contains no contradictory statements, nor such as cancel each other out. Nor does it materially alter statements, even frequently repeated statements. The šarīʿa, with its penalties and obligations, is a single consistent system.'[28]

The readings disputes concerned the use of the Qur'ān source. The use that the scholars then making appeal to the ʿAbdullāh reading had made of the ʿAbdullāh Qur'ān source had attracted criticism for making it appear that the Qur'ān contained contradictions.

> 'We used,' continues ʿAbdullāh, 'to refer our disputes to the Prophet and he would order us to recite in his presence and inform us that each was in the right. Did I know of any man more learned than

> myself in respect of what God has revealed, I would seek him out and add his store of knowledge to mine. I learned the recitation of seventy sūras of the Qur'ān from the very mouth of the Prophet and I was aware that the Qur'ān was reviewed annually, every Ramaḍān, and twice in the year he died. When he had completed the review, I would recite to him and he would inform me that I was right.
>
> 'Let therefore whoever recites after my reading not abandon it nor lose taste for it. Whoever recites according to any of these other forms, let him not abandon his reading either. But whoever denies a single verse of the Qur'ān denies the entire Book.'[29]

It is a somewhat confused ḥadīth which conflates the 'seven forms' remark attributed to the Prophet with the varying results achieved in the interpretation of another, the 'seven abwāb', ḥadīth.[30] The report insists in a defensive tone upon the correctness of the legal doctrine documented from the Qur'ān on the basis of the ʿAbdullāh codex, which it simultaneously strives to vindicate by reference to the Prophet's late-period endorsement. The ḥadīth alludes to disagreements on legal conclusions, but denies that these can be urged to argue inconsistency in the Qur'ān itself.

Disagreements are the perfectly natural outcome of the appeal by the different lawyer groups to different Qur'ān recensions.

Although the claim is obviously enough made that the codex of ʿAbdullāh carried the Prophet's repeated and, more important, his late-period approval, the report somewhat inconsistently shrinks back from insisting that the disagreements should be limited by the imposition of textual uniformity.

No serious harm need be anticipated from the multiplicity of Qur'ān codices, providing only that all recensions are treated as equally valid. Division in the ranks of the Muslims would result only from a narrow-minded insistence that there can be only one authentic Qur'ān tradition which its proponents would seek to enforce upon the whole community. Public contention about the reading of a single verse is unbelief.

This is how one group of Muslims sought to defend and vindicate their right to employ Qur'ān variants.

In view of the reported complacency of the Prophet, ʿAbdullāh can be projected as undoubtedly correct.

Equally, ʿUthmān, if the squabbles over the readings bid to destroy the very unity of Islam, had acted from motives of the highest expediency in insisting upon a single uniform text, to achieve which he set his mind upon the destruction of every other documentary record of the revelations.

The Prophet had not irrevocably commanded the preservation of the variant readings. He had merely countenanced them as a gracious concession. Were it otherwise, and were the 'seven readings' understood to have represented an obligatory injunction laid by the Prophet upon his community, knowledge of each and every one of them would have come to be regarded by the Muslims as an integral and indispensable element in the transmission of the entire corpus of the divine revelations, to be passed on undiminished to the successor generations. That this had not occurred, however, was for Ṭabarī the clearest evidence that the 'seven *aḥruf*' had been alternative texts. ʿUthmān could therefore, in no sense, be accused of having derelicted from his duty either to the Qur'ān or to the community.[31]

> The Muslims abandoned recitation after six of the forms which their just leader insisted they abandon, until they lost all knowledge of them and all trace of them became quite obliterated. There is today no possibility of reciting them on account of their having quite vanished, and on account of the agreement among the Muslims to reject their recitation without, however, any reflection upon their individual correctness or that of any fraction of any one of them. No recitation today is possible for the Muslims other than on the basis of that one consonantal text which their solicitous leader selected for them.

The connection through Ḥudaifa to the variant pre-ʿUthmān Qur'ān traditions, associated in the *Ḥadīth* with the names of ʿAbdullāh, Ubayy, Miqdād/?Muʿād, Abū Mūsā, ʿĀ'iša, Ḥafṣa, Umm Salama and others, is not, in Ṭabarī's way of seeing things, so much broken as suddenly duplicated. What has been abandoned, what has vanished and become quite obliterated so that its recitation is no longer in fact possible, can be quite ignored for all but antiquarian purposes.

It was now inevitable that, where they continued to be alleged, variant readings, even variant codices, were seen by the scholars to be mere variants of the ʿUthmān text. Goldziher was right after all.

The alleged pre-ʿUthmānic Companion *muṣḥafs* had no historical, merely a theoretical identity, partly explicable by the necessity to provide a rational explanation for

ʿUthmān's having had to act at all.

Abū Bakr or ʿUmar had already collected the texts, but neither had taken steps to disseminate the text universally. Thus were the Companion readings/*muṣḥafs* explained. The reports settled upon ʿUthmān as the caliph who had despatched a unique text throughout the empire. Two collections having been reported, two motivations had to be assumed, with all the implications that strictly logical thinking would cause to follow.

The error of the Nöldeke-Schwally conclusions lay in their looking for only a single collection. As between Abū Bakr and ʿUmar and ʿUthmān, their preference fell on the ʿUthmān *ḥadīth* series and the Abū Bakr/ʿUmar series had to be explained away.

Admittedly, we too have seen that there existed a single *ḥadīth* strain which attributed to ʿUthmān the merit of having been the first to complete a collection of the Qur'ān *ab initio*. That view had not, however, prevailed among the Muslims. Harmony and rationalisation was their way with conflicting *ḥadīths*. The Muslims looked therefore for at least two collections in the period following the death of the Prophet, and to each they allotted a separate motivation.

The two occurred, successively, under Abū Bakr-ʿUmar and then under ʿUthmān. The aim of the first was the earliest collection of the scattered fragments of the individual revelations into one central place. The aim of ʿUthmān was the collection of the Muslims, that is, uniting the Muslims of every region throughout the empire on the basis of a single text. To do this he merely needed to arrange for the despatch of copies of the assembled Abū Bakr-ʿUmar text to the provinces. Typical of this view of the matter are the following:

> The reading of Abū Bakr, ʿUmar, Uthmān, Zaid, of the *Muhājirs* and the *Anṣār* was one and the same. All used a common reading that had been employed by the Prophet before them. This text Muḥammad had read over twice with Gabriel in his final year, on the occasion of the last check-reading of the Qur'ān texts. Zaid attended the final review and taught the reading endorsed on that occasion to the Muslims until he died. That is why Abū Bakr commissioned Zaid to assemble the corpus of the revelations and why ʿUthmān engaged him to copy out the *muṣḥafs* that were despatched to the regions.[32]

> Zaid b. Thābit attended the final review and in the course of it what had been removed from the Qur'ān and what remained was explained to the Prophet. Zaid wrote out this final review text for the Prophet and read it over to him to check it once again. Zaid thereafter taught this text to the Muslims. That is why Abū Bakr and ʿUmar relied upon Zaid in the assembly of the Qur'ān texts and why ʿUthmān appointed him to produce the copies.[33]

These *ḥadīths* go even further than Ṭabarī, in that they fail to take any account of the existence at any time of variant readings/*muṣḥafs* attributed to ʿUthmān's contemporaries. In fact, they are more concerned with explaining Zaid's prominent role in the history of the Qur'ān texts than with ʿUthmān's motive for his collection. From what we have seen in the foregoing analysis of the collection *ḥadīths*, ʿUthmān had to have rival Companion codices to suppress in order to make the effort to unite the Muslims on the basis of a unique text.

But even the most naïve ḥadīths, which fail to assign to ʿUthmān a specific technical motive, nevertheless report his as the second collection.

Indeed, the Muslims believe that the Qur'ān had been collected on three separate occasions. The first had occurred in the lifetime and indeed in the presence of the Prophet. 'We organised the Qur'ān,' reports Zaid, 'in the presence of the Prophet.'[34]

Certain commentators suggested that this report is to be interpreted in the sense that by organisation is meant the internal arrangement of each of the sūras.

The question of the internal organisation of the muṣḥaf also gave rise to much speculation. What here concerned them was when and by whom the present arrangement of the contents had been determined. As two collections had been reported, two issues are involved. The order of the verses within the sūras was considered so intimately connected with the processes of the actual revelation, that it was concluded that this aspect of the organisation of the text must have been the work of the Prophet.

ʿUthmān reports that when lengthy sūras were being revealed the Prophet would summon one of the scribes and say, 'Place these verses in the sūra in which such-and-such a topic is mentioned.' When a single verse was revealed in isolation the Prophet would say, 'Put it in the sūra where so-and-so is mentioned.'[35]

Generally, therefore, the Muslims were agreed that the sūras were distinguished one from another and that the ordering of their verses had been fixed by the Prophet, although even here adventurous claims are occasionally met with. On the discovery of the two closing verses of Q 9, ʿUmar is said to have remarked, 'Had they been three verses, I would have made them a separate *sūra*',[36] a report which disturbed some scholars.

The statement in the *Mabānī*, that 'in the *muṣḥafs* attributed to ʿAlī and ʿAbdullāh there is discoverable no difference whatsoever relative to our *muṣḥaf*, apart from the order of the *sūras* and verses',[37] is apologetic in tone. The reference to the order of the verses goes too far, but that to the order of the *sūras* is a characteristic acknowledgment of the feeling among the scholars that if, as opposed to speaking of Companion readings, one is ready to accept that there had once existed whole Companion *muṣḥafs*, then presumably one of their hallmarks would have been a different ordering of the *sūras*.

The order of the verses in each *sūra* was generally conceded to have been the work of the Prophet. Only the order of the *sūras* therefore presented any possibility of idiosyncrasy by the individual Companion.[38]

In fact, several views have been expressed on this question. Bāqillānī reflects that 'it is possible that it was the Prophet who ordained the present arrangement. It is equally possible that we may owe the present order to the decision of the Companions.' As between the two possibilities, the *Qāḍī* finally decided that the order of the *muṣḥaf* has come down from the Prophet.[39] This was suggested by the reports on Muḥammad's having checked the Qur'ān with Gabriel. Presumably they had reviewed the texts in their present order. That was also the view of ibn al Anbārī. However, the review was said to have occurred annually. ibn Ḥajar was inclined to think it more probable that they had checked them in the chronological order of their revelation. That need apply only to the yearly reviews however. In the muṣḥaf, the sūra order bears no relation to the chronological order of the revelation of the verses and chapters. This observation may perhaps have been one of the factors encouraging the appearance of ḥadīths on the final review.

ʿAlī is said to have arranged his muṣḥaf in the chronological order of the revelation and to have included his notes on the nāsikh and the mansūkh.[40] The importance of this work would have been immense, but all Muḥammad b. Sīrīn's efforts to locate this work in Medına came to nothing. In any case, the story merely underlines the rule that the theories of naskh set no store whatever by the present arrangement.

Scholars who long assented to the view that the text we have in our hands today and the detailed arrangement of its contents were the work of Zaid and ʿUthmān, naturally asserted that the arrangement of the contents in the variant muṣḥafs ascribed to some of the Companions had been different. The Qāḍī ʿIyyāḍ reports that in the night prayer the Prophet recited Q 4 before Q 3 and that that was the order of the two chapters in the muṣḥaf of Ubayy. This led the Qāḍī to conclude that the sūra order had not been fixed by the Prophet, but had been left to the discretion of the Companions.[41]

Bāqillānī, noting that the order of the sūras is not

insisted upon for the purposes of prayer, private study or public instruction, supposed that this explained the different ordering reported to have occurred in the Companion codices.

We find, therefore, in various studies on the subject, varying versions of the order of the sūras occurring in the Companion codices. The difficulty arises here that arises elsewhere in Muslim literature, namely, that the reports are seldom in agreement. 'I have seen,' reports the author of the Fihrist, 'a number of codices alleged by those who had copied them to be the muṣḥaf of ʿAbdullāh. No two of them, however, agreed with each other.'[42]

The most recent scholar to attend to the reports on the Companion codices was Professor Jeffery who, with admirable perseverance, collected an impressive body of material for a projected history of the text of the Qur'ān. The most striking feature of this work is the regularity with which the reader encounters expressions of Jeffery's scepticism concerning this or that aspect of the reports he is considering. For example, he thought it 'unfortunate that not sufficient has survived to enable us to get a real picture of the text of any one of the pre-ʿUthmānic codices'.[43]

He recognises that,

> The older variants, even though they were known to be represented in some of the older codices, for the most part survived only in the works of two classes of savants: firstly, certain exegetes interested in the theological implications of such variants; and secondly, the philologers who quoted them as grammatical or lexical examples.[44]

Jeffery admits that

> the question arises, of course, as to the authenticity of the readings ascribed to these old codices. In some cases, it must be confessed, there is a suspicion of readings later invented by the grammarians and the theologians being fathered on these early authorities, in order to gain the prestige of their name. This suspicion is perhaps strongest in the case of distinctly Šī'a readings that are attributed to ibn Mas'ūd and to the wives of the Prophet. It is felt also in regard to the readings attributed to ibn 'Abbās, who as Übermensch des Tafsīr, tended to get his authority quoted for any and every matter connected with Qur'ānic studies. On the whole, however, one may feel confident that the majority of readings quoted from any reader really go back to early authority.[45]

It is not clear from anything that Jeffery, Schwally or Bergsträsser has said in any of their specialist works on the Qur'ān why anyone should feel this degree of confidence. 'The traditions as to the sūra-order in 'Abdullāh and other of the old codices come, argues Jeffery, 'from persons who were familiar with the 'Uthmānic sūra-order, but knew that the material was differently disposed in the others.'[46]

First 'feel' and now 'knew'! Alas for his use of this 'knew'. Surely what is meant is just 'alleged'.

'It is evident that we cannot place any reliance on the Ubayy sūra-order which, as in the case of the lists for ibn Mas'ūd's codex, must be regarded as later formations, not based on the original codex.'[47] It is remarkable to Jeffery how often Ubayy's 'variants agree with ibn Mas'ūd's against the 'Uthmānic codex'.[48]

On ibn 'Abbās' codex, Jeffery remarks,

> From the exalted position which ibn ʿAbbās holds in Muslim exegesis, where he figures as '*tarjumān al Qur'ān*', '*al baḥr*' and '*ḥeber al umma*', one would have expected his codex to be as famous in Qur'ānic literature as that of ʿAbdullāh. The rarity of its mention in his case serves as an argument for its genuineness, for, had it been an invention, we should have found it running as wildly through the Commentaries as his supposed school of exegesis.
>
> His fame in exegesis, however, belongs to a later stage in his career, when he was interested in utilising Jewish and Christian material for the elucidation of the Qur'ān, but, as his exegesis is obviously based on the text of the official ʿUthmānic edition, we must place his collection of the material for his codex in the days of his youth.[49]

It is very much to be regretted that Jeffery did not place all these observations side by side and thus co-ordinate his individual acts of scepticism.

One is appalled at the results for European scholars of their too ready acceptance of all that they read in the Muslim reports on this or that aspect of the discussions on the Qur'ān. Remembering that all such reports are, after all, merely *ḥadīths* which must therefore be treated no differently from the other *ḥadīths* we daily have to deal with, we can confidently conclude that it was only because the Muslims had alleged that ʿAbdullāh and Ubayy had prepared personal codices which differed from the ʿUthmānic text, that it next became necessary for them to report the different *sūra*-order in those different codices. To do this they had, of course, to depart more or less from the order of the *muṣḥaf* they had in their hands, the *muṣḥaf* they had attributed to ʿUthmān. There was no need to depart too radically, merely enough to implant the idea of differentness. It cannot be any wonder that no two lists agree. To do that, they would have had to be describing something that really existed.

THE TAWĀTUR OF THE MUṢḤAF

If the Companions had possessed muṣḥafs privately prepared for their personal use which differed from the universally acknowledged text, now attributed to a Companion, ʿUthmān, in respect of the sūra order, was there any other respect in which they might have varied from ʿUthmān? A reasonable suggestion would be that perhaps they had differed also in length, both from ʿUthmān and from each other.

Some were longer and some were shorter. Despite the statement attributed to ʿAbdullāh that he who denies a single verse of the Qur'ān denies the entire revelation, ʿAbdullāh is depicted in the literature as having denied three whole chapters of the Qur'ān!

The codex ascribed to ʿAbdullāh is said to lack three of the sūras present in our (the ʿUthmānic) text. The codices ascribed to ibn ʿAbbās, Ubayy and Abū Mūsā are said to contain two sūras which the ʿUthmānic text lacks.[50]

The Muʿtazilī scholar al Naẓẓām is reported to have impugned ʿAbdullāh's memory on the ground that he had denied two sūras (sic) which are part of the Book of God.[51] This is a reference, says ibn Qutaiba, to Q 113 and Q 114, and for his attitude ʿAbdullāh had justification. Men may opine and opine wrongly. This is possible for prophets and for ordinary mortals more possible still. What induced

ʿAbdullāh to refrain from recording the two sūras in his muṣḥaf was that he observed that the Prophet used the chapters as charms to invoke the divine protection upon his grandsons, al Ḥasan and al Ḥusain.

A similar cause led Ubayy, on the contrary, to copy into his muṣḥaf the two qunūt prayers which he noted the Prophet reciting at the ritual service. ʿAbdullāh, taking two chapters to be prayers, thought them to be no part of the Qur'ān, while Ubayy, taking two prayers to be sūras, thought that they were part of the Qur'ān.

Of the two reports, it was that concerning ʿAbdullāh's supposed omission of Q 113 and Q 114, but more especially his refusal to record the first sūra, the Fātiḥa (to which, curiously, there is no reference in ibn Qutaiba's comment) which provoked the more serious discussion among the scholars.

The trouble with the reports is that they clash with a fundamental doctrine - the tawātur of the Qur'ān. The universally acknowledged muṣḥaf of ʿUthmān had been the unanimous bequest of the entire generation of the Prophet's contemporaries. In this connection, one might refer to the observations of Fakhr al Dīn al Rāzī,

> The reports transmitted in certain ancient books to the effect that ibn Masʿūd denied that the Fātiḥa and the two charm sūras are part of the Qur'ān are troublesome. If we accept that a mutawātir tradition had been achieved in the days of the Companions, then the three chapters are part of the Qur'ān and ʿAbdullāh's denial amounts to disbelief [kufr]. If, on the other hand, we hold that tawātur had not been achieved in the days of the Companions, it follows that the Qur'ān is not mutawātir. What

springs most readily to mind is that the reports from ʿAbdullāh are quite unfounded. This cuts the knot of that dilemma. The Qāḍī Abū Bakr said, 'It is not soundly reported from ʿAbdullāh that these three chapters are not part of the Qur'ān. Such a statement has not been reported from him. What he did was merely to erase these chapters and omit them from his text since he did not approve of their being written. This does not imply that he denied that they were part of the Qur'ān. The Sunna in his view was that they should record only what the Prophet had commanded to be recorded and ʿAbdullāh did not have information that the Prophet had himself recorded these *sūras* or commanded that they be recorded.'

al Nawawī says in his commentary on the *Muhaddab*, 'The Muslims are unanimously of the opinion that the three *sūras* are part of the Qur'ān and that anyone who denies one of them is an unbeliever. What has been reported about ʿAbdullāh is groundless and thoroughly unsound.'

ibn Ḥazm said in the *Muḥallā*, 'The thing is a lie fathered upon ʿAbdullāh. Only the reading from ʿAbdullāh as transmitted from ʿĀṣim from Zirr from ibn Masʿūd is authentic and in that reading, the three *sūras* are present.'[52]

But ibn Ḥajar in the *Fatḥ* accepts the reports about ʿAbdullāh as sound. He states that both Aḥmad and ibn Ḥibbān report that ʿAbdullāh would not write these chapters in his *muṣḥaf*. Aḥmad's son, in the supplement to the *Musnad*, al Ṭabarānī and ibn Mardawaih all report from al Aʿmaš from Abū Isḥāq from ʿAbdul Raḥmān b. Yazīd al Nakhaʿī that he said, 'ʿAbdullāh used to erase the two charm *sūras* from his records saying, "They are not part of the Book of God."' Similar reports are related by al Bazzār and al Ṭabarānī with the addition that, as he erased them, ʿAbdullāh said, 'The Prophet merely commanded that they be used as charm prayers.' ʿAbdullāh never recited them in his ritual prayers.

al Bazzār adds, 'None of the Companions concurred with this view of ʿAbdullāh's. Further, it is ascertained that the Prophet recited them at his ritual prayers.' ibn Ḥajar concludes that the allegation that the whole thing is a lie fathered on ʿAbdullāh must be dismissed. Attacks upon _ḥadīths_ of unexceptionable _isnād_ are quite unacceptable in the absence of further evidence. Since the _isnāds_ of these reports about ʿAbdullāh are sound, they must be accepted without further ado. A means ought to be sought whereby they might be interpreted. The _Qāḍī_ and others took the reports to show ʿAbdullāh's reluctance to write these _sūras_ into the _muṣḥaf_. Here is an interpretation which commends itself, excepting that the sound report states that ʿAbdullāh said, 'The charm prayers are not part of the Book of God.' Now, if one construes the words, 'Book of God' as a reference to the _muṣḥaf_, this complements the interpretation.

Some who have reviewed the drift of the reports felt this harmonisation to be somewhat far-fetched. ibn al Ṣabbāġ added that ʿAbdullāh was not quite certain as to the status of the three chapters at the time when he first made his remarks. The consensus of the Companions as to the contents of the _muṣḥaf_ was first reached after that time. The three _sūras_ were first declared _mutawātira_ during ʿAbdullāh's lifetime. It was simply that they had not at first been _mutawātira_ in his private opinion.

ibn Qutaiba, resuming his comment on ʿAbdullāh's view of the matter, refrained from expressing any opinion as to whether ʿAbdullāh or the Companions were right or wrong. As for the reports that he had omitted the _Fātiḥa_ from his _muṣḥaf_ on the grounds that that chapter was not part of the Qur'ān God forbid!

ʿAbdullāh took the view that the Qur'ān was to be recorded and to be assembled between the two covers to preclude any doubt and to obviate any forgetting, any addition or any loss. ʿAbdullāh could see that all these things were quite inconceivable in respect of the *Fātiḥa*, on account of its brevity and given the fact that every Muslim is required to memorise it for the purposes of prayer.[53]

10 General conclusions

It must now have become abundantly clear how little assistance is to be hoped for from the Muslim accounts of the history of the collection of the Qur'ān texts.

The reports are a mass of confusions, contradictions and inconsistencies. By their nature, they represent the product of a lengthy process of evolution, accretion and 'improvement'. They were framed in response to a wide variety of progressing needs.

Nöldeke-Schwally isolated reports of several incompatible contentions: that the Qur'ān had first been collected by Abū Bakr; that it had first been collected by ʿUmar; that the collection had been begun by Abū Bakr and completed by ʿUmar; that it had been begun by ʿUmar and completed by ʿUthmān; that it had been solely the work of ʿUthmān.

They failed to detect the distinction between jamʿ al Qur'ān and jamʿ al maṣāḥif. They thus took all these reports to be competitive attributions through the maze of which they hoped to find safe passage in clinging fast to the detail of the ṣuḥuf of Ḥafṣa.[1]

Schwally, and since his day all his imitators, decided that this was the one sure fact in a morass of contradictions. The security derived from the frequency of the mention of these *ṣuḥuf* has led to an unfortunate tendency to exaggerate their significance to the Muslims.

Schwally may well have been correct in his surmise that the unpopularity of the figure of ʿUthmān had induced the Muslims to reduce his stock by attributing the first collection of the sacred texts to his more revered predecessors, Abū Bakr and ʿUmar, who had been erected by Muslim sentiment into models of semi-legendary piety and energy respectively.[2]

Nor was he wrong in detecting in the *ṣuḥuf* of Ḥafṣa a motif for linking the ʿUthmānic with the ʿUmar collection. His error consisted simply in the oversimplification of the nature of that link, and hence the exaggeration of the role played in the Muslim reports by Ḥafṣa's *ṣuḥuf*. This he did, not merely by regarding the work ascribed to ʿUthmān as limited to simply copying out the *ṣuḥuf* of Ḥafṣa, but, in addition, by treating the pre-ʿUthmānic codices attributed to the several Companions as no more than merely copies similarly derived from those *ṣuḥuf*.[3]

Relying solely upon one single series of *ḥadīths*, to be subjected to an exclusively literary analysis in the light of his personal intuition, Schwally achieved a conclusion which effectively is no more than an endorsement of certain fourth-century Muslim attitudes. This resulted from his procedure of treating the Qur'ān as a literary monument. The Qur'ān, we have seen more than once, is and was much more to the Muslims than simply a document. Much more significant in its history has been the role it was called on to play as the primary source for the derivation of the Law.

It follows that the reports on its collection must logically be submitted to a test of precisely the same canons that were applied by the Muslims to their second source, the Sunna. We cannot, therefore, avoid applying to all statements on the Qur'ān the test of the use to which the Qur'ān has traditionally been put in the Islamic sciences, and especially, since it has been treated as a primary source, the use to which it has been put in the Islamic source theory.

In this light, it soon becomes apparent that, far from being identical with the so-called ʿUthmānic text, the suḥuf of Ḥafṣa, like the suḥuf of ʿĀ'isha or the suḥuf of a third widow of the Prophet, Umm Salama, played a role analogous to that conferred upon the muṣḥaf of ʿAbdullāh, of Abū Mūsā, of Ubayy, of Miqdād (or Muʿāḏ). Like all of these, Ḥafṣa's codex had occasional exegetic value in the scholars' attempts to decide issues left 'unclear' in the ʿUthmān text. Use has also been made of the suḥuf of Ḥafṣa in the interest of attempted interpolation relative to the universally acknowledged Qur'ān text of the (ʿUthmān) muṣḥaf.

In the Qur'ān sphere, as in the Sunna sphere, appeal was still allegedly possible to information provided in the names of prominent contemporaries of the Prophet.

Again in the Qur'ān sphere, as in the Sunna sphere, attempts had early been set in train to regularise the position created by the apparent conflict of sources. This was done by the application to the Qur'ān of the principles of abrogation which had been applied to the Sunna and which, by definition, involved consideration of isnāds. For the purposes of 'settling' exegetical disputes, certain circles, it would appear, were not above attributing unambiguous Qur'ān readings to senior Companions. The opposing position could always be restored by appeal to the authentic Qur'ān texts and attributing them to equally eminent Companions of later date of conversion. That was the mechanism by which Zaid b. Thābit achieved his central role in all versions of the *ḥadīths* on the various aspects of the recording and the collecting of the Qur'ān revelations.

In this connection, it should be noted that Zaid's name is more prominent and more consistently used than that of Ḥafṣa. It also perhaps should be noted that Zaid and Ḥafṣa shared roughly the same late death-date. The fact of their both having survived the major Companions mentioned in connection with Qur'ān matters doubtless accounts for the frequency with which both names occur. They both occur, as has been seen, as links connecting the alleged ʿUthmān collection with the alleged Abū Bakr-ʿUmar collection.

In order to provide this ʿUthmān collection with a rationale, the Muslims argued that it had become necessary to avoid the dangers of sectionalism and faction tearing asunder the unity of Islam, as the different regions and localities proclaimed their allegiance to this or that Companion codex.

But if, as has now been argued, appeal to the Companion codices is a common exegetical and especially an *uṣūlī* device, aimed at countering, elucidating, or even evading the ʿUthmān text, the so-called Companion codices could only have been posterior, not prior, to the ʿUthmān text. That would rob the ʿUthmān codex of its entire raison d'être and indicates that, as a matter of historical fact, it need never have occurred.

The Abū Bakr-ʿUmar collection likewise had its distinct motive, succinctly differentiated in the literature from ʿUthmān's: Abū Bakr was the first to collect the Qur'ān texts into a single volume on the occasion of the deaths of the remembrancers at Yemāma; ʿUthmān was the first to collate the _muṣḥafs_ and to produce a _textus receptus ne varietur_. Abū Bakr collected the texts; ʿUthmān collated the texts.

The Muslim sources are thus quite clear that Abū Bakr and ʿUmar were responsible for the first collection of the Qur'ān texts following the death of the Prophet. Discordant voices were nonetheless heard, 'Abū Bakr died and the Qur'ān had not been collected; ʿUmar was killed and the Qur'ān had not been collected.'

The existence of such reports makes it clear that the Muslims were confused. The earliest stage of the traditions on the collection of the Qur'ān did consist in incompatible attributions of the first collection: to Abū Bakr, to ʿUmar, to ʿUthmān.

Only when the belief that the unpopular ʿUthmān had been responsible for the first collection became general might it have been felt desirable to lessen his merits by transferring the piety attaching to this sacred undertaking to his predecessors, the representatives of the ideal caliphate. When this happened, it was consequentially necessary to introduce linking motifs, perhaps even to distinguish the objectives underlying what was coming to be seen as a two-fold collection.

Yet, if, perhaps owing to prevailing anti-Umayyad feeling, ʿUthmān's credit were deliberately minimised in this fashion, why, one may ask, had a caliph so closely identified with the unpopular dynasty ever been given the merit of any association with the collection of the Qur'ān? Schwally thought it was because the first to have collected the Qur'ān had been ʿUthmān and that it was impossible ever to suppress the fact.

My suggestion is that that attribution had resulted from even more interesting technical considerations. To guarantee an ancient and a mutawātir transmission, the collection of the Qur'ān must necessarily be attached to the name of one of Muḥammad's immediate successors. We have seen the varying results of the attempts to identify that successor in the attribution of a Qur'ān collection to each of Muḥammad's four immediate successors - the khulafā' al rāšidūn.

This led to the attempts to harmonise these conflicting attributions: Abū Bakr had initiated the sacred undertaking, ʿUmar acquiring the merit of having completed it; ʿUmar is credited with initiating the undertaking, ʿUthmān is grudgingly allowed the lesser merit of completing the work of his pious and energetic predecessor.

The circumstances in which the task was first taken up were such in which loss of Qur'ān materials is very easily conceivable, yet the task is presented as having been executed with such supererogatory care that the promulgated text was projected as having been beyond doubt complete.

The two motifs concretise the forces pulling in

opposite directions in the minds of the Muslims on the question of the completeness/incompleteness of the Qur'ān, according as they were engaging in external or in internal polemic. Further, the question arises internally from the implications of the exegesis of certain verses apparently referring to the Prophet's forgetting/being caused to forget certain unspecified parts of the revelation.

When framing the reports on the collection of the Qur'ān, there was the further need to take into account the still circulating *ḥadīths* relating the loss, withdrawal, or forgetting of this or that 'verse' said to have been revealed to the Prophet but not now figuring in the *muṣḥaf*. The *ḥadīths* had been the weapons with which the ancient exegetical dispute about precisely those 'forgetting' verses had been won.

The traditions on the collection of the Qur'ān are not, in fact, as Nöldeke-Schwally supposed, contradictory. They form a perfect harmony, for the most striking feature of all the Muslim discussions on the collection of the Qur'ān texts is the deliberate exclusion of the figure of the Prophet. This exclusion was both stressed and repeated in the principal *ḥadīth* on the supposed Abū Bakr collection. Indeed, the one common motif shared by every single Muslim account of the collection of the Qur'ān, uniting all the *ḥadīths*, whatever the details of their other conflicts, is precisely this allegation that, whoever it may have been who for the first time in the history of Islam had brought together the Qur'ān texts, it was certainly not the Prophet.

The exclusion of the Prophet from the task of

collecting and promulgating the revelations has even been rationalised into the very impossibility of his doing so, on the ground that as long as he remained alive, a safe and certain recension of the valid revelations was unthinkable. With naskh (withdrawal) a daily possibility, the extent to which the Qur'ān would continue to have valid applicability for the Law could confidently be recognised only with the Prophet dead and silent.

Having considered the Muslim theories of naskh, we have learned that two such theories referred exclusively to the Qur'ān texts and necessarily implied omissions from the Qur'ān: 1. the suppression of both the wording and the ruling, and 2. the suppression of the wording, but not of the ruling. The muṣḥaf is thus not co-extensive either with the fullness of the revelation made to Muḥammad or with the Qur'ān as this bears upon the Islamic Fiqh.

In view of the implications for their view of the history of the Qur'ān texts of this second theory of naskh especially, the Muslims simply could not afford to be found or to find themselves in possession of a Qur'ān document that had been edited, checked and promulgated by its Prophet-recipient. That was because they argued that certain elements of Islamic Law, derived from revealed and still-surviving Qur'ān revelations, were nowhere referred to in the muṣḥaf.

This motive induced the Muslims to exclude their Prophet from the history of the collection of their Qur'ān texts. It was a compelling motive. It was their only motive.

Nöldeke-Schwally, although fully informed on the three-fold modality of naskh and arguing that amidst the confusion of details in the Muslim accounts of the collection of the Qur'ān - those that are in agreement as much as those that are in clear conflict - we must throughout be on our guard against tendentious colouring of reports, given the central significance of the Qur'ān to the religious system now developing on the basis of the Book's claims and contents, nevertheless concentrated their considerable intellectual powers on the various aspects of the reports in total isolation one from another. The Qur'ān source and the Qur'ān document was a distinction they failed to exploit.

They therefore recognised in the discussion of the Qur'ān only two of the alleged three modes of naskh. The significance of the third mode, the suppression of the wording alone, to the framing of the reports on the collection they quite overlooked, despite their realisation that in all our analyses of the Muslim reports, the sole unreservedly certain point of departure must be the present condition of the Qur'ān texts.[4] Their analysis, in short, was exclusively literary.

Far too much weight has been given in European studies to alleged omissions from the Qur'ān texts owing to the tendency of European scholars to accept with uncritical naïvety the Muslim allegation that such omissions are already rationalised in the Qur'ān, and thus presumably by the Prophet.[5]

We must learn this simple wisdom: one must either accept all ḥadīths impartially with uncritical trust, or one must regard each and every hadīth as at least potentially guilty of a greater or lesser degree of inherent bias, whether or not this is immediately visible to Western eyes.

We cannot in our arrogance continue to presume that guided by mere literary intuition we can safely pick our way, selecting or rejecting hadīths on the excuse that where no motive for any particular statement is discernible by us, none was therefore intended.[6] Schwally, for example, could detect no motive for the selection of Zaid as the redactor of the ʿUthmān muṣḥaf.

The need for circumspection applies with particular force to the Muslim exegetical tradition, more especially to statements bearing upon any aspect of our present concern, the condition of the Qur'ān texts at the moment of Muḥammad's death. Nöldeke held the view that a complete recension of all the revealed texts even in the lifetime of the Prophet was already scarcely possible.[7] In the earliest days of his mission when the number of his following was insignificant, Muhammad might not have troubled to write down his revelations.[8] As the numbers of his adherents increased, the revelations would continue to be preserved solely in the memories of the faithful. Amid his manifold state responsibilities Muhammad could not always himself remember the precise wording in which he had given out certain revelations. This is how different Companions received their slightly differing versions, although all were received direct from the Prophet himself. Certain verses Muḥammad forgot outright, others he summarily altered.[9] With his own hand he had cancelled yet other verses.[10]

How far the reader will concur with these views will depend on how far he agrees with Nöldeke's model of Muḥammad as the author of the Qur'ān. Nöldeke also relied upon Ḥadīth and tafsīr. But the traditions in question here are devices all too transparently designed, in apparently innocent references to incidents in the Prophet's life, to document a Muslim contention that to the 'replacement' definition of the term naskh, adopted from Q 2.106 by the uṣūlīs to lend the appearance of Qur'ānic support to their theories that certain verses or certain sunnas had superseded other verses, must now be added a second meaning, 'omission', derived from Q 22.52.

To this end, the scholars made subsidiary references to Q 87.6-7 and to other verses. Nöldeke's references to the Qur'ān are to the self-same verses, Q 2.106 and Q 87.6-7. Hence his reasoning is circular.

What is ironic in these Muslim procedures is that the term naskh in both its occurrences in the Qur'ān, but especially in the verse from which they derived their technical term naskh, Q 2.106, where it is coupled with the term nunsi, 'we cause to forget or abandon' (taraka) can mean only 'suppression'. The irony is even clearer in the awkwardness of the three naskh formulae:

1. naskh al ḥukm wa al tilāwa, the suppression of both wording and ruling;
2. naskh al ḥukm dūna al tilāwa, the suppression of the ruling but not of the wording;
3. naskh al tilāwa dūna al ḥukm, the suppression of the wording but not of the ruling.

These formulae were forced upon the scholars by their own realisation that the term naskh, the technical term adopted into the science devoted to the study of the supersession of Qur'ānic or Sunna provisions, in fact actually meant suppression.

Naskh nevertheless proved the more popular term since the only possible Qur'ānic alternative, tabdīl (Q 16.101) raised even more awkward theological problems.[11]

The apodosis of Q 2.106, 'We shall bring one better than it or one like it', in association with Q 16.101, 'When We substitute one āya for another', provided an apparently impregnable basis in the divine revelation, the Word of God, for medieval Islam's assertion that its doctrines on abrogation could claim Qur'ānic and Prophetic sanction.

The connection between the lawyers' theories and the Qur'ān rests, however, solely upon the assertion that in both these contexts the term āya refers to a verse of the Qur'ān. Reflection upon both sūras may, however, suggest that this is by no means certain.

Q 2.106 occurs immediately before a series of sweeping changes, rather modifications, introduced by Muḥammad in both the ritual and the legal spheres. The verse thus precedes a change in the qibla (verses 115,177, 124-151); in the pilgrimage rites (verse 158); in the dietary laws (verses 168-74); in the law relating to the talio (verses 178-9); in bequests (verses 180-2); in the fast (verses 183-7); and again in the pilgrimage (verses 191-203).

Similarly, Q 16.101 is followed by allusions to

modifications in the dietary laws (verses 114-19), and in the Sabbath laws (verse 124).

What seems more likely, in view of the contexts in which each of these key verses occurs, is that, in each instance, the notoriously difficult term āya refers to an individual ritual or legal regulation established and hallowed in one religious tradition, the Jewish, and now modified in a later tradition, the Islamic.

Q 2.106 would now read, 'Whatsoever legal or ritual regulation We suppress or cause you to forget [or abandon] We shall bring in its stead another superior to the first, or at least its equal.'

Whatever may be thought of this suggestion, at least its possibility must work against the kind of dogmatic certainty with which the Muslims insist on this verse as the Qur'ānic legitimation of their theories, and that with which Nöldeke and others confidently pronounced on the incompleteness of our Qur'ān texts.

The proof that would establish rationally that the Qur'ān in actual historical fact is incomplete must be sought elsewhere than in a science which teaches the incompleteness of the Qur'ān texts that have reached us,[12] and which pretends that 'supersession' is the same as 'suppression'.

Moreover, although Nöldeke-Schwally were aware of the three modes of naskh, they argued that when we consider the present contents of the Qur'ān, we find that we have to deal with only two modes: either with cases where, on a given topic, both abrogated and abrogating texts are present, or only the one or the other.[13]

They further recognised that there are two classes of abrogated verses: those whose wording remains in our texts, only their rulings having been set aside; and those verses whose wording does not appear in our texts, having been omitted at the instance of the Prophet himself.

This also is oversimplification, for, as already pointed out, verses once revealed, but 'omitted' from our texts fall likewise into two classes: verses whose rulings have lapsed on account of the suppression of their wording; and verses whose rulings have not lapsed, despite the suppression of their wording.

The principal representative of the last class of verses is the so-called stoning 'verse'. The conclusions of Schwally on its reliability mark a considerably more matured and reasoned judgment than that expressed originally by Nöldeke.[14]

What above all is regrettable is that these two scholars, who rendered outstanding services to our study of all aspects of the Qur'ānic sciences, never once brought this second type of supposed Qur'ān omission into close comparison with the central overall contention inspiring all versions of the Muslim accounts of the history of the collection of the Qur'ān texts, namely that the collector had been anybody but Muḥammad.

If we now reject both classes of alleged Qur'ān omissions, we become capable of stepping over the one barrier that the Muslims themselves had erected which alone prevented them from conceiving of a Qur'ān text collected, edited and promulgated by their Prophet.

The motives underlying the ʿUthmān collection of the Qur'ān have been shown to derive from the schools' attempts to smuggle into the Qur'ān texts unwarranted interpolations designed to support local opinion on certain debated topics and calculated to swing the argument in their favour. Without this motive (i.e. without Companion codices to suppress) ʿUthmān's collection collapses. With it, Abū Bakr-ʿUmar's collection collapses. The implications are momentous.

The single vigorous Qur'ān text that throughout the ages has successfully withstood the assaults of both the exegetes and the uṣūlīs, stoutly retaining its textual identity in the face of countless attempts to insinuate interpolations through exploitation of the alleged codex of this or that Companion, is none other than the unique text of the revelations whose existence all their tricks betoken, the text which has come down to us in the form in which it was organised and approved by the Prophet.

So far as they have been examined to date, all Qur'ān MSS exhibit throughout the 'ʿUthmānic text'.[15] But, if the ʿUthmānic collection collapses, as never having occurred, this means that only one text of the Qur'ān has ever existed. This is the universally acknowledged text on the basis of which alone the prayer of the Muslim can be valid. A single text has thus already always united the Muslims.

We have isolated and neutralised the only motive for excluding Muḥammad from the editing and promulgating of the Qur'ān texts. In those processes, Muḥammad at last must now be once more re-instated. What we have today in our hands is the *muṣḥaf* of Muḥammad.

Works cited

In the case of major standard works reference to specific editions is unnecessary.

al Alūsī, Abu al Faḍl Šihāb al Dīn Maḥmūd b. ʻAbdullāh. Rūḥ al maʻānī, 6 vols., idārat al ṭabāʻa al mūnīriya, Cairo, n.d.

al Āmidī, Abu al Ḥasan Saif al Dīn ʻAlī b. abī ʻAlī b. Muḥammad. K. al Iḥkām fī uṣūl al Aḥkām, 4 vols., Cairo, 1332.

ibn al ʻArabī, Abū Bakr Muḥammad b. ʻAbdullāh. Aḥkām al Qur'ān, 4 vols., Cairo, 1957/1376.

al Asfarā'inī, Abū ʻAbdullāh. K. al nāsikh wa al mansūkh, MS Dār al Kutub, Taimūr majāmīʻ no. 297.

al Baiḍāwī, ʻAbdullāh b. ʻUmar. Minhāj al wuṣūl ilā ʻilm al uṣūl, MS Istanbul, Bayazit, no. 1019.

al Baihaqī, Aḥmad b. al Ḥusain. al Sunan al Kubrā, 10 vols., Haiderabad, 1925-38/1344-57.

al Bājī, Burhān al Dīn, Jawāb, MS Dār al Kutub, Taimūr majāmīʻ no. 207.

Baron, S.W. A Social and Religious History of the Jews, 12 vols., New York, 1952.

Bell, R. Introduction to the Qur'ān, Edinburgh, 1953.

al Bukhārī, Muḥammad b. Ismaʻīl. al Ṣaḥīḥ.

al Dānī, Abū ʿAmr ʿUthmān b. Saʿīd. K. al Muqniʿ, ed. O. Pretzl, Istanbul, 1932.

al Dārimī, Abū Muḥammad ʿAbdullāh b. ʿAbdul Raḥmān. K. al Sunan, Cairo, 1966/1386.

Abū Da'ūd, Sulaimān b. al Ašʿath. K. al Sunan, 2 vols., Ḥalabī, Cairo, 1952/1371.

ibn abī Da'ūd, Abū Bakr ʿAbdullāh. K. al Maṣāḥif, ed. A. Jeffery, Cairo, 1936/1355.

al Farrā', Abū Zakariyā Yaḥyā b. Ziyād. Maʿāni al Qur'ān, 2 vols. to date, Cairo, 1955- /1374- .

al Ġazālī, Abū Ḥāmid Muḥammad b. Muḥammad. K. al Mustaṣfā, 2 vols., Bulāq, 1322.

Goldziher, I. Muhammedanische Studien, 2 vols., Halle, 1889-90. Eng. tr. by C.R. Barber and S.M. Stern, Muslim Studies, 2 vols., London, Allen and Unwin, vol. 1, 1967; vol. 2, 1971.

Die Richtungen der Islamischen Koranauslegung, Leiden, 1952.

ibn Ḥajar, Aḥmad b. ʿAlī b. Muḥammad al ʿAsqalānī. Fatḥ al Bārī, 13 vols., Cairo, 1939/1348.

al Hamḏānī, Abū Bakr Muḥammad b. Mūsā b. ʿUthmān b. Ḥāzim. K. al Iʿtibār fi al nāsikh wa al mansūkh min al āthār, Haiderabad, 1319.

ibn al Jawzī, Abu al Faraj ʿAbdul Raḥmān b. ʿAlī b. Muḥammad. K. nawāsikh al Qur'ān, MS Topkapisarai, Aḥmad III, no. 192.

Jeffery, A. Materials for the History of the Text of the Qur'ān, Leiden, 1937.

Two Muqaddimahs, Cairo, 1954.

Mālik b. Anas, al Muwaṭṭa'.

Mekkī, Abū Muḥammad Mekkī b. abī Ṭālib al Qurṭubī. K. al nāsikh wa al mansūkh, MS Istanbul, Sulaimaniya, Šahīd ʿAlī, no. 305.

al Naḥḥās, Abū Jaʿfar Muḥammad b. Aḥmad b. Ismaʿīl, al Ṣaffār. K. al nāsikh wa al mansūkh fi al Qur'ān al Karīm, [Cairo?] pub. Zakī Mubārak, n.d.

ibn al Nadīm, Muḥammad b. Isḥāq b. abī Yaʿqūb. al Fihrist, Cairo, 1929/1348.

Nöldeke, Th. Geschichte des Qorans, Göttingen, 1860. GdQ1. 2nd edition, ed. Fr. Schwally, 2 vols., Leipzig, 1909-19. GdQ2.

Die Geschichte des Korantexts, ed. G. Bergsträsser and O. Pretzl, Hildesheim, 1961. GdQ3.

al Qurṭubī, Abū ʿAbdullāh Muḥammad b. Aḥmad al Anṣārī. al Jāmiʿ li aḥkām al Qur'ān, 30 vols., Cairo, 1952/1372.

ibn Qutaiba, Abū Muḥammad ʿAbdullāh b. Muslim. K. ta'wīl mukhtalif al Ḥadīth, Cairo, 1966/1386.

al Ṣaʿīdī, Abū ʿAbdullāh Muḥammad b. Barakāt b. Hilāl b. ʿAbdul Wāḥid. K. al Ījāz fi al nāsikh wa al mansūkh, MS Dār al Kutub, tafsīr, nos. 1015,1085.

al Šāfiʿī, Abū ʿAbdullāh Muḥammad b. Idrīs al Muṭṭalibī. al Risālah; K. Ikhtilāf al Ḥadīth; K. al Umm, 7 vols., Bulāq, 1321-4.

al Sarakhsī, Abū Bakr Muḥammad b. Aḥmad. Uṣūl, 2 vols., Haiderabad, 1372.

al Mabsūṭ, 30 vols., Cairo, 1324.

Schacht, J. The Origins of Muhammadan Jurisprudence, Oxford, 1950.

al Suyūṭī, Jalāl al Dīn ʿAbdul Raḥmān b. abī Bakr. al Itqān fī ʿulūm al Qur'ān, 2 vols., in 1, Ḥalabī, Cairo, 1935/1354.

al Ṭabarī, Abū Jaʿfar Muḥammad b. Jarīr. Jāmiʿ al Bayān ʿan ta'wīl āy al Qur'ān, ed. Šākir, 15 vols. to date, Cairo, 1954- .

al Ṭabā'ṭabā'ī, Muḥammad b. ʿAlī al Hāšimī al ʿAlawī. Mafātīḥ al wuṣūl fī uṣūl fiqh al Šīʿa, MS Alexandria, Baladiya, no. 1031.

al Ṭayālisī, Sulaimān b. Da'ūd. Sunan, Haiderabad, 1904/1321.

al Thaʿālibī, ʿAbdul Raḥmān. al Jawāhir al Ḥisān fī tafsīr al Qur'ān, 2 vols., Algiers, 1905.

al Ṭūsī, Abū Jaʿfar Muḥammad b. al Ḥasan. al Tibyān, 10 vols., Najaf, 1957.

abū Yūsuf, Yaʿqūb b. Ibrāhīm al Kūfī. K. al āthār, Haiderabad, 1355.

Zaid, Muṣṭafā. al naskh fi al Qur'ān al Karīm, 2 vols., Cairo, 1963/1383.

al Zarkašī, Badr al Dīn Muḥammad b. ʿAbdullāh. K. al Burhān fī ʿulūm al Qur'ān, 4 vols., Ḥalabī, Cairo, 1957/1376.

al Zurqānī, Muḥammad ʿAbdul ʿAẓīm. Manāhil al ʿIrfān fī ʿulūm al Qur'ān, 2 vols., Ḥalabī, Cairo, 1954.

Notes

CHAPTER ONE: INTRODUCTION

1 I. Goldziher, *Muhammedanische Studien*, 2 vols. (Halle, 1889-90), vol. 2, pp. 1-274, Über die Entwickelung des Hadith.

2 J. Schacht, *The Origins of Muhammadan Jurisprudence* (Oxford, 1950).

CHAPTER TWO: THE ISLAMIC LEGAL SCIENCES

1 Abū Bakr Muḥammad b. ʿAbdullāh b. al ʿArabī, *Aḥkām al Qur'ān*, 4 vols. (Cairo, 1957/1376), vol. 1, p. 46.

2 Q 2.142-3.

3 Abū Jaʿfar Muḥammad b. Aḥmad b. Ismaʿīl al Ṣaffār, al Naḥḥās, *K. al nāsikh wa al mansūkh fi al Qur'ān al Karīm*, ([Cairo?] pub. Zakī Mubārak, n.d.), pp. 6-7.

4 Abū Bakr Muḥammad b. Mūsā b. ʿUthmān b. Ḥāzim al Hamḏānī, *K. al Iʿtibār fi al nāsikh wa al mansūkh min al āthār* (Haiderabad, 1319), p. 25.

5 Abū ʿAbdullāh Muḥammad b. Idrīs al Šāfiʿī, al Muṭṭalibī, K. Jimāʿ al ʿilm, in *Umm*, 7 vols. (Bulāq, 1324), vol. 7, pp. 250-64.

6 Šāfiʿī, *Risālah*, (Bulāq, 1321), p. 16.

7 al Hamḏānī, *Iʿtibār*, pp. 24-5.

8 *Umm*, vol. 7, p. 254.

9 *Risālah*, p. 17.

10 *Umm*, vol. 7, p. 251; Q 59.7.

11 Risālah, p. 15.

12 Umm, vol. 7, p. 251.

13 Risālah, p. 17.

14 al Hamdānī, I'tibār, p. 25.

15 Risālah, p. 17.

16 Abū Zakariyā Yaḥyā b. Ziyād al Farrā', Ma'āni al Qur'ān, 2 vols. to date (Cairo, 1955- / 1374-), vol. 1, p. 95.

17 Abū Ja'far Muḥammad b. Jarīr al Ṭabarī, Jāmi' al Bayān 'an ta'wīl āy al Qur'ān, ed. Šākir, 15 vols. to date (Cairo, 1954-), vol. 3, p. 230.

18 Ṭabarī, Tafsīr, vol. 1, p. 52.

19 Ibid. p. 54.

20 Abū Ḥāmid Muḥammad b. Muḥammad al Ġazālī, K. al Mustaṣfā, 2 vols. (Bulāq, 1322), vol. 1, p. 102.

21 Umm, vol. 7, p. 60.

22 Ġazālī, vol. 1, p. 102.

23 Abū Bakr Muḥammad b. Aḥmad al Sarakhsī, Uṣūl, 2 vols. (Haiderabād, 1372), vol. 2, p. 81.

24 Abū Bakr 'Abdullāh b. abī Da'ūd, K. al Maṣāḥif, ed. A. Jeffery (Cairo, 1936/1355), p. 53.

25 Jalāl al Dīn 'Abdul Raḥmān b. abī Bakr al Suyūṭī, al Itqān fī 'ulūm al Qur'ān, 2 vols. in 1 (Ḥalabī, Cairo, 1935/1354), pt 1, p. 82.

26 Ibid.

27 Risālah, p. 6; p. 33.

28 Itqān, pt 1, p. 82.

29 Ibid.

30 Ibid.

31 Ibid. p. 47.

32 Ibid.

33 _Itqān_, pt 1, p. 82

34 _Ibid_. p. 47.

35 _Maṣāḥif_, p. 54; _Itqān_, pt 1, p. 76.

36 _Ibid_.

37 _Risālah_, p. 15.

38 _Itqān_, pt 1, p. 57.

39 _Maṣāḥif_, p. 54.

40 Cf. _Umm_, vol. 5, p. 217 with al Sarakhsī, _Mabsūṭ_, 30 vols. (Cairo, 1324), vol. 6, p. 32.

CHAPTER THREE: THE SUB-SCIENCE OF _NASKH_

1 M. Zaid, _al naskh fi al Qur'ān al Karīm_, 2 vols. (Cairo, 1963/1383), vol. 1, pp. 284-5.

2 _Itqān_, pt 2, pp. 20-7.

3 _Ibid_. p. 26.

4 _Ibid_. p. 20.

5 Ṭabarī, _Tafsīr_, vol. 2, p. 428.

6 _Risālah_, p. 17.

7 _Ibid_. p. 32.

8 _Ibid_. p. 17.

9 _Risālah_, p. 16; _Umm_, vol. 7, p. 271.

10 _I'tibār_, p. 26.

11 Abū Muḥammad Mekkī b. abī Ṭālib, al Qurṭubī, _K. al nāsikh wa al mansūkh_, MS Istanbul, Sulaimaniya, Šahīd 'Alī, no. 305, bāb naskh al Qur'ān bi al Sunna al mutawātira.

12 _Mustaṣfā_, vol. 1, p. 125.

13 _Risālah_, p. 17.

14 _Mustaṣfā_, vol. 1, p. 125.

15 'Abdullāh b. 'Umar al Baiḍāwī, _Minhāj al wuṣūl ilā 'ilm al uṣūl_, MS Istanbul, Bayazit, no. 1019, _faṣl_ 2.

16 *I'tibār*, p. 24.

17 ibn al 'Arabī, *Aḥkām*, vol. 1, p. 361.

18 *Itqān*, pt 2, p. 20.

19 *Risālah*, p. 17.

20 Ṭabarī, *Tafsīr*, vol. 2, p. 535.

21 *Ibid*. p. 475.

22 *Ibid*. p. 479.

23 'Abdul Raḥmān al Tha'ālibī, *al Jawāhir al Ḥisān fī tafsīr al Qur'ān*, 2 vols. (Algiers, 1905), vol. 1, p. 95.

CHAPTER FOUR: THE BACKGROUND TO THE EMERGENCE OF THE THIRD MODE OF *NASKH*

1 Ṭabarī, *Tafsīr*, vol. 10, pp. 301-46.

2 S.W. Baron, *A Social and Religious History of the Jews*, 12 vols. (New York, 1952), vol. 5, pp. 240-1.

3 *Umm*, vol. 4, p. 129.

4 *Risālah*, p. 20.

5 Aḥmad b. al Ḥusain al Baihaqī, *al Sunan al Kubrā*, 10 vols. (Haiderabad, 1925-38/1344-57), vol. 8, p. 210.

6 Sulaimān b. Da'ūd al Ṭayālisī, *Sunan* (Haiderabad, 1904/1321), p. 79.

7 Aḥmad b. 'Alī b. Muḥammad al 'Asqalānī, ibn Ḥajar, *Fatḥ al Bārī*, 13 vols. (Cairo, 1939/1348), vol. 12, p. 103.

8 *Ibid*. p. 123.

9 Ṭayālisī, p. 6.

10 *Muwaṭṭa'*, K. al Ḥudūd.

11 Ibid.

12 *Fatḥ*, vol. 12, p. 115.

13 Baihaqī, vol. 8, p. 213.

14 *Fatḥ*, vol. 12, p. 119.

15 Baihaqī, vol. 8, p. 210.

16 Sulaimān b. al Ašʿath, Abū Da'ūd, *K. al Sunan*, 2 vols. (Ḥalabī, Cairo, 1952/1371), vol. 2, p. 456.

17 *Muwaṭṭa'*, K. al Ḥudūd; cf. *Fatḥ*, vol. 12, p. 119.

18 *Mabsūṭ*, vol. 9, p. 36.

19 *Fatḥ*, vol. 12, p. 119.

20 Baihaqī, vol. 8, pp. 210-11.

21 GdQ2, vol. 1, p. 251, n. 3.

22 Ṭayālisī, p. 540.

23 *Itqān*, pt 2, p. 25.

24 *Fatḥ*, vol. 12, p. 119; *Itqān*, pt 2, p. 26.

25 *Fatḥ*, vol. 12, p. 131; *Itqān*, pt 2, pp. 26-7.

26 *Ibid*.

27 *Ibid*.

28 *Ibid*.

29 *Itqān*, pt 2, p. 25.

30 *Ibid*.

31 Burhān al Dīn al Bājī, *Jawāb*, MS Dār al Kutub, Taimūr *majāmīʿ* no. 207, f. 17.

32 *Itqān*, pt 2, p. 25.

33 *Ibid*.

34 *Bājī*, f. 18.

35 Abu al Faḍl Šihāb al Dīn Maḥmūd b. ʿAbdullāh al Alūsī, *Rūḥ al maʿānī*, 6 vols., idārat al ṭabāʿa al mūnīriya (Cairo, n.d.), vol. 1, p. 315.

36 Ṭayālisī, no. 1983.

37 Bukhārī, K. al Tafsīr, ad Q 2.106.

38 *Itqān*, pt 2, p. 25.

39 Bājī, f. 10.

40 Mekkī, bāb aqsām al naskh.

41 Bājī, f. 15.

42 Ikhtilāf al Ḥadīth, margin of Umm, vol. 7, p. 251.

43 Umm, vol. 5, pp. 23-4.

44 Umm, vol. 7, p. 208.

45 Mekkī, bāb aqsām al naskh.

46 Ibid.

47 Risālah, pp. 20-1; 35-6.

48 Ibid. p. 21.

49 Ibid. pp. 20,21.

50 Naḥḥās, pp. 6-7.

51 Fatḥ, vol. 12, introduction to K. al Muḥārabīn.

52 Mekkī, bāb lā yajūz an yakūn al naskh illā qabla wafāt al nabī.

53 Abū Muḥammad ʿAbdullāh b. Muslim, ibn Qutaiba, K. ta'wīl mukhtalif al Ḥadīth (Cairo, 1966/1386), pp. 310-15.

54 Badr al Dīn Muḥammad b. ʿAbdullāh al Zarkašī, K. al Burhān fī ʿulūm al Qur'ān, 4 vols. (Ḥalabī, Cairo, 1957/1376), vol. 2, p. 41.

55 Mekkī, bāb lā yajūz an yakūn al naskh illā qabla wafāt al nabi.

56 Uṣūl, vol. 2, p. 58.

57 Itqān, pt 2, p. 22.

58 Zarkašī, vol. 1, p. 235.

59 Uṣūl, vol. 2, p. 78.

60 K. al Mabānī, in A. Jeffery, Two Muqaddimahs (Cairo, 1954), p. 89.

61 Cf. Naḥḥās, p. 9; Umm, vol. 7, p. 251.

62 Mabānī, p. 89.

63 Cf. Naḥḥās, p. 9; Umm, vol. 7, p. 251.

64 Mabānī, p. 78.

65 Ibid. p. 81.

66 Ta'wīl, p. 314.

67 Umm, vol. 7, p. 251.

68 Itqān, pt 2, p. 26.

69 The term used, munsa'/mansa', derives from reading Q 2.106 as: aw nansa'.

70 Muḥammad ʿAbdul ʿAẓīm al Zurqānī, Manāhil al ʿIrfān fī ʿulūm al Qur'ān, 2 vols. (Ḥalabī, Cairo, 1954), vol. 2, pp. 115-16.

71 Ibid. pp. 92-3.

CHAPTER FIVE: THE MUṢḤAF: AN INCOMPLETE RECORD OF THE QUR'ĀN

1 Abū ʿAbdullāh al Asfarā'inī, K. al nāsikh wa al mansūkh, MS Dār al Kutub, Taimūr majāmīʿ no. 297, f. 102.

2 Abū ʿAbdullāh Muḥammad b. Barakāt b. Hilāl b. ʿAbdul Wāḥid al Ṣaʿīdī, K. al Ījāz fi al nāsikh wa al mansūkh, MS Dār al Kutub, tafsīr, 1015,1085, f. 42.

3 Abu al Ḥasan Saif al Dīn ʿAlī b. abī ʿAlī b. Muḥammad al Āmidī, K. al Iḥkām fī uṣūl al Aḥkām, 4 vols. (Cairo, 1332), vol. 2, p. 185.

4 Muḥammad b. ʿAlī al Hāšimī al ʿAlawī al Ṭabā'ṭabā'ī, Mafātīḥ al wuṣūl fī uṣūl fiqh al Šīʿa, MS Alexandria, Baladiya, no. 1031, bāb naskh al kitāb bi al sunna.

5 Abu al Faraj ʿAbdul Raḥmān b. ʿAlī b. Muḥammad, ibn al Jawzī, K. nawāsikh al Qur'ān, MS Topkapisarai, Aḥmad III, no. 192, f. 67.

6 Ṭabarī, Tafsīr, vol. 8, p. 80.

7 GdQ2, vol. 1, p. 45.

CHAPTER SIX: THE FIRST COLLECTION

1 _Itqān_, pt 2, p. 25.

2 _Fatḥ_, vol. 9, p. 9.

3 _Ibid_.

4 GdQ2, vol. 2, p. 22.

5 _Maṣāḥif_, p. 10.

6 _Fatḥ_, vol. 9, p. 12.

7 _Ibid_. p. 9.

8 _Itqān_, pt 1, p. 58.

9 Bājī, f. 14.

10 _Maṣāḥif_, p. 10.

11 _Fatḥ_, vol. 9, p. 10.

12 _Mabānī_, p. 39.

13 _Maṣāḥif_, p. 6.

14 _Ibid_.

15 _Ibid_. p. 5.

16 _Ibid_. p. 6.

17 _Ibid_. p. 10.

18 _Fatḥ_, vol. 9, p. 9.

19 _Maṣāḥif_, p. 10.

20 _Fatḥ_, vol. 9, p. 10; _Maṣāḥif_, p. 10.

21 GdQ2, vol. 2, p. 15, n. 2.

22 _Fatḥ_, vol. 9, p. 12.

23 _Itqān_, pt 1, p. 57.

24 _Maṣāḥif_, p. 10.

25 _Ibid_. p. 9.

26 _Fatḥ_, vol. 9, p. 18.

27 _Maṣāḥif_, p. 30.

28 _Fatḥ_, vol. 9, p. 11.

29 _Maṣāḥif_, p. 22.

30 _Ibid_. pp. 23-4.

31 _Ibid_. p. 29.

32 Zarkašī, vol. 1, p. 234.

33 _Fatḥ_, vol. 9, p. 12.

34 _Ibid_. p. 11.

35 The published text ought here to be amended: for _fa lammā jamaʿa Abū Bakr_, I propose to read: _wa lammā yajmaʿ Abū Bakr_, to follow: _lam yuktab_.

36 _Maṣāḥif_, p. 23.

37 _Fatḥ_, vol. 9, p. 12.

38 _Ibid_. p. 11.

39 GdQ2, vol. 1, p. 45.

40 Bukhārī, K. Faḍā'il al Qur'ān, bāb nisyān al Qur'ān.

41 _Fatḥ_, vol. 9, p. 53.

42 _Itqān_, pt 1, p. 61.

43 _Fatḥ_, vol. 9, p. 9. The reference is to Q 15.9.

44 Zarkašī, vol. 1, p. 235.

45 GdQ2, vol. 1, pp. 47-8.

46 Zaid, vol. 1, pp. 284-5.

CHAPTER SEVEN: THE ʿUTHMĀN COLLECTION

1 _Fatḥ_, vol. 9, p. 18.

2 Abū ʿAmr ʿUthmān b. Saʿīd al Dānī, _K. al Muqniʿ_, ed. O. Pretzl (Istanbul, 1932), p. 9.

3 _Ibid_. p. 7.

4 _Maṣāḥif_, pp. 18-19.

5 Ṭabarī, _Tafsīr_. vol. 1, p. 60.

6 _Maṣāḥif_, p. 13.

7 *Ibid*. p. 11.

8 *Fatḥ*, vol. 9, p. 15.

9 *Maṣāḥif*, p. 21.

10 *Ibid*. p. 22.

11 *Ibid*. p. 36.

12 *Mabānī*, p. 78.

13 *Maṣāḥif*, pp. 23-4.

14 *Muqniʿ*, p. 7.

15 var. *maṣāḥif*.

16 *Maṣāḥif*, p. 13.

17 *Ibid*. p. 14.

18 Ṭabarī, *Tafsīr*, vol. 3, p. 507.

19 *Ibid*. vol. 1, p. 25.

20 *Ibid*. p. 32.

21 *Ibid*. pp. 23-4.

22 *Itqān*, pt 1, pp. 90-1.

23 Ṭabarī, *Tafsīr*, vol. 1, p. 24.

24 *Ibid*. The final sentence derives from Q 73.20. Use of Q 73.20 is common in *Fiqh* quarrels over the night prayer. Its use there, as here, is artificial.

25 Ṭabarī, *Tafsīr*, vol. 1, p. 22.

26 *Fatḥ*, vol. 9, p. 16.

27 *Itqān*, pt 1, p. 47; *Maṣāḥif*, p. 11.

28 Ṭabarī, *Tafsīr*, vol. 1, p. 66.

29 Yaʿqūb b. Ibrāhīm al Kūfī, Abū Yūsuf, *K. al āthār* (Haiderabad, 1355), p. 44; *Itqān*, pt 1, p. 47.

30 Ṭabarī, *Tafsīr*, vol. 1, p. 35.

31 *Itqān*, pt 1, p. 47.

32 *Ibid*. p. 50.

33 *Maṣāḥif*, p. 11.

34 *Fatḥ*, vol. 9, p. 7.

35 *Ibid*.

36 *Ibid*. p. 22.

37 *Itqān*, pt 1, p. 60.

38 *Ibid*. Cf. *Fatḥ*, vol. 9, p. 18.

39 *Itqān*, pt 1, p. 47.

40 GdQ2, vol. 2, p. 22.

41 *Ibid*. p. 21.

42 R. Bell, *Introduction to the Qur'ān* (Edinburgh, 1953), p. 40.

43 *Ibid*. p. 44.

44 GdQ2, vol. 2, p. 56. Bell, *Introduction*, p. 44.

CHAPTER EIGHT: THE QUR'ĀN COLLECTIONS: A REVIEW

1 *Itqān*, pt 1, p. 60.

2 *Uṣūl*, vol. 2, p. 81.

3 *Itqān*, pt 1, p. 60.

4 *I'tibār*, p. 4.

5 *Itqān*, pt 1, p. 60.

6 *Ibid*. p. 65.

7 A. Jeffery, *Materials for the History of the Text of the Qur'ān*, (Leiden, 1937).

8 *Ibid*. p. 17. Cf. Abū Muḥammad ʿAbdullāh b. ʿAbdul Raḥmān al Dārimī, *K. al Sunan* (Cairo, 1966/1386), p. 55.

9 Bukhārī, K. al Tafsīr, ad Q 2.106.

10 Abū Jaʿfar Muḥammad b. al Ḥasan al Ṭūsī, *al Tibyān*, 10 vols. (Najaf, 1957), vol. 1, p. 397. Cf. Zarkašī, vol. 2, p. 40.

11 *Maṣāḥif*, p. 14.

12 *Maṣāḥif*, p. 17.

13 *Ibid*.

14 *Ibid*. p. 15.

15 *Ibid*. p. 35.

16 *Ibid*. p. 39.

17 *Ibid*. p. 36.

18 *Ibid*. p. 33.

19 I. Goldziher, *Die Richtungen der Islamischen Koranauslegung* (Leiden, 1952), p. 35.

20 Muḥammad b. Isḥāq b. abī Yaʿqūb, ibn al Nadīm, *al Fihrist* (Cairo, 1929/1348), al maqālat al thāniya.

21 Q 58.4.

22 *Mustaṣfā*, vol. 2, p. 102. Cf. Sarakhsī, *Uṣūl*, vol. 2, p. 81.

23 GdQ3, pp. 77 ff.

24 *Maṣāḥif*, p. 53.

25 Bukhārī, K. al Tafsīr, ad Q 2.106 and commentaries.

26 *Umm*, vol. 7, p. 219 and previous reference.

27 Goldziher, *Muhammedanische Studien*, vol. 2, p. 12.

28 *Itqān*, pt 1, p. 77.

29 *Fatḥ*, vol. 9, p. 21.

CHAPTER NINE: THE *ISNĀD* OF THE QUR'ĀN

1 GdQ2, vol. 2, pp. 22-3.

2 Ṭayālisī, no. 618.

3 *Umm*, vol. 1, pp. 108-10.

4 *Risālah*, p. 37.

5 Ṭayālisī, p. 44.

6 *Ibid*. p. 59.

7 Ṭabarī, *Tafsīr*, vol. 1, p. 24.

8 Bukhārī, K. Faḍā'il al Qur'ān, bāb kāna Jibrīl ya'riḍ al Qur'ān...

9 Fatḥ, vol. 9, pp. 35-6.

10 Cf. Itqān, pt 1, p. 50.

11 Fatḥ, vol. 9, pp. 35-6.

12 Abū 'Abdullāh Muḥammad b. Aḥmad al Anṣārī al Qurṭubī, al Jāmi' li aḥkām al Qur'ān, 30 vols. (Cairo, 1952/1372), vol. 1, p. 57.

13 Itqān, pt 1, p. 50.

14 Fatḥ, vol. 9, p. 25.

15 Itqān, pt 1, p. 50.

16 Ibid. p. 61.

17 Fatḥ, vol. 9, p. 36.

18 Itqān, pt 1, p. 70.

19 GdQ1, p. 43; GdQ2, vol. 1, p. 47, vol. 2, p. 44.

20 Q 2.106; Q 87.6-7.

21 Maṣāḥif, p. 33.

22 Fatḥ, vol. 9, p. 15.

23 Ibid. p. 7.

24 Itqān, pt 1, p. 49.

25 Ṭabarī, Tafsīr, vol. 1, p. 22.

26 Itqān, pt 1, pp. 46-7.

27 Ṭabarī, Tafsīr, vol. 1, p. 29.

28 Ibid. p. 28.

29 Ibid.

30 Itqān, pt 1, pp. 45-9.

31 Ṭabarī, Tafsīr, vol. 1, pp. 64-5.

32 Zarkašī, vol. 1, p. 237.

33 Itqān, pt 1, p. 50.

34 Ibid. p. 57.

35 *Itqān*, pt 1, p. 60.

36 *Ibid*. p. 61.

37 *Mabānī*, p. 33.

38 *Itqān*, pt 1, p. 64.

39 *Ibid*. p. 61; cf. *Fatḥ*, vol. 9, p. 34.

40 *Itqān*, pt 1, p. 58.

41 *Fatḥ*, vol. 9, p. 32.

42 *Fihrist*, bāb tartīb al Qur'ān fī muṣḥaf ʿAbdullāh.

43 *Materials*, p. x.

44 *Ibid*. p. 2.

45 *Ibid*. p. 15.

46 *Ibid*. p. 23.

47 *Ibid*. p. 115.

48 *Ibid*. p. 116.

49 *Ibid*. p. 193.

50 *Itqān*, pt 1, p. 65.

51 ibn Qutaiba, *Ta'wīl*, p. 31.

52 Cf. Jeffery, *Materials*, p. 21.

53 *Itqān*, pt 1, p. 79.

CHAPTER TEN: GENERAL CONCLUSIONS

1 GdQ2, vol. 2, p. 21.

2 *Ibid*. p. 22.

3 *Ibid*. p. 46.

4 *Ibid*. p. 5.

5 *Ibid*. p. 3.

6 *Ibid*. p. 23.

7 GdQ1, p. 36; GdQ2, vol. 1, p. 47.

8 GdQ1, p. 34; GdQ2, vol. 1, p. 45.

9 GdQ1, p. 36; GdQ2, vol. 1, p. 47.

10 GdQ1, p. 43; GdQ2, vol. 1, p. 54.

11 _Uṣūl_, vol. 2, p. 54.

12 GdQ2, vol. 2, p. 3, n. 2.

13 GdQ1, p. 42; GdQ2, vol. 1, p. 54.

14 GdQ2, vol. 1, p. 251; vol. 2, p. 45. GdQ1, p. 186; p. 194.

15 GdQ3, p. 97.

General Index

abrogation (see also forgetting; _al nāsikh wa al mansūkh_; _naskh_; _n s y_; replacement; substitution; supersession; suppression; _tabdīl_; withdrawal), 27, 47-51,57,161-3

of Qur'ān by Qur'ān, 49,52,58,61,93,162

of Qur'ān by Sunna, 50-9,71,89,92,105-7,134,162,166

of Sunna by Qur'ān, 50,55,58,61,134,166

of Sunna by Sunna, 43,49,58,91,134,180,203

theories of, 18,50,59,180,186-9,193,227,236

Abū Bakr, 75-7,98-102,118-27,137-46,155-61,165,190-2,196, 200-1,206,212,225-30,239

reading of, 122,192,213

Abū Mūsā al Aš'arī, 83-5,147,165-7,190,201-5

reading of, 142,146,167-8,181,192,211,220,227

adultery,

penalties for, 69-76

'_aḥruf_', the seven, 148-56,193-4,206-11

'Ā'iša, 12,16,30-2,37,84-7,94-100,106,150,165;

reading of, 37,181,211,227

'Alī, 37,75,120-2,130,139,144-5,149-50,165-8,191-3,200,206, 215-16

aqra' (Q 87.6-7), 82-3,107,124,133,148,151,166,193,199

asbāb al nuzūl, 15,68-70,147,150,185

ʿ*asīf* ('hired hand'), 75,90-2,102

Baṣra, 147,194

Bell,R., 158

Bergsträsser,G., 172,174,178,218

Companions (see also conflict; *muṣḥaf*; Qur'ān variants),

illiteracy of, 39,153

conflict

of Companion information, 34; for Qur'ān, 34,41-4,81,168, 180-4,189,193,200-2,227; for Sunna, 34,41-4,168,180-4, 199-202,227

of evidence, 17,31-2,60

of exegesis, 32,62,65-7,103-4,199,227,231

of *ḥadīths*, 43,95,126,135,160,166,170-2,180,191,212,217, 225

inter-*madhab*, 36,42-4,56,60,182-6,201-2,209,239

of sources, 14,50,60,81,227; *Fiqh*-*Fiqh*, 17,37,41,60,150; *Fiqh*-Qur'ān, 17,31-2,61,72,75,81,135-6,163,204; *Fiqh*-Sunna, 17,135-6; Qur'ān-Qur'ān, 18-21,42,97 Qur'ān-Sunna, 16,25,27,32,52,82,117,161,197; Sunna-Sunna, 16

conversion, date of, 43-4,166,180,189-97,203-5,228

dialects, 37,141,147,152-6,170,188,200-1,206-8

exegesis, 22,48,63,105,147,219,239

of Prophet, 33

jam' (see also Qur'ān, collection of)

al maṣāḥif, 139-140,225-9

al nās, 139

al Qur'ān, 122,139,225-9

Jeffery,A., 217-18

Karā'ites, 71

Khawārij, 93

kitāb allāh (the Book of God), 3,21,48,51,54,68,70-1,75-9, 99-103,111,120-3,138,145-7,152,157,191,201,220,222

Kūfa, 147,169,194,208

Kufans, 166

Law, Islamic (see also Fiqh), 3-6,121,232

regional origins of, 6-9

sources of, 40; relative primacy of, 9

Mālik b. Anas, 31,70,75,78-9,81,88,94-5,104,164

mansūkh, 57,65-6,84-5,88-9,93,216,237

mithl, 52-4,58,102-3,237

Mu'āḏ b. Jabal, 148,165,190,196,211,227

Muḥammad (see also Prophet), 3,22,41,55,69,98,106,118,121, 129-30,140,142,148,150

muṣḥaf (pl. maṣāḥif), 30,35,40-1,48,50,64,66,70,77,79-85,89, 111,121-2,125,135,139,144,163,185,192,223

completeness of, 119-21,130-1,165,190,230; denial of, 67, 82,86,93,97,104,106,110-12,117-21,126-7,129-31,145, 160-5,184,204,232,237

prayer,
shortening of, 55,149
use of Qur'ān at, 39-40,42,57,84-6,96,102,122,130,151,161, 175,183,203,211,217,221-4,239
Prophet,
amanuenses of, 4,118,120,124,145,159,164,201,214
illiteracy of, 4
reading of, 43

<u>qibla</u>, 7,24,55,59,236
Qur'ān document, 40,44,47,66,82,84-5,111,135-6,161,163,175, 178,187,203,205,208,226,232-3
additions to, 77-9,92,101,108,122,152,176,189,224
alteration of, 30,52,54,98,132,234
collection of, 5; history of, 6,18,42,47,86,109,117, 132-6,139-40,159-65,189,192,197,200-1,206,214,225, 231,238; commissions, commissioners, 154, 157,200; first to collect, 110,112,119-26,146,153-7,160,187, 190-1,212,225-30; ideological basis of, 7,110,131, 134,160-3
divine authorship of, 20,51
direct knowledge of (<u>samā'</u>), 82,104,120-8,141,145-6,157, 166-9,179,193,209,234
punctuation of, 149,186
review of (see also Gabriel)
annual, 193,195,209,215; final, 153,194-8,209,213, 216
science of, 9,203,238
text of, 85,148,165; improvement of, 32,41;

Index of Qur'ānic references